D1242928

The Lessons
of Recent Wars
in the Third World,
Volume II

The Lessons
of Recent Wars
in the Third World,
Volume II

Comparative Dimensions

Edited by

Stephanie G. Neuman
Columbia University

Robert E. Harkavy
The Pennsylvania State University

Lexington Books
D.C. Heath and Company/Lexington, Massachusetts/Toronto

Library of Congress Cataloging-in-Publication Data
(Revised for vol. 2)

The Lessons of recent wars in the Third World.

Vol. 2 edited by Stephanie G. Neuman, Robert E. Harkavy.
   Includes bibliographies and index.
   Contents: v. 1. Approaches and case studies—v. 2. Comparative dimensions.
   1. Military art and science—Developing countries—History—20th century. 2. Military
history, Modern—20th century. 3. World politics—1975–1985. 4. Developing countries—
Armed Forces. I. Harkavy, Robert E. II. Neuman, Stephanie G.
U43.D48L47   1987   355'.0332'1724   81-47912
ISBN 0-669-06765-2 (v. 1 : alk. paper)
ISBN 0-669-09852-3 (v. 2 : alk. paper)

Copyright © 1987 by D.C. Heath and Company

All rights reserved. No part of this publication may be reproduced or transmitted in any
form or by any means, electronic or mechanical, including photocopy, recording, or any
information storage or retrieval system, without permission in writing from the publisher.

Published simultaneously in Canada
Printed in the United States of America
Casebound International Standard Book Number: 0-669-09852-3
Library of Congress Catalog Card Number: 81-47912

The paper used in this publication meets the minimum requirements of American National
Standard for Information Sciences—Permanence of Paper for Printed Library Materials,
ANSI Z39.48-1984.

87 88 89 90 8 7 6 5 4 3 2 1

To Elena and Michael

Contents

Acknowledgments

The editors wish to thank a number of people whose assistance helped make this book possible, with the usual caveat that they are excused from blame for its shortcomings.

This book emerged from a conference held at, and financially supported by, the Strategic Studies Institute of the U.S. Army War College, Carlisle Barracks, Pennsylvania, September 20–22, 1984, under the aegis of the Institute's director, Colonel Thomas Stone. The editors wish to thank Colonel Stone and the staff of the institute for their administrative efforts as well as the institute's former director, Colonel Keith Barlow, for his help in the germination of the project and his subsequent support and encouragement.

Administrative assistance for the publication of the book was provided by Pennsylvania State University's Center for Research in International and Strategic Studies (CRISS) and the political science department. Secretarial assistance at Pennsylvania State was provided by Joanne Ostergaard and Melanie Romig.

Administrative support also came from Columbia University's Comparative Defense Studies Program. Dawit Toga and later Leonard Kreynin, both graduate assistants in the Program, provided much help during the production phase of this book. Marjean Knokey of the Research Institute on International Change gave generously of her time and organizational skills.

Finally, we would like to add a word of appreciation to Jaime Welch-Donahue, our editor at Lexington Books, who gave the moral support and cooperation, not to mention patience and good humor, necessary for achieving smooth, efficient, and rapid publication.

1
Introduction

Robert E. Harkavy

The project that led to *The Lessons of Recent Wars in the Third World* was conceived, not coincidentally, in the wake of the nearly simultaneous cluster of conventional wars ongoing in 1982: Lebanon, the Falklands, Iran versus Iraq. There then followed a spate of press and journal articles devoted to "lessons learned"; indeed, there arose virtually a new vogue in "lessons learned." Old government hands in the Pentagon and CIA might, of course, have smiled ruefully at this apparent discovery of "lessons learned" and would at any rate have seen this sudden burst of activity as a mere bump on a line graph. The government had all along conducted massive "lessons learned" exercises (many of them classified) amid and after important wars such as those in the Middle East in 1967 and 1973 and, of course, in Vietnam.

In their various ways, all three of the aforementioned wars provoked great interest in ever evolving military strategy, tactics, and weapons. The Lebanon war was claimed by some to have initiated a truly new era of electronic warfare; Edward Luttwak deemed it the single most important war, regarding lessons, since 1945.[1] Naval buffs were of course fascinated by the Falklands war, which saw the first real major naval combat since 1945 entailing, additionally, an important role for submarines. The seemingly primitive slaughter near the Shatt-al-Arab seemed a throwback to some, a reminder of things thought perhaps forever past; it inspired comparisons with Chancellorsville and Fredericksburg, Verdun and the Somme. The fact that such things could still occur in an era some thought had heralded the "irrelevance of military force" was itself a sobering lesson.

Interest in these wars was not merely prurient or specific to the immediate regions and nations involved. These wars were watched carefully by analysts of the NATO–Warsaw Pact military balance in Central Europe. Did the smaller limited arena of the Lebanon air war negate any inferences to possible Central European scenarios? Was the performance of British subs and Argentine antiship missiles indicative of what might one day occur in the Norwegian Sea?

Many writings on lessons learned during this period brought up prominent examples from the past. There was awareness of what the Spanish Civil

War portended—or did not portend—for World War II, and likewise, awareness of the virtual ignoring in this sense of the combat in the late 1930s along the China-Siberia border between the Soviet Union and Japan. There was awareness that pre–World War I military planners in Europe divined hoped-for lessons from the Prussia-France war of 1870, but not from the Boer War nor from the 1905 Russo-Japanese conflict, and that the result was a critical misperception all around about the then current state of warfare.

Some might argue that now, in an era of nuclear weapons and the assumed near automaticity of escalation from superpower conventional warfare, such attempted applications of lessons are no longer as important. Rather, they might concede, the main basis for lessons is in the skein of unconventional wars running from Vietnam to Afghanistan to Central America, where the superpowers have been, are, or may yet be militarily engaged. And of course other types of (politico-military) lessons, if not those involved in tactics and operations, can be gained from both conventional and unconventional wars in the Third World: security assistance lessons, politics of influence lessons, coercive diplomacy lessons, and so forth. But it may also be noted that very lately there has been growing interest, evidenced in the strategic literature, in a (U.S.-Soviet) "protracted conventional phase" that might—or might not—precede a nuclear exchange.[2] Hence, to that degree, the ghost of Spanish Civil War's Lessons remains alive.

The time context of the recent vogue of lessons learned is also worth remarking upon: the fading of the "counterculture" and of the once overwhelmingly dominant "Vietnam syndrome," the shifted political mood of American universities, conservative trends among younger people, Reaganism, signs of an overall realignment of the American electorate, if not of its intellectual elites, and so on. The serious study of warfare—of actual war-fighting—had in the process become more legitimate, at least within a critical mass of American intellectual life. Almost by definition, conservative political trends implied legitimacy of the belief that the institution of war was and is presumably ineradicable. If so, it behooved scholars to study it in a nonemotional and conceptual way.

This bring us back to the niche in the scholarly literature intended—or hoped—for this work by the editors. Needless to say, the literature is hardly lacking in attention to the subject of war. Indeed, recent decades have witnessed a truly massive expansion of the volume of writings on war and peace issues. These have ranged from the general to the specific, from the "functional" to the regional. Many in their comprehensiveness have stemmed from the seminal tradition of Quincy Wright: typologies and various dimensions of warfare, its causes and suggested remedies, and the crosscutting disciplinary perspectives thereon.[3] Recent works by, among others, Singer and Small, Kende, Lebow, Bueno de Mesquita, Beer, and Levy represent extensions of this tradition.[4] Within this tradition, emphasis ranges along a spectrum, from large-scale aggregate data presentation and events data analysis, to mixed use of hard data and historical/descriptive materials, to a more traditional approach. The bulk of these are, however, reflective of modern social science methodologies and modes of analysis. There is of course extensive topical coverage of nuclear deterrence and arms control, overshadowing that of conventional warfare.

There is in all of this, as we have noted previously, a vast gulf between the worlds of military history and, by contrast, military-related social science.[5] These remain not only distinct fields, but different worlds of endeavor and interaction. Few social scientists are well versed in the works of the more prominent contemporary military historians such as Michael Howard, John Keegan, Jay Luvaas, and Martin van Creveld. Military historians on their part tend to evidence almost open disdain for social science, for anything smacking of quantitative manipulation, empirical methodologies, or comparative (by country, region, or time) analyses. Indeed, John Keegan, perhaps the most prominent and renowned of contemporary military historians, has gained his deserved reputation for meticulous attempts at recreating battle history, for a form of extreme imputed realism intended to be devoid not only of pomp and glory, but of any theorizing as well.[6]

The editors set forth in this project to help bridge this gap. As a result, the work was intended, even with recognition of the practical inseparability of war and politics/diplomacy, to lean toward a more *military* analysis of recent wars. But, that being said in a general way, there remained serious questions about an appropriate mix of approaches and angles in an edited volume intended to provide variety, even competing types of analysis.

Hence, in our first volume, the first section was devoted to laying out various general approaches to the study of lessons learned. One chapter, by Harvey Starr and Benjamin A. Most, was devoted to aggregate data analysis at a macro level (frequency, intensity, and types of wars, their distribution by region, time periods, and so on). In the process, the reader was encouraged to think about the evolving nature of contemporary warfare, specifically, about the shift toward "unconventional" wars in the Third World. Another chapter by Jay Luvaas, written explicitly from the perspective of a military historian, provided great detail about inappropriately applied lessons over a lengthy swath of history; the reader was cautioned about the need for humility in divining lessons rather than merely "insights gained." Still another chapter by T.N. Dupuy provided a methodology—at a micro level—for gauging combat effectiveness, that is, a guide to explaining who wins and who loses wars, and for what reasons. Particularly, such an analysis compels the reader to focus on the comparative—rather, combined—effect of the quantitative and qualitative elements of military power. And, although no such chapter was provided, the editors were aware that one might have been included on the role of luck or chance—in essence, a perhaps more extreme view of randomness, or the relative absence of the possibilities for empirical analysis, than that typically asserted by military historians.[7]

The section on approaches stressed the various levels of analysis applicable to lessons learned, that is, the several angles from which the subject could be approached. The contribution on macrolevel data stressed the complementarity of case studies, comparative analysis (functional dimensions), and longitudinal analysis. With regard to academic disciplines, it was clear that there are somewhat distinct approaches favored, variously, by historians, political scientists, psychologists, and so forth. From the perspective of the professional military—but, again, crosscut by macro- and microlevel distinctions—there are the telescoped but still discrete strategic, operational, and tactical levels of analysis.

The second section of the first volume was devoted to case studies. Some of those discussed—Iran versus Iraq, Lebanon, the Falklands, the People's Republic of China (PRC) versus Vietnam, the Horn war—were predominantly traditional, conventional wars, perhaps best defined in terms of identifiable "battlefronts." Three—the Western Sahara, Central America, Afghanistan— were more readily described as unconventional. The editors had early on decided to use the mid-1970s as a baseline. This focus upon the most recent wars would best facilitate truly comparative analysis, as the wars have taken place within a particular era of superpower relations and of other aspects of world politics (the high watermark of OPEC, for instance) and have all been based on one specific generation of extant weapons technology.

If the editors had chosen to extend backward the period under analysis, the major conventional wars of 1971 (India-Pakistan) and 1973 (Israel-Arabs) could of course have provided additional perspective on the more recent ones. Not without good reason these wars are at any rate taken into account by some of our authors. We decided to focus on the more intense and destructive of the recent unconventional wars. If we had chosen to move farther along a spectrum toward low-level, brief, or sporadic guerrilla or low-intensity conflicts, some others might have merited attention: Angola, Chad, Vietnam in Cambodia, Tanzania's invasion of Uganda, the civil war in South Yemen, and so on. Steven David, indeed, provides us some analysis in volume 2 of the Angolan conflict as an example of the use of surrogate forces.

The case studies and methodological vantage points presented in volume 1 seemed, to the editors, to raise a host of questions demanding a more explicitly comparative treatment. So, volume 2 was born.

Many of these questions were raised, directly or indirectly, in Dr. Neuman's conclusions to volume 1—they can be understood as acting somewhat in the manner of dependent variables. How many wars and of what types? How have the wars been fought, at the various levels of strategy, operations, and tactics? Why and how did they start, and with what kinds of mutual assumptions and/or misperceptions? Who won and why, and with what consequences? How did the wars end (if they did), and what were the ramifications?

As "independent" variables in relation to those general questions a number of "functional" areas were chosen for comparative study. These were in turn clustered or ordered in the subsequent chapter outline so as to provide a certain coherence to our overall analysis, or at least to highlight or underscore certain key relationships.

First off, we provide in volume 2 a section on (the very heart of traditional military analysis) the conjunction of weapons, strategies, tactics, and doctrines. Herein are raised anew such fundamental questions as the role of changing weapons technology in shifting advantage to offensive or defensive operations.

At what would appear to be the core of comparative analysis as it is applied to war—particularly as regards the relatively more subjective elements determining who prevails—we chose comparative geography, culture, and economics. These appear fruitfully to comprise a mix of disciplinary perspectives that span the social sciences. And, despite their importance, these subjects, in a comparative sense as applied to war-fighting, have received scant attention from scholars. The efforts here, we think, are both venturesome and important, even if they raise more issues than they resolve.

Finally, we have provided several selections that dwell on the external linkages of these wars, for the most part involving the political/military relations of the combatants with their major power allies or protectors. Even here, as applied to our format, there are some fundamental disagreements among scholars. Some appear to consider most Third World wars as virtually adjuncts—almost as sideshows—to the main event of superpower competition just because their outcomes cannot often fundamentally shift the overall military balance between the superpowers. Others tend rather to see competition for influence in the Third World as increasingly *the* most important element of that competition just because the nuclear balance of terror stalemates that competition at a "higher" level. It is not clear whether these varying perspectives on the meaning of Third World conflict emerge primarily from contrasting ideological perspectives that are then translated into would-be empirical positions.

At any rate, we have provided selections here on security assistance (arms resupply), indigenous Third World arms industries, and surrogate forces, which together provide a panorama of the relationship of the big powers' competition to Third World warfare. The chapter on Third World arms industries reminds us as well of a shifting global system in which some middle-tier states are becoming more important actors, involving new roles as supporters of one or another side to Third World conflict.

The inclusion of a chapter on war termination speaks for itself, perhaps all the more so as virtually none of "our wars" has conclusively been terminated. In a related vein, we could perhaps have used a chapter on the origins or initiations of some of these conflicts. Lacking that in a focused way, the reader will nonetheless note that some attention is paid to that matter within the interstices of other analyses; for instance, the chapter on geography raises some questions about the spatial imperatives for preemptive warfare in some cases, while that on economics looks at the role of domestic economics as a possible cause for some wars.

In the process of editing these two volumes, the editors themselves learned a few lessons. One of them was that, in a rather gradual and somewhat unanticipated way, some key research questions began to emerge amid the nearly overwhelming blizzard of detail. It became obvious, for instance, that far more attention needs be paid to the possible blurring of the traditional distinction between conventional and unconventional warfare, heretofore dealt with as wholly separate traditions of military analysis. Next, the seemingly nearly consistent inability of most Third World combatants to sustain long-range offensive operations—that is to say, to project military power even relatively modest distances outside their own borders—cried out for further analysis. The strictly geographical aspects of guerrilla war—topography, cover, weather, size of theater of operations—clearly had received insufficient attention. So too, on a more historical note, the question of whether patterns of war terminations—rather, the absence of definitive, conclusive endings—were unique to the modern era or were instead reminiscent of some periods of the past. Comparative culture as applied to Third World wars appeared to need more attention, as did the matter of dominant historical images—Munich, Pearl Harbor, Vietnam, Sinai—that determine defense planning as well as interpretations of wars' lessons. We shall return to these questions and others in our concluding, summary chapter.

Notes

1. Edward Luttwak, "Gauging Soviet Arms," *New York Times*, December 31, 1982, p. A19.

2. See Douglas Hart, "Soviet Approaches to Crisis Management: The Military Dimension," *Survival* 26 (September–October 1984): 214–23.

3. Quincy Wright, *A Study of War*, rev. ed. (Chicago: University of Chicago Press, 1965).

4. See J. David Singer and Melvin Small, *The Wages of War, 1816–1965* (New York: Wiley, 1972), and *Resort to Arms: International and Civil Wars, 1816–1980* (Beverly Hills, Calif.: Sage, 1982); Istvan Kende, "Twenty-five Years of Local Wars," *Journal of Peace Research* 8 (1971): 5–27, and "Wars of Ten Years (1967–1976)," *Journal of Peace Research* 15 (1978): 227–41; Richard Ned Lebow, *Between Peace and War* (Baltimore: Johns Hopkins University Press, 1981); Bruce Bueno de Mesquita, *The War Trap* (New Haven: Yale University Press, 1981); Francis Beer, *Peace against War* (San Francisco: W.H. Freeman 1981); and Jack S. Levy, *War in the Modern Great Power System, 1945–1975* (Lexington: University Press of Kentucky, 1983).

5. This is elaborated upon in Walter Emil Kaegi, Jr., "The Crisis in Military Historiography," *Armed Forces and Society* 7 (Spring 1981): 291–316.

6. John Keegan, *The Face of Battle* (London: Jonathan Cape, 1976).

7. For an example of such a perspective, see Jeffrey Record, "Fortunes of War," *Harper's* 260 (April 1980): 19–23.

2
Distant Battles

Eliot A. Cohen

A chieving an understanding of wars in the Third World is difficult. Records are few, inaccurate, and often unavailable; governments frequently have every reason to wish to conceal both success and failure, and to misrepresent the conditions of both; the long-range implications of any action may demand many years to reveal themselves—whether, for example, the Israeli occupation of southern Lebanon in 1982 succeeded or failed depends partly on one's point of view, but partly on the future repercussions of that war. The scholars of contemporary wars should find it sobering to realize that students of a conflict as massively documented and researched as the First World War still argue over the "lessons" of that war. They cannot establish, for example, whether the slaughter on the Western Front reflected inept leadership or the inescapable conditions of early twentieth-century warfare; they cannot agree whether the British expedition to the Dardanelles demonstrates how brilliant strategy can falter through poor organization and tactics, or, conversely, how even courage of the most desperate kind cannot redeem an irretrievably flawed concept of operations. In the face of such uncertainty, some humility about the drawing of lessons is clearly in order.

On the other hand, we have little choice but to make the best judgments we can about the international order under which we live. Three kinds of judgments interest American students of wars in the Third World: those that pertain to conflicts between Third World states; those that may instruct us on the nature of contemporary warfare (and more narrowly, the U.S.-Soviet military balance); and those that can help us understand the peculiar problems the United States may face in conducting wars *against* Third World states. Of these purposes, the first and third strike me as the most likely to prove fruitful, since war does not wear a uniform hue throughout the world in a given epoch, and the political circumstances in which a war occurs, not the tools with which

The author is grateful for comments by Stephanie Neuman, Robert Harkavy, Stephen Rosen, and Williamson Murray on earlier drafts of this article. The views expressed in this article are the author's own and do not necessarily reflect those of the Naval War College or any other government agency.

men wage it, shape its nature. This line of thought, expressed most clearly by Clausewitz, informs the discussion that follows.

It begins with a discussion of strategy—the relationship between politics and war—rather than hardware. We must bear in mind, however, that war is a whole, in which the state of technology, tactical doctrines, and logistics react upon strategy and modify it. From these premises, it would appear that we cannot hope simply to draw up lists of *purely* strategic, or *purely* logistical, or *purely* tactical lessons from any war. Clausewitz himself proceeded analytically, that is, breaking the nature of war down into its fundamental parts, beginning with strategy. At the same time, however, he reminded his reader that "in war more than in any other subject we must begin by looking at the nature of the whole; for here more than elsewhere the part and the whole must always be thought of together."[1]

The first task of a student of war as well as of those responsible for its conduct is, as we have said, to understand the political conditions and context that call it forth.[2] This ordering departs from the practice of many Western journalists who often focus on the technical rather than the strategic lessons of recent wars. Yet such technical assessments may mislead as much as they inform. For example, the 1982 Lebanon war might tell us a great deal about the relative merits of U.S. and Soviet military hardware. On the other hand, the outcome of that war might reflect instead the skill of Israeli and Syrian military organizations, the former operating the latest U.S. technology, the latter operating older Soviet systems, and all taking place in a politically and geographically confined environment. The Lebanon campaign may, in short, have no lessons to offer concerning future air battles in Central Europe.

Strategic considerations, depending as they do on the forms of government and on the basic patterns of international politics, have a more constant aspect than technical ones. Fundamentalist theocracies pursue peculiar ends in particular ways whether their soldiers drive Chieftain tanks or trucks loaded with high explosives. Moreover, and perhaps more importantly, strategic considerations dominate all others: war is about politics; hence, it is with politics that we must begin. If we do not begin our analysis with a discussion of strategy, we will find ourselves reduced to making such trivial observations as that war is becoming more dangerous, or more complex, or briefer—all common assertions found in Western journals, observations that are neither helpful nor accurate.

Strategy

What, then, are the strategic characteristics of recent wars in the Third World? The first and most important observation is that most of these wars—for example, the Lebanon war, the Falklands war, the Sino-Vietnamese war, and the Iran-Iraq war—are all thoroughly postcolonial, or even post-postcolonial. These conflicts have not (even in the case of the Falklands, despite the posturing of the Argentine junta) taken place between an occupying European power in retreat and a movement of "national liberation" (as in Algeria), or between a European power seeking to aid an ex-colonial dependency and a newly independent rival (as in Britain's skirmishes with Indonesia in the early 1960s), or between a European power and a newly independent state over the immediate legacy of colonial rule (as in the case of the Suez war of 1956). The disputes do not stem from the continuation of a colonial war of independence (as in Vietnam) or from civil war in a newly independent state (as in Biafra, or during the early stages of the Arab-Israeli conflict).

Rather, these postcolonial wars have taken place between states that have demonstrated formal and substantive independence for at least several decades. Where fighting *has* occurred between European and Third World states, the old colonial disproportion of power (embodied in Hilaire Belloc's ditty, "Whatever happens/We have got/The Maxim Gun/And they have not") no longer exists. Few observers (particularly British soldiers and sailors) would argue that the Falklands war was a walkover or that the Third World state involved in it lacked the material wherewithal for an even fight. Moreover, the leadership in virtually all of the countries concerned comes from the postcolonial generation. In other words, those conducting these wars did not, for the most part, begin their political lives by leading their nations to independence. In this respect, for example, we can expect the Arab-Israeli conflict to enter shortly a new phase, as the post-1948 generation of·leaders replaces the founding generation in Israel. (In the Arab countries, for the most part, this generational change has already occurred.)

This emergence of a postcolonial world order means that the purposes for which Third World nations fight wars, the means that they have available to them, and the international system in which such wars take place have all changed radically. Wars in the Third World no longer occur in the context of an irresistible dissolution of colonial empires. Even where wars of "national liberation" continue, the enemy (for the Eritreans, Ethiopia, for example) is no longer a distant, internationally isolated, and domestically divided European power, but a local state. The fragile consensus of the neutralist bloc of the 1950s and 1960s has vanished and with it some real inhibitions on the use of force to settle disputes. Instead of a large and superficially united front of Third World states, animated by a common opposition to (largely Western) imperialism, by a common embarrassment over internal squabbles, and by a common fear of border changes, we now see something quite different, the collision of states operating in subsystems of international politics. Instead of a spurious adherence to common principles and views, we see emerging long-term antagonisms between Third World states, for example, Iran versus Iraq, Somalia versus Ethiopia, Morocco versus Algeria, China versus Vietnam. These antipathies—no longer moderated by the presence of a common, Western enemy—will last.

In many regions of the world, we see a pattern familiar to students of Franco-German relations from 1870 to 1914, namely, an enduring suspicion and preparation for war, carefully nursed fears and resentments, a perpetual competition for potential allies, and a constant jockeying for marginal advantages.

These bipolar animuses can, in many instances, feed off recent memories of invasion and counterinvasion—themselves products of the return to conventional warfare characteristic of interstate war. The young nationalisms of the Third World feel violations of national territory with exceptional keenness; in some cases, the magnitude of destruction wrought (in the case of the Iran-Iraq war, some one million casualties on the two sides) further embitters these relations. The operational pattern of most wars in the Third World—the limited-objective surprise attack—results from and in turn enhances these suspicions. Henceforth, in many parts of the world, regional politics and, hence, regional warfare will have as their pivots the mutual hostility of two states, about which all else will revolve.

The intensity of these antipathies, and the fact that the key actors are states rather than guerrilla or political movements, brings other states into the orbit of conflict. Most of the recent wars in the Third World have become coalition wars. Not only do Third World states successfully exploit superpower rivalries in order to gain economic and military support from Washington or Moscow; they have also managed to induce (occasionally, coerce) the aid of other regional powers. The fighting in the Iran-Iraq war takes place between the armed forces of those two states, but the war in the broadest sense—the contest for power, influence, and prestige—takes place between an alliance of Iran, Syria, and Libya, on the one hand, and Iraq, the Gulf States, Egypt, and Jordan, on the other. The same kind of coalition formation takes place in other conflicts as well, principally, though not exclusively, in the involvement of the superpowers as bankers, arms suppliers, ultimate guarantors, or simply influential friends. The Lebanon war involved both superpowers, at least in the form of arms support, and the Sino-Vietnamese war similarly involved the superpowers, although in less dramatic ways. The Algerian-Moroccan conflict involves the United States, as well as Libya, and Mauritania, and so on.

The fact of coalition warfare colors the strategy of those who fight these wars. First, it shapes strategic objectives and the conditions of victory. As Winston Churchill observed in his discussion of the strategy of World War I:

> At the summit true politics and strategy are one. The maneuver which brings an ally into the field is as serviceable as that which wins a great battle. The maneuver which gains an important strategic point may be less valuable than that which placates or overawes a dangerous neutral.[3]

During the Falklands war, the skill of British statesmen in securing the economic support of the European states, the active logistical support of the United States, and the uneasy neutrality of Latin America played as important a role in securing victory as did the undeniable skill and valor of the fleet that went to the South Atlantic. Similarly, the ability of Iraq's Saddam Hussein to bully and wheedle billions of dollars from his Persian Gulf neighbors has kept his state and its war alive despite initial fiascoes and the virtual collapse of his main source of revenue, oil exports. In coalition warfare, a shrewd strategist will make his strategic objective the integrity of the enemy's alliance system, rather than his capital or army.[4] Observers of these wars (and, for that matter, participants in them) will misjudge them if they focus on the clash of two nations' armies rather than on the larger whole.

Coalition wars have usually taken years or decades to run their course; often they come to inconclusive ends. This flows from the simple fact that the real resources on both sides may be greater than first appears, and from the changing political complexion of such wars, in which the success of one side may cause other states to join the opposition or, if already committed, to intensify their participation in the war. Thus too in wars in the Third World. The Iran-Iraq war has lasted for five years; the Sino-Vietnamese conflict for longer yet; and similarly for the Israeli-Syrian confrontation. As in the wars of the eighteenth century, short periods of intense fighting punctuate much longer periods of uneasy truce, during which the primary antagonists (in the eighteenth century, England and France) rebuild their forces and attempt to attract new allies. Even the Falklands war has not really ended, as Britain's construction of "Fortress Falklands" has demonstrated, and it is hardly inconceivable that a new Argentine government (or even the current one, under the right conditions) might renew the battle with various forms of harassment or even outright invasion. In order to understand these wars, therefore, we must take a far longer view than that taken by technological lessons-seekers.

A third strategic characteristic of recent wars in the Third World concerns the unusual advantages Third World leaders have in conducting these wars. Western analysts often regard wars in the Third World as inferior, miniature copies of the real thing—war between the Great Powers. Insofar as this assumption refers to the technology and operational art of such wars, they may often (though not necessarily always) be right. But insofar as strategy goes, the very reverse might be true. Leaders in the Third World have certain innate advantages in the formulation of strategy that considerably outweigh those of their Western contemporaries.

For one thing, Third World leaders have the tremendous advantage of having relatively narrow horizons. They know their enemies and can turn their full attention to coping with them. Their armed forces know (or in theory can know) exactly where and whom they will fight and, within limits, how they will fight. As a result, we see a concentration of attention that countries such as the United States and even the Soviet Union simply cannot hope to duplicate. The Argentines could score a remarkable success in their occupation of the Falkland islands because they had only two potential enemies to consider: Chile and Great Britain. The British, on the other hand, even in their much shrunken international role of the early 1980s, had other international troubles to concern them and divert their attention. President Hafez al-Assad of Syria adroitly outmaneuvered the United States in Lebanon in 1983 in part because he could give his full attention to the manipulation of that exceedingly complex situation; President Reagan could not. In short, in wars in the Third World, strategy making really can exist, in a way that it cannot in the chancelleries of world powers preoccupied with crisis management.

Moreover, Third World leaders often have the capacity to take the initiative, to act offensively rather than reactively, that their counterparts in the First World do not. Where U.S. and Soviet leaders, for example, must weigh the potential for a cataclysmic nuclear confrontation between the superpowers, Third World leaders live with no such incubus. In addition, the extreme centralization of power in many Third World states makes it possible for one man, or at the most a very small group of men, to take far-ranging decisions with a minimum of consultation or consensus making. The Argentine seizure of the Falklands (an episode as instructive and almost as impressive as the subsequent British counterattack), the Iraqi invasion of Iran, the Egyptian and Syrian attack on Israel in 1973, the Israeli invasion of Lebanon in 1982—each required a decision by no more than two or three men at the very top.

Finally, modern Third World states often can rely on what Michael Howard has termed the social basis of strategy for at least the opening stages of a conflict.[5] Sometimes society gives this support freely; at other times governments must extort it by terror. The peculiar cast of wars in the Third World attributable to the nature of public support will be discussed below.

Operations and Tactics

Strategy refers to the relationship between political ends and military means; operations fall into the area between strategy and tactics (the conduct of specific battles). To use a Soviet definition, operations refer to "the theory and practice of preparing for and conducting combined and independent operations by major field forces or major formations of services."[6] For our purposes, operations refer to actions by large formations and combined service operations. We will begin by looking at the latter problem of "triphibious warfare," as General Eisenhower once called it, and then examine the peculiar operational patterns of wars in the Third World.

The nearly universal division of armed forces into three services, land, sea, and air, reflects not simply the accidental evolution of parochial and self-interested bureaucracies, but the existence of three distinct forms of warfare. Environmental conditions shape the technological level and organizational culture of the three services that wage these forms of warfare, and this holds as true in the Third World as anywhere else. What is remarkable about most wars in the Third World is the predominance of ground warfare, the ineffectiveness (with one or two remarkable exceptions) of air warfare, and the virtual absence of naval warfare. To some extent, this reflects the intrinsic decisiveness of land warfare: only armies can occupy capitals or subdue and police populations. Nonetheless, the weakness of the two other forms of warfare requires explanation.

The usual explanation has it that air and naval warfare require high levels of technical expertise not available to most Third World states. But, as we shall see below, a scarcity of technical expertise in a narrow sense does not characterize all or even most Third World armed forces. Rather, the difficulty in using naval and air power stems from several causes, most notably the strategic context of most wars in the Third World, that is, the prevalence of wars of limited political objectives. Naval and air warfare play a large role in the outcome of conflicts with total objectives, where the tools of blockade, large-scale amphibious landings, and the destruction of an enemy's economic infrastructure contribute to his final collapse. Most wars in the Third World, however, have far more limited objectives; hence naval and air forces serve as adjuncts to the ground forces, which attempt to seize decisive bits of territory for political advantage.

The very nature of air and naval warfare, however, and not simply the complexity of the weapons involved, also affects the ways in which Third World states can use them. Table 2–1 illustrates some of the outstanding differences among the three forms of warfare.

We notice naval engagements in wars in the Third World (with the exception of the Indian Navy's operations during the 1971 war with Pakistan) primarily for their absence. Part of the explanation for this phenomenon has to

Table 2–1
Three Forms of Warfare

	Land	*Sea*	*Air*
1. Number of units	Many	Very few	Few
2. Dependence on special basing	Low	Medium	High
3. Officers are mainly	Leaders	Leaders/ technicians	Fighters
4. Enlisted men are mainly	Fighters	Technicians/ fighters	Technicians
5. Operational penalties for minor organizational or technical failures	Low	Very high	High
6. Degree of centralized operational control required	Low	High	High
7. Time required to reconstitute organization and equipment after defeat and/or heavy losses	Short	Very long	Long

do with the highly centralized character of naval battles. Naval engagements and campaigns require extremely close coordination of a handful of major units. Admirals can order their forces at sea to maneuver with a degree of expectation that their wishes will be fulfilled about which a general on land can only dream.[7] However, without adequate control, the scope for disaster at sea (loss of a fleet) far exceeds that on land. An inept attack on land may cause heavy casualties, but it may not lead immediately to disaster, and unless the generals have conceived the attack extraordinarily badly, the opponent will suffer damage as well. At sea, however, wins and losses usually take a very lopsided form—the sinking of the *Belgrano,* for example (or, for that matter, Trafalgar or Midway). Third World admirals have only a few ships (Argentina, for example, had barely a dozen major combatants) and, reasonably enough, feel loath to risk them in major naval engagements.[8] Hence the preference for naval guerrilla warfare conducted by small craft or by a handful of submarines. Rarely, however, can such means achieve command of the sea (ability to use the ocean safely for one's own shipping) or even deny its use to the enemy.

Other considerations hamper naval operations as well. First, any conflict that might spill over into international waters runs the risk of offending the great maritime powers, particularly the United States. These states have substantial interests in the free flow of shipping, and possess both the wherewithal to protect that shipping and the will to do so. The discrepancies between the maritime power that the United States can project anywhere in the Third World and the capacity of indigenous states to resist that power far exceeds the comparable differences on land. A second element that may restrain long-range naval operations is the failure of most countries to develop adequate naval air power, projected either from extremely expensive aircraft carriers or from land bases. In the latter case, few countries in the Third World have managed to resolve the inevitable battle between air forces and navies for control of such aircraft. Third, conduct of prolonged naval operations (as opposed to the kind of coastal raiding characteristic of the Arab-Israeli wars and the Iran-Iraq war) requires a kind of logistical depth that very few states possess. This matter will be discussed further below. Finally, small but inferior navies can often preserve themselves by holing up in well-defended harbors or by simply leaving the theater of operations, yet still exercise some influence on the course of the war by their very existence—what Mahan termed the fleet-in-being strategy. Air and ground forces find it more difficult to avoid battle and have fewer strategic consolations (or rationalizations) for inaction.

Air campaigns can only achieve decisive results under one of two conditions: if a central leadership wields air power against one or two target systems, or if an air force can win and exploit utter and undisputed air superiority. The desultory air campaigns of the Iran-Iraq war, the virtual absence of aerial combat in the Sino-Vietnamese conflict, the ultimate failure of the Argentine Air Force, and even the inability of the Israeli Air Force to turn Arab defeats in

1973 and 1982 into routs, all point to a surprisingly small role for air power in wars in the Third World. This should not surprise us, since air operations had a major effect in World War II under only one of two operational conditions: when a particular target system (railroad marshaling yards, oil plants, or cities, for example) received intense and carefully directed blows day after day for months, or when one side could exploit complete air superiority over an enemy's rear areas for comparable periods of time.[9] To achieve the former, an air force needs the ability to sustain high levels of daily operational readiness, for speed and concentration of destruction, and not simply its weight, determine success. This readiness must continue despite steady losses and the strain of continued operations. For the latter operational condition (air superiority), one must often physically destroy an enemy's air force, and have fliers willing to fly low, braving antiaircraft fire to shoot up road convoys, bridges, and supply dumps.

Third World states can only rarely pursue either strategic bombing or tactical air dominance. Although pilots may have the requisite skills to perform these missions, the organizations that must support them may lack the skilled maintenance manpower and the stocks of spare parts and ammunition to sustain them in prolonged combat. Often, the sheer numbers of aircraft involved are too small to tolerate even relatively low levels of attrition, since Third World states can rarely replace their aircraft from current or near-term production. An air force of 150 frontline aircraft, each of which flew three sorties a day and suffered an attrition rate of 2 percent, would have fewer than 70 operable planes left at the end of two weeks—losses that the high command of a Third World state might find as distressing because of the low *absolute* number of aircraft that would remain as the *relative* loss of strength suffered. The diffusion of antiaircraft technology in the Third World—simple heat-seeking missiles and rapid-fire antiaircraft cannon—ensures that except in unusual cases, even when an enemy air force has succumbed, its ground forces will still exact a toll from one's own air force. The diffusion of even simpler defensive technologies (concrete shelter construction, for instance) makes it increasingly difficult to obliterate an enemy's air force on the ground, as the Israelis did in 1967 and the Indians did in East (though not West) Pakistan in 1971.

Air warfare in the Third World, therefore, may resemble naval warfare more than it has at any time in the past. During the 1940s, for example, aircraft, like tanks, could be produced in large numbers, that is, the thousands. Today, however, this is not the case. Syria and Israel, for example, currently maintain tank inventories of approximately the same size as those maintained by France and Germany before World War II; their air forces, however, are an order of magnitude smaller. (Even in the last decade the Syrian plane-to-tank ratio has gone from 0.2 to 0.12, the Israeli ratio from 0.17 to 0.15, using International Institute for Strategic Studies' *Military Balance* figures).[10] Moreover, where pilot training took approximately a year during World War II, today it takes much longer—three years or more. As a result, both the machines and the men who fly them are scarcer and more expensive commodities than in the past. The Third World air force general, like his naval counterpart, may choose low-attrition operational doctrines in order to avoid losing the small absolute number of irreplaceable (at least in the short term) men and machines under his command.

Even assuming that a Third World country has the steadiness of nerve and material ability to sustain the kinds of losses that a serious bombing or air superiority campaign requires, it may lack the ability at the highest levels to conduct such a campaign properly. Third World air forces rarely have the kind of centralized operational control that World War II history suggests they would require. In many countries, the ground forces dominate the other two and hence can insist on a priority to ground support rather than comprehensive air superiority. In other cases, operational centralization of any kind poses too great a threat to a regime's survival for a prudent government to allow it. Finally, decisive air campaigns require not only men, planes, munitions, and mainte-nance support, but highly efficient and prompt intelligence services that can use many intelligence sources to gather targeting and damage assessment in-formation, analyze it, and provide the results in usable form to operational staffs. Third World states may lack these capabilities.[11]

It is therefore not surprising that land power—protean, reconstitutable, fault-tolerant, and relatively cheap—appeals most to Third World states, and plays the greatest role in their wars. This is not to say that air power, in par-ticular, plays no part in the conduct or outcome of such wars, but rather to say that it does not play a decisive one. As for naval power, with the important exception of littoral warfare, it seems to have played a negligible role thus far, and there seems little prospect of a change in that respect.

What of the second aspect of operational art in wars in the Third World, namely, patterns of war conduct? We can distinguish four trends that seem par-ticularly important for the course of future wars, all of which flow from the strategic conditions of war discussed above. The first of these is the predom-inance of the surprise, set-piece, but limited offensive (as opposed to a meeting engagement or a blitzkrieg, aimed at decisive victory). The Chinese invasion of Vietnam, the Iraqi invasion of Iran, the Argentine seizure of the Falklands, the Israeli invasion of Lebanon, and earlier, the Indo-Pakistani war of 1971 (which opened with a remarkably feeble Pakistani attack on India) all fit this pattern. Third World states can often achieve surprise but frequently find themselves frustated by their inability to exploit it. They do not pursue, by and large, what Hans Delbrück termed *Niederwerfungsstrategie,* or the strategy of overthrow, and rely instead on what he called *Ermattungsstrategie,* the strategy of exhaustion.[12] The limited but sudden offensive enables its user to seize a piece of strategic territory and then assume the operational and tactical defensive, in the hope that the attacker will find himself unable to regain his position, since the tactical defense is intrinsically the stronger form of war. The Egyptian assault on Israel's Bar-Lev line in 1973 provides a classic example of this combination of strategic offense and tactical defense which served Egypt's political ends—breaking a political deadlock—superbly. The Iraqi attack on Iran in 1980 achieved similar initial successes, although it quickly bogged down, for reasons that include sheer operational incompetence and unexpected resistance from the inhabitants of Khuzistan. In each case, the attacker assumed that possession of a politically significant slice of territory would considerably improve his bargaining position in the peace negotiations that followed.

The second operational characteristic, attrition warfare, follows from the first. The initiator of the limited offensive assumes that a period of counterattacks may follow but hopes that they will prove fruitless and end with a favorable settlement. When, as in the case of the Iran-Iraq war, the attacker miscalculates badly, prolonged attrition warfare results. Third World states by and large lack the supporting infrastructure to carry out true blitzkrieg warfare—the kind of war that shatters an enemy's entire armed force at a stroke and leaves the enemy homeland completely defenseless. Even when a state could, in theory, conduct such a *Niederwerfung* campaign (Israel, for example), it finds itself constrained by the coalitional nature of modern warfare. In the case of the Middle Eastern wars, the intervention of the superpowers has swiftly brought to an end (and will continue to do so) any such attempt to fight a modern campaign in the style of 1866, 1870, or 1940. Increasingly, however, Third World states do have the ability to stick out a long period (years or more) of low-level conflict, punctuated by shorter bursts of intense fighting.

Wars of attrition need not end with a whimper. The greatest one of them all, World War I, ended with the collapse of almost every combatant, with the exception of the British (barely) and the United States. Indeed, one can say that the victor in such wars is simply the state that collapses last. The victory thus won, as the example of World War I should remind us, may take as complete and thorough a form as any war brought to an end by blitzkrieg. Thus far, however, only one war in the Third World has followed this pattern of attrition and collapse, namely, the Vietnam War (or more precisely, its civil component). The enormous losses suffered on both sides in the course of the Iran-Iraq war, however, may lead to just such an outcome, rather than (as many commentators expect) a mere petering out of the conflict. Even then, this collapse would probably take the form either of major regime change in one of the two principal belligerents, rather than the physical occupation by one of the other.

Attritional warfare produces long periods of seeming stalemate, during which both sides seek means of achieving a decision by resorting to radically new weapons or doctrines, as well as by simply increasing the weight of their current efforts. The third operational pattern, therefore, is the resort to unconventional means of warfare as a supplement (not alternative) to the conventional ground offensive. The use of chemical weapons in the Iran-Iraq war and, it would appear, in Southeast Asia provides one example of this. Far more frequently, the warring states encourage insurgencies or terrorist activity behind the enemy's lines. India's use of the Mukhti Bahini in East Pakistan, the manipulation of the Kurdish insurgency by both sides in the Iran-Iraq war, Chinese support for Cambodian insurgents, and Syrian support for Palestinian and now Shiite terrorists in the war with Israel—all of these unconventional means help divert an opponent's resources and attention before a conventional conflict and (the attacker hopes) paralyze his movements during it. Western analysts often accept far too easily the distinction between conventional and unconventional warfare, as in the current U.S. debate on the pointless question, "Was the Vietnam War a conventional war or an insurgency?" As in so many wars in the Third World today, it had both dimensions, and those on the other side treated insurgency as but another weapon in their armory.

Although few wars have yet had an explicitly nuclear dimension, we have seen preemptive strikes directed against an Iraqi reactor and possibly against an Iranian one. Whether future wars in the Third World will take place under a nuclear shadow we cannot predict, but in a number of conflicts between nuclear weapons and nonnuclear weapons states (the Falklands, Arab-Israeli wars, Sino-Vietnamese wars), atomic weapons have played no role. The open use of poison gas by Iraq provides a much more open and dangerous precedent for the use of unconventional weapons.

A fourth pattern, and an odd one, is the urbanization of warfare. A surprising number of major (that is, large and politically important) battles have occurred in cities; Khorramshahr, Beirut, and Lang Son are only three examples. Why should this be the case? In the first part, the limited offensive followed by the war of attrition often has a highly political operational objective, best served not by slaughtering a fixed number of enemy soldiers but by capturing and retaining a politically important piece of real estate. In classic Clausewitzian thought, the enemy's army, not his territory, was the most usual (although not under all conditions the most appropriate) object. Clausewitz saw that only by disarming the enemy, rendering him helpless and harmless, could a government gain decisive objectives.[13] The German panzer divisions did not immediately enter Paris in 1940, preferring instead to consummate the destruction of the French army first. In another total conflict, the American Civil War, the end for the Confederate States did not come until Northern generals concentrated on the destruction of the Confederate armies rather than on the capture of Richmond.

When governments wage war for limited rather than total objectives, however, the capture of a city can achieve the purpose they desire. The Chinese wished to capture a provincial capital in order to demonstrate to the Vietnamese and their patrons their ability to inflict pain on North Vietnam. The Iraqis evidently expected the capture of the main cities of Khuzistan to induce the Iranians to come to terms, or the local Arab residents of those towns to desert their Persian rulers.

Sometimes, as in the case of Beirut, and possibly in the Khuzistan campaign, the weaker side may actually prefer to fight in the city, where irregular infantry armed with cheap antitank rockets and machine guns can fight a more ponderous mechanized opponent on equal terms. Urban warfare is dispersed and unusually chaotic warfare, and with few exceptions allows the defender to impose heavy casualties on his opponent. In some cases, moreover, city fighting gives a defender a chance to create his own civilian martyrs for the benefit of both a domestic audience and an international one (that is, anyone within reach of television). To some extent, too, the new phenomenon of urban warfare simply reflects the growing urbanization of the Third World, which parallels that of the industrialized world.

Technology

Students of conventional arms transfers often sound the alarm over the transfer of high technology weapons—sophisticated jet fighters and cruise missiles—to the Third World.[14] Conventional arms transfers can elevate tensions and ultimately provoke war (as in the 1956 war between Israel and Egypt, touched off in part by the 1955 sale of large quantities of Czech arms to the latter country). And in some cases, they may put a supplier in the uncomfortable position of having his own weapons turned against him—as the British very nearly discovered in the Falklands.

On the other hand, two contradictory views of arms sales to the Third World—that the weapons increase the lethality of war and that their new owners find them too complicated to handle—are both incorrect. The great killer in all of the wars under discussion has been the simplest of technology, the artillery round, which is not greatly different from its ancestor of World War I (with the possible exception of cluster bomb units, which, however, do not differ that greatly in *conception* from the shrapnel shell of the beginning of the war). The high-technology Exocet missile, for example, has caused only a handful of casualties in the Persian Gulf war, barely managing to sink a single ship; in the Falklands, the iron bomb dropped by brave, low-flying pilots caused far greater damage.[15] Indeed, some kinds of high-technology weapons probably *decrease* lethality. The evidence from the two wars in which Exocets have been used suggests that pilots understandably tend to launch their weapons at very long ranges, in order to maximize their own chances of survival. This practice, however, although safer for the pilot than direct bombing, also appears to be safer for the ship's crew as well, which may (by luck or because of adroit countermeasures) avoid or destroy the missile. In one case in the Falklands, one of the Argentine Exocets struck a merchant ship rather than one of the two British aircraft carriers.

On the other hand, Western analysts seem consistently to have underestimated the ability of Third World states to handle advanced technology. When President Sadat of Egypt expelled Soviet advisers from Egypt in 1972, Western news accounts suggested that the Egyptian surface-to-air missile (SAM) system would no longer operate efficiently. More recently, neither French nor British intelligence analysts appear to have predicted that the Argentines would be able to fit their newly acquired Exocet missiles to their fighter-bombers, a delicate task.[16] Iranian ingenuity in using F-14 aircraft that had been partially disabled (mainly through a lack of spare parts) as miniature airborne warning posts, and their skill at countering Iraqi missile attacks on shipping in the northern Gulf, speaks equally well of the technical ability of Third World states to handle modern weaponry, even under difficult conditions.[17] Indeed, in some cases high technology proves more appropriate to certain Third World states that have a constricted manpower pool and think (not without reason) that they will do well to minimize their disadvantages by using the very best weapons poorly, rather than mediocre weapons well.[18]

By and large, the level of technology has not proved decisive in wars in the Third World, although in one case (that of Israel) technological superiority clearly goes hand-in-hand with organizational skills of a high order. The most murderous technologies have proved to be some of the oldest—the RPG-7 (the Soviet unguided antitank rocket), for example, the mortar, the gun-howitzer. Even when such basic weapons as these and others (land mines, for example) have been improved by modern technology, they remain cheap and relatively simple and hence attractive to Third World states.

What has changed, however, is the widespread availability in quantity of the basic *consumables* of war. The dispersion of weapons manufacturing technologies to the Third World has begun to attract critical attention, yet more important than the growth in the number of states that can manufacture jet aircraft is the increase in the number of states that produce basic types of ammunition.[19] Most basic types of artillery conform either to Soviet or NATO standards, and the same is true of small arms and mortars. The Indochina wars, the Middle East wars, the oil wealth of the Persian Gulf and Libya, and the use by both Western and Eastern states of arms sales to increase influence, expand their military-industrial production base, and make money have flooded the world with large inventories of modern artillery pieces, small arms, and tanks. Commentators often remark on the rise of Third World producers of sophisticated military hardware such as tanks, light aircraft, and artillery such as Brazil and Israel; equally important, however, are the burgeoning arms industries of Egypt, Pakistan, China, Singapore, and South Africa, which do a good business making ammunition and refurbishing old equipment.

The resulting *quantitative* change in the availability of basic weapons and ammunition has, in the long run, important *qualitative* ramifications. Wars in the Third World have become high firepower wars, in which armies deluge their opponents with volumes of small arms fire and barrages that would have been inconceivable twenty years ago.[20] High rates of fire have several consequences, among them high casualty rates and collateral damage; the reemergence, as a consequence, of extensive field fortifications (mutually supporting strongpoints linked by minefields, barbed wire, and other obstacles, all echeloned in depth); and ponderous rates of advance, caused not only by the difficulty of securing a breakthrough, but by the need for supply that commanders accustomed to lavish support begin to believe they need.[21] The result is a battlefield that a poilu of 1917 would have found depressingly familiar.

In addition, as long as countries can raise the cash (and sometimes even if they cannot), they can usually purchase ammunition from a growing number of suppliers. No longer will a few weapons producers be able (as in the 1950 Tripartite Agreement in the Middle East) to control the armament levels or the readiness rates of Third World states. Moreover, states will less frequently find themselves unable to find for political reasons a supplier state. The implications of this development are discussed further below.

Logistics

"The amateurs discuss strategy; the experts discuss logistics." This well-known jab at contemporary military criticism has much to support it. For military analysts, including newspaper readers, whose understanding of war is shaped by maps on which a thirty-mile mountain road occupies less than an inch of space, logistics is the excuse given by bad generals for their failures. It is, in fact, a matter of critical importance, and one to which military historians have only belatedly begun to give due attention.[22]

It is in respect to logistics—the art of moving men and material into battle and sustaining them there—that Third World military forces face their gravest problems. Many of the wars that have not occurred, such as an Egyptian invasion of Libya in the 1970s, have been stymied by difficulties of supply and maintenance. The one example of a Third World army whose chief commander concentrated on logistics gives us the exception that proves the rule. Douglas Pike remarks that an essential element in Vietnamese Communist strategy is

> infinite, meticulous, endless attention to mundane matters of logistics and administration. Moving troops rapidly is one of General Giap's unique abilities, made possible by the careful stockpiling along the route of arms, ammunition, food, and medical supplies, often involving unbelievable effort.[23]

Indeed, only the persistence of the Viet Cong and North Vietnamese forces coupled with this kind of mastery of logistics accounts for the victory of an armed force that time and time again exposed itself to enormous human losses against a materially superior foe. On the other hand, the Vietnamese have taken many years to develop these abilities, and have not always proved capable of sustaining major offensives (in the early 1950s against the French, in 1965–66, in 1968, and 1972).

The magnitude of Giap's achievement, and of the difficulties faced by his counterparts in other Third World states, can only be understood if we understand the nature of the logistical difficulties faced by Third World armies. The motorization and mechanization of Third World armies, and the quantum rise in ammunition consumption referred to above, have vastly increased the logistical problem involved in supporting and sustaining large military operations. Although Third World armies may have simpler equipment than Western armies do, and their soldiers fewer wants, the burden of training, feeding, housing, and sustaining them remains immense.[24]

Logisticians have always faced a critical problem known as "the logistic snowball," a kind of Parkinson's Law of military operations, which holds that logistical difficulties increase geometrically when the size of the forces involved, or their activities, increase arithmetically. One particularly acute student of this problem identifies two subproblems, "the under-planning over-planning sequence" and the problem of second-rate personnel. In the first instance, a narrow escape by a logistically overstretched commander leads him to overestimate his needs in a particular area (for example, diesel fuel). Comfortable surpluses in another area, however (for example, rifle ammunition), do not normally lead to compensating reductions in requirements.[25]

As for the quality of support personnel, Eccles observes:

> The supply of highly efficient officers, men, and civilian employees is always limited in war. If inefficient personnel are involved, it is likely that many of them will spend their time doing useless tasks, and each administrative unit and staff, accordingly, will expand in order to get the work done. This results from a lowering of quality, which in turn leads to sluggishness in response and to a generally lower quality of planning and administration. This, again, leads to a demand for more personnel with the corollary increases in transportation, housing, messing, medical, and management personnel.[26]

Acute as this problem may be in Western armies, it is far worse in Third World armies, which almost by definition face an acute shortage of the kind of managerial expertise needed. It may not be entirely surprising, therefore, that the logistically adept Vietnamese have managed to cripple their national economy, in part because most of the high-quality managerial personnel serve in the Vietnamese Army.

The shortage of high-quality leaders (many of whom will be siphoned off into the more prestigious combat arms) causes one kind of logistical difficulty;

the socio-political structure of many Third World countries (familiar to many students of socialist economies as well) further inhibits logistical effectiveness. One study of Middle Eastern military organizations found no "*absolute* barriers to training operations and logistics support personnel for sophisticated weapons." Rather,

> Supply systems provide ample illustration of organizations where traditional patterns of authority and responsibility have constrained efficient performance. The reluctance to release accumulated hoards, the insistence on face-to-face transactions, the fascination with forms and stamps, and the disposition to seek higher-level approval for trivial decisions means, for example, that a parts inventory may remain in excess in one location while equipment is grounded for want of the same item at a nearby base.[27]

The operational pattern described above—preplanned limited offensive followed by a war of attrition—helps Third World states minimize the logistical friction that afflicts them. Yet even so, the bogging down of the Iraqi and Chinese attacks and the Argentine army's acute problems of distributing food to its forces in the Falklands testify to the problems Third World armies have in conducting operations over long distances or in difficult terrain. The absence of adequate roads and rail networks in much of the Third World, of course, further exacerbates the difficulty of logistical support.[28]

In addition to problems of logistics narrowly defined, Third World armies also find themselves hard pressed by difficulties of maintenance. This in turn stems from two phenomena: dependence on external suppliers for spare parts (true even for the most militarily autarkic Third World states), and inadequate organizational depth to maintain complex supply and maintenance systems. Simply put, most Third World states can provide pilots to fly their planes, but have difficulty developing adequate ground crews, stocks of spare parts, and maintenance facilities to serve them during intensive operations. In the Falklands war, for example, the British were able to fly many more sorties than their Argentine opponents, in part because their airplanes operated closer to the battlefield (although the Argentine advantage of having large land bases partially compensated for this), but also because of the skill and abilities of their maintenance crews. Planes conducted up to six sorties a day, at which point pilot fatigue, not maintenance problems, grounded the planes. Similarly, in all of the Arab-Israeli wars, the Israeli Air Force relied as much on the ability of its ground crews swiftly to reprovision and maintain airplanes as it did on the skills of its pilots.[29]

Third World air forces in particular, then, often lack the kind of organizational depth required for prolonged and effective operations. Not only do they lack the sheer numbers and production base required to build the necessary airplanes, they also lack the pilot and ground crew training, the reserves of spare parts, and the maintenance depots to do more than keep up a low operating tempo.

Such vulnerabilities do not manifest themselves, however, until fairly late in a war; during the opening days of a limited objectives offensive (as in the case of the Arab attack on Israel in 1973), such air forces may carry out their missions successfully.[30]

The difficulty of sustaining the operation of complex military organizations such as air forces contributes to the reliance on ground forces noted above and to the dominance in war of such simple but robust weapons as gun-howitzers and multiple rocket launchers. By turning to defensive operations, a Third World army can greatly ease its logistical difficulties—hence the preference for the tactical defense in the wake of a surprise attack.[31] The diffusion of basic ammunition and spare parts manufacturing technologies means that a country can hope to take advantage of a lull in the fighting to rebuild stocks of these items either from local production or through imports. Unlike previous wars, future conflicts in the Third World need not come to a sudden end because national logistics have failed completely, but rather because of temporary logistical crises at both the theater and national levels.

The experience of wars in the Third World suggests that the logistic intervention of outside states—the resupply efforts of the United States and the Soviet Union in the Middle East wars, or Soviet resupply and logistic efforts in the Somali-Ethiopia war—offers the superpowers the greatest leverage over the outcome of such wars. This last point harks back to our discussion of the coalition nature of most wars in the Third World. By and large, the "teeth" of Third World armies outstrip the "tail" required to support them. Tempted or encouraged to invest heavily in such visible and high-prestige items as aircraft or tanks, Third World armies find themselves suddenly dependent in wartime on urgent external resupply of spare parts and even the technicians to install them. When they cannot get such resupply (as in the case of Pakistan in 1965, Argentina in the Falklands, or Somalia in the latter stages of the war with Ethiopia), a military collapse or at least an abrupt halt in the fighting occurs. This pattern, however, may not continue indefinitely, as Third World militaries begin stockpiling ammunition and spare parts. (For the foreseeable future, however, only the superpowers will be able to afford the stockpiling of major weapon systems such as aircraft.)

Finally, a sound maxim of logistics holds that:

> A logistical system should be in harmony with its supporting economic system. Among other things, this implies that for the greatest effectiveness and efficiency the military should make the maximum practicable use of civilian equipment and techniques.[32]

The logistical slack of the British merchant marine in the Falklands and the harmony between civil and military transportation and maintenance sectors in Israel clearly strengthened those two states in their recent conflicts. In that respect, as in others, a healthy economy contributes to military power *during* wars, as well as in the periods of buildup that precede them.[33] Thus, the notion that modern warfare is strictly a "come as you are" affair, that is, one in which the underlying strength of an economy comes into play only before the war but not during it (a view often expressed by U.S. military leaders), seems incorrect.

Society and Psychology

In all of the wars under discussion, in only one case (the Falklands war) has defeat or a major setback caused a government to fall. The reason for that collapse was obvious: a military dictatorship becomes a laughingstock when it appears manifestly incompetent at the one thing its leaders can claim to be good at. The Turkish invasion of Cyprus caused the similar dissolution of the Greek junta in 1974. Yet in other cases—most noticeably those of Somalia, Syria, and Iraq—heavy losses and battlefield defeats in wars that those states had started did *not* lead to a change in government. One lesson of recent wars in the Third World, therefore, is that most civilian regimes display astonishing resiliency and control in the face of defeat. This was not always the case: the Egyptian government after 1949 and the Syrian government after 1967 fell to coups d'état soon after their defeats. What accounts for this change?

The basic reason appears brutally simple: many Third World states have become quite good at suppressing dissent. The technical and organizational skills required to terrorize opponents into submission, coupled with centrally controlled propaganda machines that flood a country with images of an omnipotent and omniscient president, have kept leaders in power who might otherwise have lost office and life in a swift coup. Third World leaders might be vulnerable to assassination, perhaps (the death of Anwar Sadat is an example), but such conspiracies must be small in order to survive and are as a result incapable of seizing state power. By and large, the secret police apparatuses of modern Third World states—often trained by outsiders from the Warsaw Pact, Western states, or some of the more sophisticated Third World states— protect leaders against medium-sized revolts, the kinds of coups that bedeviled the Vietnamese government in the last years of Diem until the rise of President Thieu, for instance. Genuine revolutions will not, perhaps, easily succumb to such measures (as the Shah of Iran discovered), but the early manifestations of revolutionary activity can. The leveling of the Syrian town of Hamma in 1982 by government forces seeking to crush the activities of the Moslem Brotherhood seems to have temporarily, at any rate, paralyzed the opposition to the Assad regime. In the words of one Western journalist:

> The Assad regime wanted to send a message to its residents and the rest of
> Syria on what would happen to those who challenged its leadership, and the

message got through loud and clear. There has been no anti-government activity of any note in Syria since. I remember being struck by the fact that during the whole day I spent in Hamma, I saw only one Syrian soldier. After
what the Syrian army had done to the city, that was probably all the government needed to keep the peace—one soldier.[34]

Not all regimes in the Third World play by "Hamma rules," but many will,
if pressed, act with equal if more selective ruthlessness.

In addition to using sheer repression and terror, Third World leaders often
protect themselves by maintaining personnel promotion systems and organizational rivalries that inhibit coup making. Frequent rotation of top-level commanders, the creation of special (and hated) presidential guard units, split lines
of authority, exploitation of ethnic rivalries, and selection of subordinates on
the basis of political reliability or kinship rather than professional expertise—all
help shield Third World leaders to a remarkable degree from the consequences
of their failures. These practices exact a price, of course, in terms of military
efficiency, which may help contribute to the problem in the first place.
Nonetheless, some states (Syria, in particular) seem to have found a reasonable
trade-off between reliability and efficiency. Ironically, only democratic Third
World states (for example, Israel) and Communist ones (for example, Vietnam) can rely sufficiently on orderly civilian control of the military to such
an extent that they need take few precautions against a military or joint civilian-
military putsch.

Coupled with the negative measures of control discussed above are positive
sources of support—that is, militaristic chauvinism—unfamiliar to most contemporary Western states. As Michael Howard once remarked, the experience
of World War I "de-bellated" Western societies. These societies could accept
war as a grim necessity, perhaps, but never again would they march off to it
singing, as they did in 1914. Despite short fits of militaristic patriotism (as
in Britain during the Falklands war), Western societies (and the same would
probably be true of the Soviet Union) can treat only minor conflicts with such
exuberance. The prospect of large wars they face with grim determination at
best, despair at worst. This does not yet hold true in much of the Third World,
where nationalist, ethnic, and religious passions still feed nationalist fervor of
a kind quite unthinkable in the West. Whether such fervor can withstand a
prolonged slaughter, as in the Iran-Iraq war, is another matter. Nonetheless,
Third World states have a surprisingly solid social base from which to support
prolonged wars.

The ability of governments to manipulate nationalist and religious fervor
suggests that the sources of low-level cohesion and effectiveness in Third World
armies may be quite different from those of the more advanced states. It is
perhaps too easily accepted as a given in the literature on military cohesion
that small group relations, rather than broader concerns, determine a unit's

cohesiveness. While this may hold true for Western armies, it is not necessarily the case in those of the Third World—the human wave assaults of the Iranian Revolutionary Guards are a case in point.[35] We need much more thorough study of the nature of unit cohesion in Third World armies than we currently have, and we must avoid the mirror-imaging fallacy that affects our ability to understand cohesion in foreign armies more generally. One of the most unpleasant surprises experienced by American and British soldiers during World War II was the extraordinary willingness of Japanese soldiers to fight literally to the death—a characteristic found in the modern world only among some Shiites in Iran and Lebanon. At the same time, we should beware the mistake of exaggerating the advantages that accrue to Third World armies by virtue of such unsettling sources of motivation. Here, too, the experiences of the Pacific war offer interesting parallels, for the same qualities of iron determination that made the Japanese such formidable opponents also accounted for their fatal tactical rigidity, which American and British commanders learned to exploit.[36]

Conclusions

Wars in the Third World take the form of carefully planned limited offensives followed by periods of attrition; they reflect long-standing and perhaps insoluble national antagonisms, and feed off societies that are psychologically mobilized for war. They are often initiated by leaders who have some coherent strategic conception, although these leaders find themselves, like all war leaders in the past, as much at the mercy of events as in control of them. These wars no longer reflect directly the struggle for independence, but resemble, rather, the state conflicts of nineteenth-century Europe. The coalitional nature of such wars, together with the logistical limitations mentioned above, cause them to drag on for prolonged periods of quiescence or truce, punctuated by brief bouts of intense fighting.

Four observations follow from this understanding of recent wars in the Third World. First, with regard to the conduct of foreign policy, we should recognize the bipolar antagonisms described above as constants in contemporary international politics. Rather than see these conflicts as temporary phenomena, the product of mishandled decolonization or superpower interference, we should recognize them for what they are: the product of hatreds and clashes of interest as profound as those in nineteenth- and early twentieth-century Europe. The United States may exercise its influence most fruitfully by recognizing the primacy of these disputes in the minds of local governments and acting accordingly.

Secondly, military analysts (professional and amateur) must reconsider how they go about figuring out the implications of recent wars for the central U.S.-Soviet balance. It may be as dangerous, in other words, to study the last war too much as to study it not at all, for tactics, technologies, and operational concepts that work well in wars in the Third World may bear no relation at all to wars in the First World. This problem is not a novel one. The French Army during the Franco-Prussian War, for example, found itself disadvantaged by tactical formations adopted from experience in Algeria. A student of the Boer War might have suggested that the British Army increase its mounted infantry and light artillery, neither of which would have proved terribly useful on the Somme in 1916.

Thirdly, strategists contemplating war in the Third World must understand the nature of the gaps between the United States and Third World countries with respect to air and naval power (which are huge), on the one hand, and with respect to land power (which is much smaller), on the other. Moreover, as war in the Third World becomes more material-intensive, it may be worth our while to reconsider logistical strategies—strategies of interdiction or industrial targeting. To be sure, we must remember that such strategies work only when (as in Italy in 1944) we can force the enemy to expend large quantities of ammunition and supplies—when, in other words, he cannot resort to passive or evasive defense. Nonetheless, the "conventionalization" of Third World armies may operate to our benefit, by allowing us to make greater use of our strongest assets, air and naval power. U.S. air operations in Korea and Vietnam have not received a good press; under certain conditions, however, we may be well advised to use blockade and air interdiction to sap the strength of opponents who may (unlike our light infantry opponents of 1951 and 1967) require large quantities of ammunition and spare parts.

Finally, scholars studying wars in the Third World should consider the longer-term implications of many of these conflicts. If we think of the enormous social, economic, and political changes wrought by the Civil War or either of the world wars, we will realize that these wars may have consequences that extend far beyond the location of a boundary or the rise and fall of a ruling elite. Universal military service, refugee movements, lopsided industrialization, losses of large numbers of young men—all will exercise an influence on the development of Third World states in ways that we can only guess at, but which, in the long run, may be the most important consequences of these distant battles.

Notes

1. Carl von Clausewitz, *On War,* trans. Michael Howard and Peter Paret (Princeton: Princeton University Press, 1976), 75 (book I, chapter 1).
2. Ibid., 606 (book VIII, chapter 6B), Clausewitz writes: "The first, the supreme, the most far-reaching act of judgment that the statesman and commander have to make is to establish by that test the kind of war on which they are embarking; neither mistaking it for, nor trying to turn it into, something that is alien to its nature. That is the first of all strategic questions and the most comprehensive." Ibid., 88–89 (book I, chapter 1).

3. Winston S. Churchill, *The World Crisis,* vol. 2, *1915* (New York: Scribner's 1923), 6.

4. Clausewitz, *On War,* 484–87, 595–96 (book VI, chapter 27; book VIII, chapter 4).

5. See his essay, "The Forgotten Dimensions of Strategy," in *The Causes of War* (Cambridge: Harvard University Press, 1983), 101–15.

6. V. Kulikov, cited in Harriet Fast Scott and William F. Scott, *The Armed Forces of the USSR,* 3d ed. (Boulder, Colo.: Westview Press, 1984), 75.

7. I am indebted to Gen. Paul Gorman (USA, ret.) for a fascinating discussion of this matter. See also Martin van Creveld, *Command in War* (Cambridge: Harvard University Press, 1985), for a discussion of command in land warfare. It is regrettable that the author did not compare command on land warfare with that at sea.

8. This aversion to risk characterizes the navies of advanced states as well. During the Falklands war, some British soldiers are reported to have criticized the Royal Navy's task force commander for not wishing to bring his ships close to shore to support them, echoing complaints as old as joint operations themselves. Antony Preston, *Sea Combat off the Falklands* (London: William Collins, 1982), 120–21. Even the most daring of naval powers, the Japanese at the beginning of World War II, did not launch follow-up attacks on Pearl Harbor out of fear of exposing their most precious ships.

9. See R.J. Overy, *The Air War 1939–1945* (New York: Stein and Day, 1980), especially 102–26; Walt W. Rostow, *Pre-Invasion Bombing Strategy* (Austin: University of Texas Press, 1981); Charles P. Kindleberger, "World War II Strategy," *Encounter* (November 1978): 39–42; Solly Zuckerman, "Bombs & Illusions in World War II," *Encounter* (June 1979). The two *decisive* target systems of World War II in Europe were oil production and the transportation system. As for the implications of total tactical air supremacy exploited to its fullest, see Erwin Rommel, *The Rommel Papers,* trans. Paul Findlay, ed. B.H. Liddell Hart (New York: Harcourt Brace, 1953), 282–86, 476–77, 489–92. In North Africa, Italy (in late 1944), and in Normandy, Allied domination of the air paralyzed German movements—but this required the continuous efforts of thousands of tactical aircraft, which took heavy losses from German flak.

10. I have used the International Institute for Strategic Studies figures from *The Military Balance, 1975–1976* and *The Military Balance, 1984–1985* (London: IISS, 1975 and 1984, respectively). In 1940, the Wehrmacht had slightly more tanks than planes on the frontline; even the French had something on the order of three tanks to one plane, or a plane/tank ratio of around 0.3. See Alistair Horne, *To Lose a Battle* (Boston: Little, Brown, 1969), 182–85.

11. The great exception to all of these strictures, of course, is the Israeli Air Force. The IAF compares favorably to many Western air forces; the Israeli intelligence services are in fact capable of supporting these kinds of air operations (in 1967 by supplying extremely accurate information on the workings of Egyptian air bases, in 1982 by monitoring Syrian planes as they took off from their bases). Of course, whether Israel is a Third World state, in fact, as opposed to a mislocated European one, is open to debate.

12. See Gordon Craig, "Delbrück: The Military Historian," in *Makers of Modern Strategy,* ed. Edward Meade Earle (Princeton: Princeton University Press, 1943), 260–86.

13. Clausewitz, *On War,* 90–99, discusses the centrality of the destruction of the enemy's forces (book I, chapter 2).

14. See, for example, Michael T. Klare, "The Unnoticed Arms Trade: Exports of Conventional Arms-making Technology," *International Security* 8, no. 2 (Fall 1983): 68–90.

15. See "Exocet Tries Again," *The Economist* (June 30, 1980), 31–32.

16. Preston, *Sea Combat,* 69–70.

17. See Nick Cook, "Iraq-Iran: The Air War," *International Defense Review* 17, no. 11 (1984), 1605–7.

18. See Anthony H. Cordesman, "Defense Planning in Saudi Arabia," in *Defense Planning in Less-Industrialized States,* ed. Stephanie G. Neuman (Lexington, Mass.: Lexington Books, 1984), 86.

19. On this subject generally, see James E. Katz, ed., *Arms Production in Developing Countries* (Lexington, Mass.: Lexington Books, 1984). For good discussions of two new arms industries, see H.M.F. Howarth, "Defense Production in Pakistan—A Quest for Self-Reliance," *International Defense Review* 18, no. 6 (1985): 939–43; and Roger Frost et al., "Cairo Emphasizes Local Production," *International Defense Review* 18, no. 2 (1985): 213–22. For that matter, one may simply browse through the pages of trade journals such as *International Defense Review* or *Jane's Defence Weekly* and take in the ads for Chilean cluster bombs, South African grenade launchers, and Chinese antiaircraft guns.

20. The first occasion on which a Third World army proved capable of delivering heavy quantities of artillery fire was at Dien Bien Phu in 1954. Before the battle, French intelligence estimated that the Viet Minh would have only 25,000 rounds at their disposal; in practice, they fired over four times as many shells into the outgunned fortress. Bernard Fall, *Hell in a Very Small Place* (New York: Lippincott, 1966), 451. Ammunition shortages plagued the Pakistanis in 1965 and the Israelis in 1973, and helped contribute to those countries' strenuous efforts thereafter to stockpile munitions and build the plants to produce them. See Katz, *Arms Production,* 198, 267.

21. Knowledgeable observers of even the most maneuver-oriented army in the Third World, that of Israel, argue that it has turned too much to high firepower "American" tactics. See, inter alia, Ze'ev Schiff and Ehud Ya'ari, *Israel's Lebanon War* (New York: Simon and Schuster, 1984), especially chapter 7, "The Lame Blitz."

22. See Martin van Creveld's excellent book, *Supplying War: Logistics from Wallenstein to Patton* (Cambridge: Cambridge University Press, 1977). The official and semiofficial American histories of World War II also have valuable material. See Roland G. Ruppenthal, *Logistical Support of the Armies,* vol. 2 (Washington, D.C.: Department of the Army, 1958).

23. Douglas Pike, *War, Peace, and the Viet Cong* (Cambridge: MIT Press, 1969), 119. Precisely the same kind of attention to detail accounts for the extraordinary success of the 1975 offensive that finally ended the war.

24. According to Egypt's Chief of Staff during the Yom Kippur War, fully two-thirds of his budget went to manpower costs. Saad el-Shazly, *The Crossing of Suez* (San Francisco: Mideast Research, 1980), 88.

25. Henry E. Eccles, *Logistics in the National Defense* (Harrisburg, Pa.: Stackpole, 1959), 108–9, 138–39.

26. Ibid., 104. See also el-Shazly, *Crossing,* 48ff. on the problem of securing adequate numbers of officers and technical experts. Argentina created a class of officer/technicians in order to keep its naval vessels running. Preston, *Sea Combat,* 70.

27. Anthony Pascal et al., "Men and Arms in the Middle East: The Human Factor in Military Modernization," in *The Defense Policies of Nations,* ed. Douglas J. Murray and Paul R. Viotti (Baltimore: Johns Hopkins University Press, 1982), 412. See also 409.

28. The Argentine forces in the Falklands (and, for that matter, the invading British forces as well) faced acute logistical difficulties. See Max Hastings and Simon Jenkin, *The Battle for the Falklands* (New York: W.W. Norton, 1983), 324; and Harlan W. Jencks, "Lessons of a 'Lesson': China-Vietnam, 1979," in *Lessons of Wars in the Third World,* vol. 1, ed. Stephanie Neuman and Robert Harkavy (Lexington: Lexington Books, 1985), p. 151.

29. According to the International Institute for Strategic Studies, *Strategic Survey 1982–1983* (London: IISS, 1983), 122, the three dozen Harriers deployed in the South Atlantic generated as many sorties as did the Argentine Air Force, which outnumbered them by as many as five or six to one.

30. For an example of a highly proficient air force that suffered, nonetheless, from this absence of organizational depth (albeit on a much grander scale, and with some compensating advantages), see Williamson Murray, *The Rise and Fall of the Luftwaffe* (Washington, D.C.: Government Printing Office, 1983), especially 302–3.

31. Allied analysts during World War II exaggerated the strain that air interdiction campaigns would impose on the Germans, because they failed to realize how a relatively passive defense would enable the enemy to conserve supplies. Only when air interdiction coincided with intense ground assaults on enemy positions, forcing him to expend ammunition, did the logistic crisis hurt the enemy badly. Even then, the paralysis of the enemy's tactical movements in his rear areas played as great a role as the cutting of supply lines. See F.M. Sallagar, *Operation Strangle,* Rand R-851-PR (Santa Monica, Calif.: Rand, 1972).

32. Eccles, *Logistics,* 224. See also 194.

33. In 1973, Israel's civilian transport swiftly augmented the rather skimpy military logistic system—milk trucks carried ammunition across the Suez Canal, and El Al's passenger planes brought high-priority spare parts and ammunition to Israel from the United States. The robust high-technology industries of Israel help account for the ability of that state to absorb new weapons swiftly, to modify imported items for Israeli needs, and to design new weapons fitted to Israeli circumstances. Robert Jackson argues that India used its air force more freely in its war in 1971 with Pakistan than did Pakistan, because the Indians knew they could rely on their indigenously produced Gnat and MiG-21 fighters (and associated spare parts). The Pakistanis, however, had no source of resupply on which to fall back, or even the prospects of one. *South Asian Crisis* (London: Chatto & Windus, 1975), 122.

34. Thomas L. Friedman, "The Lessons of Lebanon: A Personal Retrospective," speech to the Council on Foreign Relations, Sept. 17, 1984. The speech appeared a few weeks later as an article in the *New York Times Magazine.*

35. For example, the North Vietnamese created an elaborate system of rewards for particularly good soldiers. They were called "Valiant American Killers." These heroes

received invitations to special Valiant American Killer Congresses, were the subject of emulation campaigns, and so on. See William Darryl Henderson, *Cohesion: The Human Element in Combat* (Washington, D.C.: National Defense University Press, 1985), 27–30, 120. One perfectly worthy book on the subject of cohesion draws almost exclusively on the experiences of European and North American armies in the last century, and makes only passing references to the questions of cohesion in Third World armies; Anthony Kellet, *Combat Motivation: The Behavior of Soldiers in Battle* (Boston: Kluwer Nijhoff, 1982). A discussion of this issue with reference to a specific war is Arthur Campbell Turner, "Nationalism and Religion: Iran and Iraq at War," in *The Regionalization of Warfare,* ed. James Brown and William P. Synder (New Brunswick, N.J.: Transaction Books, 1985), 144–63.

36. See Ruth Benedict, *The Chrysanthemum and the Sword: Patterns of Japanese Culture* (Boston: Houghton Mifflin, 1946), 1–42. Sir William Slim, *Defeat into Victory* (New York: David McKay, 1961), 445–47, sums up the strengths and weaknesses of Japanese military culture brilliantly.

3
The Geography of Wars in the Third World

Patrick O'Sullivan

T he "Third World" is not a very useful geographical category. The countries that are put in this class display an enormous range of physical and human conditions. The wars examined in this book have been fought in vastly different landscapes and settings. The tactically significant aspects of climate, landforms, and human occupation of the land vary enormously among the theaters of war in question. In the broader, geopolitical scope we are faced with a set of conflicts at various distances from the borders of the great powers and having quite different strategic foci of contention. From the geopolitical, strategic, or tactical viewpoint, then, Third World wars are not a homogeneous set of events about which we can make singular and worthwhile geographical generalizations.

What the geographer's preoccupation brings to bear on the study of war is a concern for the significance of distance and habitat and a sense of scale. The circumstances of wars need to be examined at different levels of geographical resolution in order to understand fully the effect of location and environmental variety on their outcome. There are three sets of variables that describe the relevant geographical circumstances of war. These are positional, environmental, and topographic. Each set needs to be viewed at a different focal distance. Thus, we have three scales of geographical analysis that we can roughly equate with geopolitical, strategic, and tactical levels of decision making.

The geopolitical setting of war is a matter of the locations of the antagonists, of the disputed ground, and of the other sources of military and political power in the world. These locational matters are best examined at a scope that encompasses the whole world, on a globe or on the 1:20,000,000 wall map beloved of foreign offices.

Strategy is concerned with the geographical arrangements and environmental conditions of a theater of war. A general's decisions on the deployment of men, weapons, and vehicles must respect the broad lie of the land, the terrain texture, the variety of climate and vegetation, and the disposition of the major man-made elements of the landscape, such as roads and towns. These are best scrutinized at the 1:1,000,000 scale of the headquarters wall map.

When it comes down to the realities of fighting, tactical success often rests on a superior appreciation of the topographic detail of the combat zone. What Harkavy calls the "idiosyncrasies" of geography are best grasped at the company commander level with the help of a 1:50,000 scale map.[1] In the last resort the outcome of a fight may depend on the peculiarities of the lie of the land and how these may be exploited to defend against or to attack an enemy.

The landscapes in which the wars selected here were fought do have something in common. They have relatively scanty populations. The Third World does contain areas of dense rural population and enormous cities. Many of the open conflicts of the last four decades, however, have occurred in the lightly populated fringes between core areas. The majority of any set of small wars would probably have such a setting. In the particular set we are concerned with the land is too dry, too wet, or too rugged to sustain much in the way of intense cultivation or commerce. Thus, these lands lack the immense superstructures of manufacturing and service employment supported by the surplus of commercial agriculture, and as a consequence, the extensive urban infrastructure of Europe, North America, and Japan. For this reason mechanized, remotely controlled armies are at a disadvantage in these undeveloped settings. Climate and terrain that inhibit commerce do the same for massed military might. The texture of these landscapes hampers mechanized operations and often provides a multiplicity of niches for guerrillas, requiring a great number of regulars to carry out successful sweeping actions.

The remove between the theaters of war we are looking at and the industrial core regions of the world implies long supply lines and often requires the provision from scratch of networks for communication, movement, and the distribution of water, food, fuel, and ammunition.

Whatever their similarities or differences, the geography of Third World wars is best addressed in terms of scale under the headings location, environment, and topography.

Location

At first glance there does seem to be a geopolitically significant difference among the conflicts addressed in this book in terms of the involvement of the great powers in them. Their participation does seem to vary with distance from their borders. The Soviet Union is directly involved in Afghanistan, and the United States is keenly concerned with Central America. The other wars are essentially nationalistic tussles fought at the thinning edges of hegemonic spheres of interest, where local ambitions and animosities dominate the scene. The lack of immediate interest, the difficulties of projecting force, and the potential cost of head-on confrontation far from home keep the two great powers in the background in the crush zone that lies between them.

If we try, however, to formalize the notion of a relationship between distance and great power influence, postulating an attenuation of power projected with distance, any generalization falls apart amidst the irregularities of geography. What Boulding pictured as a gradient of power[2] is in reality a somewhat untidy and irregular step function. Nevertheless, events suggest that distance does matter in military affairs, denying Wohlstetter's attempt to abolish it.[3] We can best acknowledge its significance by dividing our war zones into two groups. Afghanistan and Central America are obviously in the backyards of the great powers. The other fights are further removed geographically and politically.

Domination of Afghanistan is of symbolic rather than strategic importance to the Soviet Union. The military threat of an enemy on this border is slight, but the image of encirclement and the fear of Islamic revivalism are strong motives. Although Afghanistan contains the passes through the Hindu Kush from Central Asia to India, there is now no conceivable temptation for conquering migration through these into the Indo-Gangetic plain. There are those who claim that the Soviet government has designs on Baluchistan as a path to the Strait of Hormuz and, thus, to a stranglehold on Gulf oil traffic. But the route through Afghanistan and Baluchistan is a long, dry, rough, and visible way to that objective. Soviet entanglement here seems mostly a matter of responding to Islamic reaction and its possible ramifications in the Moslem republics of the union. The Red Army was sent in to prop up a client establishment reeling under the revolt of conservative tribesmen. The Soviets' position was not too different from that of the U.S. government and Mohammed Reza Pahlavi in Iran, except that the action was too far away for direct intervention and too massive and urban to be stalled by military means. The Soviets are left holding a rural revolt in their remote borderlands, a revolt bolstered by sympathy and support from their enemies.

The position of the United States in Central America bears some similarity to this, except that so far the United States has avoided overt, massive intervention. The major motive of the Reagan administration seems to be apprehension over political and social instability in what is deemed their own hemisphere. Strategic danger from Soviet footholds in the Americas is a very faint threat. The prospect of the Red Army's invading from the south is in the realm of fantasy. The establishment of Soviet missile bases in the Caribbean would not change the present nuclear balance dramatically. It would only bring Soviet missiles within a range similar to that of the U.S. weapons in European sites that are pointed at the Soviet Union. Khrushchev's effort to place bases on Cuba was a frantic effort to outflank the U.S. early warning network when the potential superiority of Polaris and Minuteman became apparent in 1962. This technological gap is no longer significant, and any Soviet provocation would have no obvious payoff.

The Panama Canal has no great military significance since aircraft carriers cannot get through it. The canal and the Caribbean seaways are not vital arteries to what is still a largely self-sufficient U.S. economy. Venezuelan oil and Jamaican and Guyanan bauxite are important but not indispensible to the United States.

When we look at the sources of conflict in Central America, they are obviously local. Even Jeane Kirkpatrick admitted as much when she effectively renounced her adherence to the "superpower rivalry model of the world," allowing that the Third World "is not anti-democratic, anti-West, anti-U.S. or whatever."[4] The U.S. government, however, has committed its support to the oligarchs of the last remnants of the Spanish empire, which puts it at odds with more radical desires to rearrange rights to property and power in Nicaragua, El Salvador, Guatemala, and elsewhere.

The other unconventional war on our list, that in the Western Sahara, is beyond the immediate reach of the United States and the Soviet Union, although equipment and advice is being provided by both great powers to the combatants. The United States is supplying Morocco, while the *Polisarios* are getting Land Rovers and weapons from some other bankroller. The phosphates of what was the Spanish Sahara are hardly worth a great expenditure of energy by the great powers. Having friendly command of the Strait of Gibraltar is more significant. Involvement is a matter of picking a side to discomfort your global rival, with the United States gravitating to the established order in Morocco and the Soviet Union to the insurgents. Since Libya has now reached an accord with Morocco and supposedly turned against the *Polisarios* to embarrass Algeria, we have the United States and Colonel Qaddafi on the same side, for a change.

Turning to the geopolitics of the conventional wars, these are all nationalistic tussles fought in the trough between the superpower peaks. Here, at the outer edges of hegemonic reach, local ambitions and animosities dominate the scene. The difficulties of employing force and the potential cost of head-on confrontation far from home keep the two great powers in the background.

The long, lasting war between Iran and Iraq in the lower Tigris Valley is essentially drawn along nationalist lines, despite the strong undercurrent of Sunni and Shiite contention and the existence within Iran of an Arabic-speaking population beyond the cultural divide of the Zagros in Khuzistan. National loyalties have remained largely intact in what is ostensibly a territorial dispute over the Shatt-al-Arab. The great powers have carefully kept the warring parties at arm's length. Cutting through the profusion of overlapping claims on loyalty in the Lebanon of family, religion, and language, the most obvious interpretation of the Israeli-Syrian fight there is as a nationalist battle for hegemony in the Levant. The struggle for Ogaden pitted the irredendist ambitions of the Somali ruler against the centralizing, regional imperialism of Amharic Ethiopia. The switch of clients by the great powers here is more suggestive of hegemonic gamesmanship than of ideological commitment. China's punitive attack on Vietnam has the appearance of a longer established regional power's trying to cramp the style of a neighbor that aspires to widen its radius of influence. In the case of the Falklands it seems evident that the territory in question was not worth fighting for in economic or strategic terms. The perception of a need for pride and glory on the part of national leaders seems to have been the main motive for both parties. The Argentine junta needed military glory to divert attention from the unsatisfactory state of society and politics at home. Unfortunately for them the readiest opportunity involved picking on Britain's contracted imperial power at a time when there was a strong temptation for similar domestic reasons to hang tough and show that the Royal Navy could still dish it out.

Environment

When it comes to the course of a war rather than its causes, it is evident that warfare and its outcome is not just a matter of the location of a conflict. The social and physical geography of the theaters of war comes into play, presenting opportunities or hindrances to violent ambition at the strategic and tactical levels. For fighting, the relevant chart is the topographic sheet or air-photograph, rather than the wall map. For the soldier the landscape presents openings and pitfalls for attack and defense. Hills, plains, rivers, forests, ploughland, roads, and buildings resolve into observation and firing platforms, killing ground, protection, hiding, commanding points, and lines of movement. Along with the lie of the land and its human occupation, the weather and its seasonal changes affect the ease of moving, seeing, and fighting. A snow-covered plain is a different proposition from summer fields. The rainy and dry periods of the monsoon still dictate the maneuverings of armies.

The two principal aspects of a geographic setting that bear on tactics are how far one can see and shoot, and how easy the land is to travel over. The characteristic length of sight line in an area depends on the ruggedness of the land, the vegetation, the weather, and the human additions to the scenery, like hedges, crops, and buildings. Whether the going is good in a landscape, whether men and vehicles can move easily, depends on the pattern of water courses, the slopes, the firmness of the ground, the thickness of vegetation, the types and spacing of fences, the variety of crops, and, most importantly, the density of the road network.

The landscapes of our Third World wars can be placed between two axes that capture the tactically most significant elements of the environment: ruggedness and rainfall. Figure 3–1 shows ruggedness increasing from plains to mountains on the vertical axis, and rainfall increasing from desert to rain forest conditions on the horizontal axis.

At one extreme of the terrain range lie depositional plains, desert basins, and the lower reaches of rivers. Here we find flat, low-lying conditions with sandy or marshy patches, where the going can get bogged down. For the most

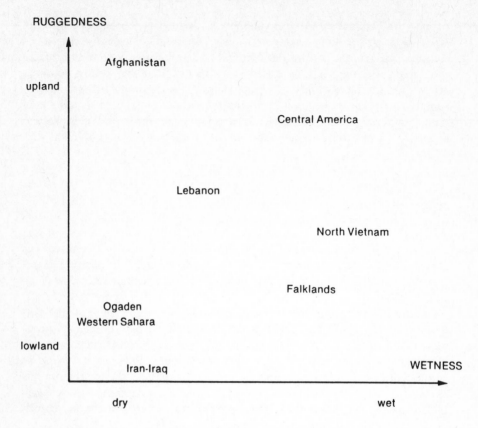

Figure 3–1. Military Habitats

part ruggedness increases with elevation as we move into more heavily eroded upland with steep-sided valleys and jagged interfluves. There are exceptions where flat plateau surfaces are raised up on crustal blocks, as in Africa or between the young, folded ridges of the Andes, for example.

The theaters of war we are considering range from the heated wetness of Central America to the harsh dryness of Afghanistan to the cool dankness of the Falklands. Combinations of altitude, latitude, distance from the sea, and prevailing winds generate a variety of temperature and moisture regimes and, thus, vegetative cover. The most important variation is in wetness. There are vast tracts of the Third World where aridity precludes a continuous vegetative mantle. This sparsity provides little to hide behind. The occasional rainfall comes in sharp downpours that can flash with devastating results down what are usually dry valleys. As rainfall increases, so the plant cover thickens through grassland, scattered trees, clumps of trees, the forest fringe, the jungle, to high canopied rain forest.

The human occupation of rain forest is too slight to provide targets or occasions for big, bloody conflicts. The setting is difficult to move and sustain large numbers of men and machinery in. The outer fringes of the equatorial forests, the lower dense growth of jungle, or the tall grass with clumps of trees of the savanna has been a more frequent scene of modern warfare. In general, the greater the density of vegetation the slower the progress of men and vehicles. A thick vegetative cover provides concealment and a setting of nearly point-blank sight lines. The seasonal shift of winds over much of the savanna-forest fringe, the monsoon, introduces a seasonal element into the landscape. The rains bring floods to lowlands, swell rivers and lakes, reduce visibility, and make action miserable.

Between these axes of physical geography, amenability to conventional warfare generally diminishes with distance from the origin of the axes in figure 3–1 as relief and rainfall increase. This must be modified, however, when we get to very dry conditions. The dust and heat of deserts take an environmental toll in mechanized warfare. The temperature plains are far less demanding of men and machines. These temperate plains lie outside the Third World, being the bread baskets of the First World. One of the widely held misconceptions about geography and warfare is that deserts provide a sealike arena for the likes of Rommel, Dayan, or Sharon to maneuver fleets of tanks in with Nelsonian élan. The realities of North Africa and Southwest Asia are, however, quite otherwise.

The going is very poor off the road in deserts. The third of desert plain that is sandy provides poor traction and lots of dust to clog engines and increase the friction on moving parts. The stark outlines of erosion in a dry climate create steeper stream banks and valley sides, which limit and funnel cross-country movement. The rock-strewn surfaces of the other two thirds of the arid plains is tough to traverse even on foot. The rocky slopes of dry uplands provide plenty of cover and concealment and restrict vehicular movement sharply. The desert landscape can, then, be turned to defensive advantage. The impression of speed and fluidity of movement in desert wars is more a reflection of small numbers operating in a lot of territory rather than of particularly easy going. The lack of vegetation, the telltale clouds of dust raised by tanks and trucks, and open fields of fire with long sight lines unhindered by trees or crops allow long-range engagement and mutual destruction of tank armies at ranges of over a mile and a half. The lack of cover and concealment leads to potential attrition rates in armored warfare far greater than those in temperate, wooded landscapes.

One thing that the regions under review here have in common by chance of selection is a comparatively low density of human occupation. What goes with this is a very slight presence of human handiwork on the land. In general, population density varies with the availability of water and with ruggedness. It varies from the emptiness of the dry and high places to the moderate rural densities of the moister climates of the lowlands, with clusters of higher density at oases and in alluvial river plains. These are mostly sparsely settled landscapes of villages connected by footpaths. Their networks of metalled roads are thin and the clutter of townscape very infrequently distributed. Beirut, Tyre, and Sidon stand out as exceptional cases of city fighting in this set of conflicts.

To set the scene for a treatment of the effect of topographical particulars on the outcome of war, we can sketch the salient environmental features of the battle-grounds of interest, working from the driest and flattest to the dampest and most rugged, considering the strategic implications of these conditions as we go.

The Western Sahara

The low western edge of the Saharan plateau is cut into hilly terrain by the valleys of intermittent rivers. The coastlands of the Western Sahara get nearly ten inches of rain a year between November and April, but rainfall diminishes with distance from the ocean. Mean monthly temperatures do not drop below fifty degrees Fahrenheit even on the coast in January, and in July and August the means are in the eighties.

The vast empty spaces of this land present logistical difficulties for a mechanized army and sufficient cover and concealment to meet the defensive requirements for guerrilla operations. It is difficult for regular forces to track down and destroy small, mobile bands of people familiar with the wadis and versed in stealth. There is little in the landscape to hold on to in the way of roads and villages from which to control space against insurgents. By the same token, the offensive component of a guerrilla campaign is impaired by a setting with too few targets to hit and to discomfort the opposition. The sparsity and distribution of activities was such that the Moroccans enclosed the vast majority of the population, the chief towns of El Aiún and Smara and the phosphate mines (which are the region's only exploited resource), with a four-hundred-mile-long berm. The approaches to this were mined and bugged. Forts and artillery emplacements were distributed along its length, with mobile reserves in the towns prepared to reinforce any section that came under attack and to chase the attackers back to their Algerian bases. This fixed defensive perimeter stymied the *Polisarios* hit-and-run offense. Their response was to become more like a regular army by recruiting and getting heavier weaponry. Coming to base their strength on population numbers and international political clout they have given up the advantages of guerrilla fluidity and thus, to some extent, the advantages of the theater of war.

The Shatt-al-Arab

The Shatt-al-Arab gets about eight inches of rain a year with a rainy season from November until April. These winter rains make off-road conditions very difficult for wheeled or tracked vehicles. In addition, the Tigris floods in spring, inundating much of the region with snowmelt water from its Anatolian headwaters. The level floodplain of the river is marshy and scored with abandoned river channels. To the north and east across the Iranian border the floodplain gives way to dry grasslands. To the north the border coincides with the foothills of the Zagros. Astride the river there is a three-mile band of date gardens crosshatched with irrigation ditches. In the floodplain to the north of the Shatt there is sporadic cultivation, but the dry grasslands are given over to grazing. Intensity of cultivation and population density has never recovered from the Mongol destruction during the thirteenth century. Population density is less than fifty per square mile through much of the area. The cities of the region have grown with the exploitation of its oilfields.

In its initial attack on Iran, Iraq had the advantage of short supply lines from its core area. Baghdad is only 75 miles from the closest point on the border and 300 miles from the Shatt-al-Arab. These miles are on the plain of Mesopotamia. By contrast, Tehran is a rugged 300 miles away from the border crossing leading to Baghdad and nearly 450 miles from Abadan. Although they caused some logistical problems, these distances did provide Iran with defensive depth, enhanced by the westward-looking wall of the Zagros. When the Iranians turned the tables, Iraq was clearly at a positional disadvantage as a defender. Basra and Baghdad have only a shallow territorial screen, and to the east of Baghdad the defenses are overlooked by uplands.

The Iraqi thrust into the Shatt-al-Arab faced the disadvantage of the theater for the offense. Lines of advance are confined by rivers, date gardens, and swamps to the few roads with choke points at bridges. The urban sprawl of Khorramshahr and the clutter of villages on the road to Abadan slowed their advance. Their operations were seasonally checked by rain and floods. In the dry season heat and dust does not help an army on the move. On this defensible terrain it is not surprising that the war ground down to an entrenched stalemate, with the occasional thrust and riposte.

The Ogaden

The low plateau of the Ogaden rises to the north and the west up the flanks of the Ahmar Mountains and the Audo Range. Seasonal rivers have carved valleys across this surface from northwest to southeast. The region gets from ten to thirty inches of rain a year concentrated in the high-sun rainy season. This is enough to support the drought-resistant acacia that dot the savanna grasslands, except where they have been cut back around the settlements of the region. Throughout the year temperatures range around eighty degrees Fahrenheit. Transhumant herding and some cultivation in the valleys supports up to ten persons per square mile.

As in the case of Iraq's invading Iran, the initial Somali aggression in the Ogaden attacked a peripheral region where the opposition had defensive depth and the advantage of the broad lie of the land. Although the Ethiopians were faced with logistical difficulties, given the distance from Addis Ababa, they could retreat to the high ground trading territory for respite. With an Ethiopian counter the Somali's short supply lines were translated into a dangerously shallow defensive zone. Mogadishu and Berbera are only two hundred miles or so from the front, and the road between them could now be cut by the Ethiopians at will, being only about twenty miles from the border in places. In the early fighting the Somalis did enjoy the benefit of familiarity with arid conditions and the specifics of the terrain, for many of their men had been fighting in the southern Ogaden as guerrillas since 1976. The Ethiopian army was in an alien and inhospitable setting. The Soviet vehicles and armor of the Somali forces were, however, not so suited to the land. This war too has reached an intermittently violent equilibrium roughly along the border between the two countries.

Lebanon

The grain of the Lebanon runs strongly from north to south. There is a narrow coastal plain interrupted by fingers of the Lebanon Mountains reaching toward the sea. The steep, dissected slopes of the Lebanon rise to ten thousand feet above sea level. On their eastern flank there is a steep drop to the fault valley of the Bekaa and the Litani River. This five- to ten-mile-wide trench with a relatively level surface is bordered in the east by the Anti-Lebanon, which rise to a ten-thousand-foot crest along which the Syrian-Lebanese border runs. The climate of the region is Mediterranean, with winter rainfall and summer drought. The coastlands get fifteen inches a year, and the slopes of the Lebanon get as much as forty inches, leaving the eastern slopes, the Bekaa and Anti-Lebanon in an arid rain shadow. The coastal plain is intensely farmed, with terracing carrying cultivation up the hillsides. The frequency of settlements and density of population here is high; cities occupying a significant portion of the land. The floor of the Bekaa is more sparsely cultivated where irrigation water is available. The mountains sustain a small pastoral population.

Apart from the obvious lines of advance along the coast and the Bekaa, Agriculture Minister Ariel Sharon's plan called for a division-strong thrust through the central spine of mountains to secure the Dar el-Baidar saddle and cut the road from Damascus to Beirut.[5] Their air and armor superiority notwithstanding, the Israeli blitzkrieg was slowed appreciably in these confined battlefields. On the coastal plain, citrus orchards, villages, refugee camps, and urban terrain blunted their drive to reach the forty-kilometer line within twenty-four hours. The central drive by Einan's division through the Shouf was slowed by narrow, winding mountain roads so that it failed to reach its objective.

The three-pronged attack in the east, up the center of the Bekaa and along its eastern and western highland flanks, turned into a narrow-fronted slogging match. The two flanking drives were retarded by steep slopes and winding narrow roads, which presented a major difficulty in getting tank trucks up to fuel the spearhead. In the valley itself the Syrians fought fiercely for each road junction, and the Israelis had no prospect of outflanking them.

Afghanistan

Afghanistan is high, dry, and rugged. Its population is scattered along the valleys that radiate from the Hindu Kush. Except in the borderlands with the Soviet Union along the Amu Darya, most of the country is over two thousand feet above sea level, jagged and rock strewn. Temperatures around Kabul range from below freezing in January to around eighty degrees Fahrenheit in July. Precipitation is about ten inches a year in Kabul, fifteen inches in the mountains, and three or four inches in the southern and eastern deserts. In winter this comes as snow, and Kabul gets a four-foot fall that only melts at the end of March. In the more favored parts of the north and east, the vegetation is short grass steppe fading into shrubby desert in the south and west. Outside the valleys there are fewer than ten people per square mile, while the highest reaches are uninhabited.

If the fragmented nature of Afghanistan's society provided the circumstances that led the Soviets to interfere directly, the fragmented nature of its landscape caused them to rue this intervention. It proved very difficult for a mechanized army geared to fight other mechanized armies in temperate plains to mount counterinsurgency operations in a mountainous land. The Hindu Kush is not tank country. Soviet control is limited to parts of the cities and the main roads in the daytime. Forays into the Panjsher Valley have failed to kill many *mujahiddin* but at a considerable Soviet loss and with no permanent extension of territorial control. The atomistic nature of the insurrection presents no target to turn on with hammer and anvil. The traditional way of life of the guerrillas prepared them to take every advantage of steep slopes, narrow defiles, and hard weather to give the maximum discomfort to any would-be conqueror.

The Falklands

The Falklands are low platforms of rock with ragged coastlines and rolling eroded surfaces. The monthly mean temperature hovers around fifty degrees Fahrenheit through the year. The wind and damp lowers sensible temperature considerably. The islands get about thirty inches of rain coming throughout the year in drizzle with overcast skies. The wind precludes trees, and the vegetation is low and damp loving. Sheep raising sustains a population of fewer than two thousand people.

At one thousand miles from Buenos Aires and over seven thousand miles from London, the fight in the Falklands was a matter of naval reach and perceptions of national will. But beyond political determination and the successful management of combined operations from a floating base, British success was based on the skillful deployment of mobile light forces in uncomfortable terrain. The environment put heavy armor out of the question. Training on foot in cold, wet conditions on broken terrain, like the Brecon Beacons, paid off handsomely. Specific skill in rock climbing and knowledge of every nook and cranny of the Falklands' coast cultivated by individual officers at their leisure, proved a boon to British efforts. Although they were better dressed for the climate, the Argentines showed no initiative in employing the habitat to their advantage.

The Vietnamese-Chinese Border

The sandstone and limestone uplands of the Vietnamese-Chinese borderlands have been carved by rivers into a maze of steep-sided hills. The climate of the region is monsoonal with over seventy inches of rain falling between May and September. The January average temperatures are below sixty degrees Fahrenheit and in July temperatures run over eighty. These rugged uplands are covered with deciduous forest, with patches of savanna and cultivated clearings. The more favorable slopes have paddy terraces cut into them. Population density runs at about one hundred persons per square mile.

The Chinese were very careful to confine their operations to the mountainous country of north Vietnam. They drove to Lang Son, which guards the main pass from the north into the Red River delta, demonstrating that they could invest Hanoi if they wished. Then they withdrew before the onset of the rainy season. In this demonstration they did not wish to get bogged down, to escalate their involvement, or draw the Soviet Union into the conflict. Chinese timing took account of geographical conditions much farther afield than Tonkin. Winter freezing and spring thawing could be counted on to keep the Soviets at bay along the Amur and Assuri border in Manchuria. To make their strike against Vietnam in mid-February gave the Chinese the greatest time span before the onset of the monsoon would curtail their operations. Not only did they limit themselves territorially but also in terms of arms. They used little air support. Not only might it have invited a stepping up of the intensity of the conflict, it would also not have been very effective in this hilly, wooded setting. Given the objective of the exercise and the nature of the terrain, Chinese operations were fluid and ephemeral, making no effort to hold what they won. Clearly recognizing the nature of this campaign the Vietnamese also limited their commitment, discomforting the Chinese where they could with little cost and employing the defensive advantages of the country to fight a delaying war until the monsoon came to their rescue in May.

Central America

Except for the Yucatan and the limited extent of coastal plain, valleys, and high basins, Central America is ruggedly mountainous. Although north and central Mexico is dry, the rest of the region is wet and forested, with over forty inches of rain a year, rising to over one hundred inches in the highest parts. The wet coastal lowlands support tropical rain forest, giving way to scrub forest with savanna openings on the drier northern margins. The middle slopes of the mountains are forested, with a transition from broadleaves to oaks to pines on the upper slopes. The population is gathered in clusters in the limited areas amenable to agriculture, with lightly populated areas between. Even the concentrations have low densities. Only the highlands of Guatemala and El Salvador and the basins of Costa Rica have much over one hundred persons per square mile. Cities in the region are few, far between, and relatively large.

Both government forces and insurgents have fanned out over the forested uplands of Central America in the 1980s in their battle for the loyalty of the population. The revolutionary strategy of the *foco insurrecional* manned by a cadre of the wholly committed in a distant, rugged, unpopulated region was abandoned for the doctrine of *guerra prolongada*.[6] According to this notion the struggle for power is best stretched out over time and space, bringing guerrilla war to peripheral but populated areas, involving a greater part of the population directly and indirectly in warfare. As a manifestation of this strategy in Guatemala the mestizo insurgents began to involve the Indians of the highlands in their doings. This has been met with a new counterinsurgency strategy, especially by Rios-Montt in Guatemala. There was a substitution of men for mobility. The flying column, the conventional mode of seeking to destroy guerrillas, was replaced by tactical combat groups. More men in many small units were scattered through the contested areas of the highlands, establishing a more permanent military presence in the villages. This cut down the logistical and manpower support for the guerrillas considerably. The Indians were armed and bribed to kill guerrillas. From the revolutionary viewpoint there is no doubt that rugged rural areas far from the big city provide a refuge from which to prolong the struggle. But to be successful guerrillas must operate an offensive defense. The incumbent power has to be at least irritated by constant and unpredictable attacks. In remote mountain areas there are few worthwhile targets. In the last resort, in order to change the government it is necessary to go to the big city. The outcome of these conflicts in Central America, then, will turn on how well governments do at gaining and maintaining the confidence and support of the urban population.

Topography

Prior to attacking or defending against an enemy in unfamiliar country, a good soldier will look for places from which he can see what is going on; possible directions of movement for himself and his opponent; obstacles to movement; where he can get a good shot at the opposition; where he can avoid being shot himself by hiding or getting out of the line of fire; and places from which the surrounding country can be dominated. Even in the age of electronic sensing and control, of missiles, fast-moving armor, air support, and deadly first-round accuracy, the outcome of battle may still depend on whoever uses the peculiarities of the lie-of-the-land to the best advantage. Time after time, the outcomes of engagements, battles, and wars have hinged on the quirks of geography and who employs them best. The successful exploitation of the general characteristics of a habitat with a particular tactic or weapon depends finally on its use on a unique piece of the earth's surface. To act successfully in the face of the idiosyncrasies of geography requires either luck or experience, trained powers of observation, and the ability to construct a mental image of the landscape. This latter talent, what Clausewitz called *Ortsinn*, involves transforming information from verbal descriptions, topographic maps, or air-photos into a picture in the mind of the landscape beyond the range of sight. Having done this, it remains to predict the enemy's response to this setting and act so as to get the upper hand on him.

Practice and experience has produced a conventional rubric for terrain analysis in the form of a checklist of militarily significant elements to look for in any particular piece of territory. When combining information from maps, photos, and his own visual impression, the soldier is advised to look for:

Points of observation

Avenues of approach

Obstacles

Fields of fire

Cover and concealment

Key terrain

It is appropriate, then, to use these as the headings for a survey of the geography of war at a tactical level.

Points of Observation

Despite the artificial aids now available for sensing the opposition, it still evidently pays to keep an eye on what is going on. There is a big advantage in seeing your enemy before he sees you. The *mujahiddin* of the Panjsher Valley are in no doubt about this when they melt into the mountains to watch the Soviets stumble about below. The Argentines put themselves at a heavy disadvantage when they did not man the highest ground around Port Stanley adequately and conceded Mount Longdon, the Two Sisters, and Mount Harriet to the British, giving them the advantage of vision, knowledge, and the initiative.[7]

Bitter engagements are still fought for a vantage point. The Israelis contested hotly to dislodge the PLO from Beaufort Castle overlooking the Litani Valley. In this case, however, the significance of the site was as much symbolic as it was operational. The Syrians and the Israelis struggled fiercely among the terraces on its flanks to command the Shemlan Ridge, which overlooks the coastal approaches to Beirut from the south and the main route to Damascus.[8]

Even in war in the air with electronic sensing aids, whether or not you can see your enemy and the ground on which you chose to keep a lookout for him, still matters. The Israelis came at the Syrian defenses in the Bekaa out of the sun. The Syrians were forced to turn to radar to sense them. Unlike the human eye, radar could not distinguish between drone and Phantoms, and thus missiles were spent on dummy targets. As an additional disadvantage, switching on radar made the missile sites vulnerable to antiradiation weapons.[9]

Avenues of Approach

To determine your own best line of movement or that of your enemy does require intelligence on road and bridge capacities and on slopes, load-bearing capacities of soil, and vegetation density off the road. To this engineering aspect of route appraisal, however, is added the need for the element of surprise in war. To be able to surprise your enemy and avoid being surprised by him can tip the balance in an evenly matched contest or magnify the potency of an inferior force. Surprise is partly a matter of timing but also of direction. Some geographical common sense is required to select the avenue that will most surprise the enemy or to predict which direction he will come from. Intimate knowledge of the route network has always been a major advantage of guerrillas fighting against an adventitious regular army. In the early stages of the war in the Western Sahara, the *Polisarios* were most successful in using the sheltered approach of wadis to hit Moroccan targets.[10]

Failure to predict the enemy's avenue of approach still accounts for many a defeat. The Argentines did not predict the most obvious British approach to Port Stanley. The landing at San Carlos, the only suitable site for such an operation, was virtually unopposed.[11]

Through much of the world, where slopes are steep, the woods thick, or the going soft, mechanized armies are virtually confined to the road. The rest of the landscape is one enormous obstacle from a military viewpoint. There are degrees in this, and the helicopter has opened up the prospect of overcoming surface obstacles in a tactic of three-dimensional envelopment. But obstacles do still present a defensive advantage. The extreme case of prohibitive terrain is Afghanistan, but even on the plains natural and man-made obstacles can channel and stymie an aggressor's movement. The Iraqi drive in the spring of

1981 to encircle and capture Abadan was blocked by the seasonally flooded land to the east of the Bahmanshir River, with the date plantations that line the river providing a dense screen protecting the road southeast from Abadan to Khosrowabad and the rest of Iran.[12] On the western arm of the Israeli advance into Lebanon, the cities and Palestinian camps of the coastal plain constituted a series of man-made obstacles to an armored drive.

Some of the greatest feats of arms have involved overcoming physical barriers, using difficult terrain as an avenue of approach so as to surprise the enemy or negate his advantage in position, in number, or in equipment. Hannibal crossed the Alps, Wolfe scaled the Heights of Abraham, and von Rundstedt and von Manteuffel thrust through the Ardennes in 1940 and 1944. Success, of course, is not guaranteed. The Iranian March offensives of 1984 and 1985 struck towards the Baghdad to Basra road through the marshes of the Hawr al-Hawizah at a time of year when flooding would offset the Iraqi superiority in armor. The Iraqis only halted these drives with great loss of life by dint of their greater fire- and air power.[13]

The significance of terrain and the availability of avenues of approach may be a matter of sheer capacity. The enormous superiority of numbers and armor of the Chinese over the Vietnamese was sharply diminished by the lack of road capacity to get through the broken, wooded terrain of the Chinese-Vietnamese borderlands. The avenues of approach were insufficient to bring Chinese preponderance to bear advantageously.

Fields of Fire

One major advantage the terrain can afford is a killing ground where the enemy can be shot with impunity. One of the objects of terrain evaluation then is to seek firing points that cover an avenue or field that the enemy cannot avoid.

The most important hang-up in the Israeli central axis of advance through the Shouf Mountains was at Ein Zehalta. The Syrians brought them to a halt here two miles short of their goal, the Beirut-Damascus road. This had wider implications in that it led Sharon to press for the air attack on Syrian missile sites in the Bekaa. The Syrians got the upper hand at Ein Zehalta by establishing a superior field of fire. Just to the north of the village the road wound down into a wadi. A Syrian brigade stationed its tanks on the north edge of the wadi and its infantry in the wadi, thus covering anything that arrived from the south hoping to cross the valley. The head of the Israeli column was hit when it arrived, with little chance of returning fire successfully.[14]

Even guided missiles are limited in their effectiveness by limitations in their field of fire. It is necessary to get locational information to direct them to their targets. If the landscape throws shadows across the sensory field from which this information is derived, then there is cover for an approaching enemy. The steep sides of the Bekaa masked the coverage of Syrian radar stations located in the valley. Israeli aircraft coming in over the mountains from the west were thus hidden from Syrian ground-to-air missile batteries until the last minute. The Israelis were, therefore, able to knock out these batteries with near impunity in 1982.[15]

Cover and Concealment

Guerrilla fighting is largely an exercise in the use of cover and concealment. The ambush and sudden hit from a stealthy approach are the chief guerrilla tactics. The thinly populated forest uplands of Central America and the virtually uninhabited, dissected mountainsides of Afghanistan provide a lot of hiding places. At the other end of the population density spectrum, the narrow alleys and jumbled structures of refugee camps provided the PLO with its only effective defenses against Israel. Even if reduced to rubble they still provided cover and concealment. The networks of shelters and bunkers in the camps on the edges of Tyre and Sidon stalled the Israeli advance for a couple of days. The PLO held out for a week in Ein Hilweh on the outskirts of Sidon.[16] Even a cultivated rural landscape can provide cover. The orange groves of Lebanon were used by the PLO to ambush tanks. The date groves of the Shatt-al-Arab are not only an obstacle for tanks, but they also provide screens for movement.

Weather still provides concealment for conventional operations. The British landing on East Falkland was delayed until fog covered the approach of the assault force to San Carlos.

The shelter and screening offered by some landscapes can nullify the effectiveness of particular weapons and leave the outcome to the balance of other arms. The forested hills of northern Vietnam provided such good protection against airplanes that neither China nor Vietnam employed air support for attack or defense. This suited the Vietnamese in terms of their equipment, and the Chinese from the political viewpoint, since they wished to limit and confine the war.

Key Terrain

Key terrain at the tactical level is merely used to denote bits of geography that provide good cover, observation, fields of fire, and lines of movement. There is a higher, more strategic sense of the notion in which places become an end of tactics rather than a means. The significance of some elements of the landscape extends far beyond the immediate fighting. There are crucial places that command the human occupation of the land over a broad geographical scope. Usually these are choke points on the road network, frequently at the limited number of points where a physical barrier is crossed. Time and again the fight for a single structure or position rivets the attention of armies.

Given the cost and limitation on the use of helicopters, bridges over rivers are often still the crucial links where one army can sever the arteries of another and bring all movement to a halt. It was not surprising then that the Israelis raced for the bridge at Kasmiye over the Litani. Passes over mountain ridges have similar significance. The *mujahiddin* were able to display their power of disruption early in Afghanistan when they took the Salang Pass, cutting off Kabul from the Soviet Union.[17] The Paitak Pass, leading through the Zagros to Baghdad, is a key in the Iran-Iraq war. The Friendship Pass, commanding the route to Hanoi, provided the Chinese with a geographical period with which to punctuate their demonstration of power to the Vietnamese. The Shemlan ridge, which overlooks both the coast road and the Damascus road, was a key position for the Syrians, providing an observatory and a commanding field of fire over access to Beirut.

In terrain where tanks are confined to roads, every road junction becomes crucial. The Israeli advance into the Bekaa was marked by a series of battles for crossroads. In a sparsely settled landscape such as the Ogaden, junctions and the only settlements coincide, and these are usually the scenes of the hottest fighting. When the Ethiopians managed to hold Harar and Diredawa, they established the basis for their comeback against the Somalis. The fighting between the Chinese and the Vietnamese mostly took place for the high ground that commanded the "dots and lines on the map."[18]

Two varieties of terrain are frequently distinguished for tactical purposes. *Close terrain* is considered to include forest and urban landscapes, while farmland and grassland are called *open terrain*. The weapons and tactics of the standing armies of the world display a preference for open terrain and a war of maneuver. Close terrain is to be avoided if possible. For the decisive battle, the commanders of mechanized, mass armies seek out open terrain where control and rapid movement are possible. Battles in close terrain tend to break up into soldiers' fights with a loss of central control. Commanders lose sight of what is going on. Line of sight, messenger and radio communications are less effective amidst trees, houses, valleys, and ridges. The advantage in close terrain lies with free-ranging, small, independent units using easily transported firepower.

In the soldiers' battles of close terrain, the range of engagement is small, often below the lower limit of sight calibration for direct-fire weapons. The pace that armor can maintain and the channels of movement are more restricted in close terrain, which therefore inhibits forces dependent on mechanized transport.

From the instances of war that have been examined here, we can see clearly that there is a spectrum of closeness or openness in the landscapes of the Third World. A simple twofold categorization of terrain and a binary tactical response would be foolish. A much finer adjustment of equipment and tactics to the geographical setting is called for. One thing that is quite plain is that mechanized armies designed to do battle in temperate farmland, or copied in weapons and organization from such models, have great difficulty in adjusting to mountains, forests, and desert, never mind to the urban landscape.

Conclusion

What are gathered together in this work as Third World wars run the whole gamut of fighting styles and weaponry from the electronic air warfare of Israel to the time-honored, Pathan ambush with a handmade copy of a Lee-Enfield .303. Their settings range from the rain forest of Central America to the tundralike conditions of the Hindu Kush.

The political conditions that generated these conflicts are so different that any generalizations about the suitability of different geographical settings for guerrilla warfare or for counterinsurgency operations only cover some circumstances. Some comments on the efficacy of different arms and tactics in this variety of habitats are probably in order, but obvious.

What is clear is that those who predicted the annihilation of distance and the irrelevance of terrain to the conduct of war were premature in their judgment. It is evident that at the strategic as well as the tactical level attention to geographical detail still pays off as a means of gaining the upper hand in armed conflict.

Notes

1. Robert E. Harkavy, "The Lessons of Recent Wars in the Third World: Toward a Comparative Analysis," in *The Lessons of Recent Wars in the Third World*, vol. 1, eds. Robert E. Harkavy and Stephanie G. Neuman (Lexington, Mass.: Lexington Books, 1985), 14.

2. Kenneth Boulding, *Conflict and Defense* (New York: Harper & Row, 1963).

3. Albert Wohlstetter, "Illusions of Distance" *Foreign Affairs* 46: 2 (1968): 242–55.

4. Jeane Kirkpatrick in a speech to the American Enterprise Institute, reported in the *Tallahassee Democrat*, Dec. 8, 1984, A1.

5. Ze'ev Schiff and Ehud Ya'ari, *Israel's Lebanon War* (New York: Simon and Schuster, 1984), 109–12.

6. Caesar D. Sereseres, "Lessons from Central America's Revolutionary Wars 1972—1984," in *The Lessons of Recent Wars in the Third World*, vol. 1, eds. Robert E. Harkavy and Stephanie G. Neuman (Lexington, Mass.: Lexington Books, 1985), 164.

7. *The Economist*, June 19, 1982, p. 32.

8. Schiff and Ya'ari, *Israel's Lebanon War*, 185–86.

9. W. Seth Carus, "Military Lessons of the 1982 Israel-Syria Conflict," in *The Lessons of Recent Wars in the Third World*, vol. 1, eds. Robert E. Harkavy and Stephanie G. Neuman (Lexington, Mass.: Lexington Books, 1985), 264.

10. William H. Lewis, "War in the Western Sahara," in *The Lessons of Recent Wars in the Third World*, vol. 1, eds. Robert E. Harkavy and Stephanie G. Neuman (Lexington, Mass.: Lexington Books, 1985), 126.

11. Harlan K. Ullman, "Profound or Perfunctory: Observations on the South Atlantic Conflict," in *The Lessons of Recent Wars in the Third World*, vol. 1, eds. Robert E. Harkavy and Stephanie G. Neuman (Lexington, Mass.: Lexington Books, 1985), 248.

12. *The Economist*, May 9, 1981, p. 31.

13. *The Economist*, March 16, 1985, p. 58.

14. Schiff and Ya'ari, *Israel's Lebanon War*, 161.

15. Carus, "Military Lessons," 266.

16. Schiff and Ya'ari, *Israel's Lebanon War,* 138.

17. Joseph J. Collins, "The Soviet-Afghan War," in *The Lessons of Recent Wars in the Third World*, vol. 1, eds. Robert E. Harkavy and Stephanie G. Neuman (Lexington, Mass.: Lexington Books, 1985), 191.

18. Harlan W. Jencks, "Lessons of a Lesson: China-Vietnam, 1979," in *The Lessons of Recent Wars in the Third World*, vol. 1, eds. Robert E. Harkavy and Stephanie G. Neuman (Lexington, Mass.: Lexington Books, 1985), 194.

4
Culture and War

Joseph Rothschild

An Operational Definition of Culture

This essay is my first foray into polemology—the study of war as a collective social phenomenon.[1] I have undertaken it at the request of Stephanie Neuman, who, in turn, extended her invitation after reading my recent book, *Ethnopolitics*.[2] This particular provenance leads me to suspect that she and her coeditor, Robert E. Harkavy, wish me operationally to define "culture" as specifically ethnonational culture, or something like national character, for the purpose of this essay. That surmise of mine is reinforced by the allusion, in Professor Harkavy's opening chapter in volume 1 of *The Lessons of Recent Wars*, to the question of whether or not attitudinal fatalism and associated "human wave" battle tactics as utilized by the Iranians in the current Iran-Iraq war are perhaps a culturally specific Shiite Moslem mode of warfare.[3] Now, if ethnonational culture, or national character, is deemed to be an intractable naturalistic trait or the product of biological-genetic constraints (which is not necessarily the intention of the poser of this question), then I start my inquiry from a stance of a priori skepticism toward such an understanding of the concept of "culture." In my support, I cite here not only the fact that the decidedly non-Shiite Moslem alumni of Eton, Harrow, and Sandhurst also resorted to human wave tactics on the Somme in July 1916,[4] but also the more general truism that societies and states with vastly different cultural heritages often tend to adopt similar military postures if they confront similar strategic problems. Thus, for example, the current military doctrines, structures, and dispositions of contemporary China, Sweden, Switzerland, and Yugoslavia all resemble each other in signaling the following military message to their respective stronger and unfriendly neighbors: "We acknowledge that you can defeat us, but we intend to render your possible victory so Pyrrhically costly to you as to make it punitively nonworthwhile." Now surely, the common denominator in the similar war plans and structures of these different actors is not any ethnonational cultural commonality, but a political-situational and political-environmental commonality. Indeed, I am tempted to go further and to suggest that war, being such a fiercely and fatally competitive activity, imposes a certain logic of imitation on those who engage in it or seriously prepare to engage in it. Thus, *toutes proportions gardées*, armed forces and their weapons tend to resemble each other at least as much as (and probably more than) they tend to express the distinct ethnonational cultures or national characters of their societies.[5] Those cultures and characters, I suspect, count for something in war, but for how much is difficult to assess, and it is probably less than the weight of other factors such as strategic tasks, force ratios, terrain, technology, training intensities, and so forth. We shall return to this delicate issue later in the chapter. Here, for now, I will confine myself to a brief preemptive response to these colleagues who may be inclined to retort that no student of warfare has ever seriously intended to impute a biological-naturalistic determinism to the notion of national character, or ethnonational culture—and that my skepticism is therefore allegedly gratuitous.[6] However, though the propensity is indeed unscientific, that is precisely what writers on warfare and on styles of belligerency have habitually done for centuries.[7]

I draw support for my a priori skepticism toward the suggestion of specifically ethnonational modes of warfare from the judicious warning of Machiavelli to those of his Rennaissance contemporaries who were then alleging, in a different but analogous context, that some peoples and nations are "naturally" endowed with martial prowess and others not. He responded that "good discipline and exercise will make good soldiers in any country, and the defects of nature may be supplied by art and industry—which in this case is more effective than nature itself. . . . Good order makes me bold. . . . Neither the Greeks nor the Romans were remarkable for their natural ferocity . . . ; they were obliged to resort to good discipline. . . . Few men are brave by nature, but good discipline and experience make them so."[8] Yet, while rejecting the notion of naturalistic ethnonational culture as supposedly determining a society's war-making talents and styles, Machiavelli was passionately committed to the alternative proposition—to which he harnessed all his intellectual, administrative, and literary energies—that culture in the sense of civic commitment, of social bonding, citizenship, piety, prudence, austerity, and the like, is organically related to military morale and hence to the combat effectiveness of armies.[9] And this argument is surely so well accepted by serious students of warfare that for me to rehearse it here would be altogether redundant.

A third possible operational definition of culture for the purpose of this chapter might be culture in the philosophical-anthropological sense of a society's historically developed implicit, even unconscious, values. A recent conversation with my Columbia colleague Warner Schilling furnishes an example. The U.S. military establishment has traditionally defined the object of war to be the defeat of the enemy's armed forces in the shortest possible time with the least loss of life to one's own forces and population. The two declared values of this definition—time and lives—are indeed usually congruent with each other for a relatively high-technology military establishment, such as the U.S. one has long been. Usually—but not always. And when they are not congruent, then philosophical-anthropological values that are prior to, and presumptively deeper than, military doctrines come into play because there is then no strictly professional military solution to the problem posed by the incongruity. An astute student of military history, Professor Schilling mentioned that in the spring of 1945, the U.S. high command faced precisely such a problem—which it perceived as a dilemma—in deciding which of two alternative strategies for bringing the war against Japan to a victorious conclusion (defined as Japan's unconditional surrender) was optimal. The first alternative was the systematic air/sea attrition of Japan through blockade and bombing. This was deemed to be relatively economical in terms of American lives, but necessarily protracted—that is, wasteful in terms of time to be expended. The alternative strategy of an early invasion of the core home islands of Japan proper was expected to be expensive in terms of American casualties, but promised an early and quick end to the war—that is, it would be economical in terms of time.[10] Eventually of course, the development of a feasible atomic bomb presented a deus ex machina escape from this dilemma, one that proved to be economical both in American lives as well as in time expended. Now the point that I wish to make here is that this problem was perceived as an authentic dilemma only within the unexamined American value-culture, which views time as a precious, scarce, and indeed fleeting resource. Change the anthropological culture to, say, Byzantium (330–1453), whose political and military elites also assigned high value to the lives of their relatively few but highly trained professional soldiers,[11] but who viewed time as literally sub specie aeternitatis, as a dimension rather than a value, then the analogous problem ceases to be a dilemma and becomes one with a seemingly obvious, straightforward, and easy solution, to wit: save lives (which are precious) and sacrifice time (which has no intrinsic value).

Military history also records many wars in which one of the belligerents believes himself to have such overwhelming technological superiority that he considers himself free of the need to choose between time and lives as his higher priority. In other words, he is confident that technology per se can restore congruity, spare him a dilemma, and assure a victory that is both quick and low-cost. Ironically, however, here too philosophical-anthropological culture often rears up as a nemesis, exposing and punishing this confidence as shallow technological hubris. That is because the over-confident belligerent often misassesses his low-technology foe's level of tolerable suffering or, to use the currently conventional terms, that foe's differential between acceptable and unacceptable damage, his "breaking point."[12] Culture is at work here in two dimensions. On the one hand, the differential between acceptable and unacceptable damage is itself culturally and societally contextual. On the other hand, its misassessment by a belligerent seeking to anticipate how the enemy will calculate this differential is itself also culture-bound in the sense of being the product of both subjective ethnocentric projection onto the foe and of ignorance about this foe's different schedule of values and pain tolerances. Among the recent wars in which such culture-bound misassessments of the foe's breaking points and pain tolerances appear to have been committed are those involving the United States and Vietnam, the Soviet Union and Afghanistan, Iraq and Iran, and Israel and Syria in Lebanon.

As contemporary social scientists, we recognize of course that the kind of value attributed to a variable such as time is not likely to differ and to change randomly and arbitrarily among different cultures and different civilizations. On balance, we would expect cultures that are predicated on pastoral, agrarian, and even artisanal modes of livelihood and of production to manifest a "natural" concept of time, while entrepreneurial and industrial cultures—be they capitalist or socialist—would be expected to develop an "economic" sense for time. And this, in turn, brings us to the elusive yet important subject of seeking correlations—beyond the obvious technological ones—between the material-economic stages of civilizations and their cultural apparatuses, including their military conceptualizations.

An example of what I am here groping toward is supplied by a recent revisionist interpretation of the American Civil War that seeks to explain the poor military performance of the Union armies—especially in Virginia—during the war's first three years. In place of the conventional allegations of the individual failings of a string of Union generals or the supposed professional fallacies of West Point doctrine, Prof. Michael Adams hazards a suggestive cultural/psychological explanation that may be synopsized as follows: Whereas today, we tend to assume that military might is correlated to industrial power, in the mid-nineteenth century, industrial, capitalist civilization still lacked self-confidence in the respectability and validity of its values as contrasted with the older, proven ones of a putatively aristocratic, honor-bound rather than profit-based, planter civilization. The capitalist ethos was decried as corrosive of the martial values of courage and self-sacrifice; the "selfish" profit motive was deplored as incompatible with the soldier's virtues of honor, service, and duty; individualistic democracy was apprehended as undermining the social cohesion that war requires. Thus the bourgeois-industrial Union—especially the Northeast—entered the Civil War with a collective, systemic, cultural inferiority complex toward the anticipated martial prowess of the Confederacy, especially the supposedly gallant cavalier civilization of the Southeast. Expecting to lose for a cluster of reasons that we today no longer deem plausible and instead regard as cultural/psychological projections, the Union officers therefore did lose.[13] Their "sin," ironically, was here the opposite of technological hubris; it was a kind of misplaced and "underweening" pessimism.

Cultural/Psychological Factors

Might analogous cultural/psychological inhibitions (or assets) have been operative in any of the eight recent wars that furnish the subject matter of the "Lessons of Recent Wars" project (that is, the wars of China and Vietnam, Argentina and United Kingdom, Iran and Iraq, Ethiopia and Somalia, Morocco and the *Polisario*, Israel and Syria, the Soviet Union and Afghanistan, and Central America)? It appears to me that in the case of the Sino-Vietnamese War of February–March 1979 it is relatively easy to answer this question affirmatively.

To begin, the very rhetoric of the Chinese side—that of "teaching a lesson" to the Vietnamese foe—is suffused with classical Confucian and Legalist overtones. Lessons, after all, are not taught to moral and cultural equals, but to minors, inferiors, probationers, transgressors, and barbarians. In this case the intent was to teach a sharp lesson to a delinquent minor whose previous behavior had violated rules of proper conduct and had broken the correct order of things, an order that is always perceived as centered on Beijing. Indeed, since the ideal of proper conduct is built into the very concept of the cosmos in Chinese culture, any violation thereof threatens the whole cosmic system.[14] But, by extending the logic of this cultural prism, we may note that it also does not require military victory in the Western sense as the only acceptable outcome to this kind of punitive-pedagogic war. The restoration of order, as defined by the Chinese side, suffices. And here I would register a mild dissent from Harlan Jencks's suggestion—whimsically stated but presumably seriously intended—that in closing their campaign in Vietnam in March 1979 the Chinese borrowed Sen. George Aiken's advice to President Lyndon Johnson in an earlier, slightly analogous situation, arbitrarily to "declare that [we] had won and to pull out."[15] The Chinese did not need Aiken to reach for such a declarative solution. Their own cultural inventory, honed during centuries of seesaw struggle against peripheral so-called barbarians, pointed them quite indigenously toward such a formula.

The Jencks chapter draws our attention to two more traditional Chinese cultural/psychological traits—one a stark liability to Western eyes, the other more problematical—which were exposed in the brief war of 1979 against Vietnam. The first of these is willful ignorance about the arms, organization, and capabilities of a foe definitionally deemed to be morally, culturally, and civilizationally their rebellious inferior. The other is the assignment of nonmilitary roles to China's own armed forces. Professor Jencks believes that this last aspect has now been ended in the aftermath of China's ambivalent experience in the war that he has studied.[16] But I would urge caution before definitively drawing such a conclusion, as the reluctance to permit the full and exclusive professionalization of the military institutions runs very deep in Chinese history and culture.[17]

As regards the South Atlantic War of April–June 1982, the evidence needed to answer my earlier question concerning the possible role of cultural/psychological factors is more ambiguous. True, the chapter in volume 1 (*The Lessons of Recent Wars in the Third World*) by Harlan Ullman shows convincingly that Britain and Argentina each initially underestimated the willingness of the other party to fight and was taken aback by that willingness.[18] But it is difficult to assess whether this pair of misperceptions about the respective foes was culture-bound—that is, was historically and structurally conditioned by deep factors analogous to those depicted by Adams as characterizing the Union side in the American Civil War—or was a more prosaic intelligence failure. My own free-floating suspicion is in the direction of the first hypothesis. Specifically, it seems that each side deemed the other to be too "modern" and thus, by extension, too "pragmatic" and "rational" to expend much blood and treasure for as relatively worthless a prize as the Falkland islands. Indeed, the tendency to impute a supposed rationality to modern industrial people characterizes us scholars as well as public-policy makers. Thus, the kind of behavior that we deem "fanatical" when engaged in by a Lebanese or Iranian Shiite driving an explosive-laden truck into a U.S. embassy or barracks, becomes a more reputable "passionate eccentricity" when exhibited by a Royal Marine commando on the glaciers of South Georgia Island.[19]

As regards the military *performances* of the two sides in this short South Atlantic war (as distinguished from the erroneous reciprocal assumptions of their respective *intentions*), it seems clear that the relatively poor performance of the Argentine Army and Navy (as contrasted with the Air Force) was in large part a reflection of "culture" in the second, Machiavellian sense that I introduced earlier—culture in the sense of civic commitment, social bonding, citizenship, and the like. The quality of this culture was low in Argentina during the last, discredited phase of military rule, and it thus corrupted military morale and diluted combat effectiveness.

Col. William Staudenmaier will, I trust, understand and forgive my saying that his splendidly austere chapter in volume 1 on the Iran-Iraq war that has been underway since September 1980 is literally tantalizing for my assignment. It teases me by hinting at valuable nuggets of cultural data—that are then held out of reach. For example, Staudenmaier intimates an exaggerated expectation by each antagonist that the other must imminently collapse, but refrains from accounting for it.[20] Other specialists have attributed an alleged Arab propensity for confusing wishes with reality to the allusive, diffuse, florid, and highly metaphorical (and beautiful) Arabic language's carrying its users into dithyrambic expressions and exalted yet vague styles of thought.[21] This alleged propensity has also been imputed to a system of cultural-social etiquette that prohibits interlocutors from explicitly disagreeing with each other and that thus drives them toward the orotund articulation of a false consensus. Staudenmaier also shows that, in stark contrast to the exaggeratedly optimistic strategic-political expectations, Iraqi operational doctrine has been extraordinarily cautious and hesitant. Given the historic fact that Arab armies virtually specialized in blitzkrieg in the heyday of their monumental sweeps across the Arabian peninsula, North Africa into the Iberian peninsula, the Middle East through the Fertile Crescent into Iran and beyond, and that this tropism was still noted by T.E. Lawrence as late as World War I, what cultural apparatus might account for the much more deliberate and cautious Arab style of warfare that Staudenmaier correctly perceives as operative against both Iran and Israel?[22] Or is the explanation not really cultural in any deep sense, but rather situational-political (mutual suspicions among Arab rulers and commanders) or pedagogical-institutional (aping Soviet doctrines)?

To my mind, the most striking cultural-military nexus that Staudenmaier's chapter suggests but refrains from making explicit is the cultural self-confidence and military resilience of a great, long-lived, land empire. We know, of course, that the Ayatollah Khomeini shuns the rhetoric of Persian pride and insists on the rhetoric of Islamic purity. And yet I am left with the strong sense that the tenacity, resilience, and basic self-confidence of the Iranian society and armed forces as manifested in the current war stem to a substantial degree from the sense of being the heirs of a great, ancient, and continuous imperial civilization, compared with which Saddam Hussein's Iraq is but a peripheral upstart. And the Iraqis know this too, and it accounts in part for their clumsy ineptness in this conflict. We saw a similar scenario in the Horn of Africa in 1977, when the rulers of Somalia—also laboring under the illusion that the regionally hegemonial Ethiopian Empire had been mortally wounded by its recent internal revolutionary turmoil (like the Iraqi rulers vis-à-vis Iran in 1980)—invaded that empire's Ogaden province.[23] Indeed, the original modern script, as it were, for this scenario was written in 1920, when newly restored Poland sought to exploit the supposed postrevolutionary weakness of the Russian Empire to seize the Ukraine.[24] In each of these three cases the empire struck back with a vengeance—and perhaps Britain in the South Atlantic and Morocco in the Western Sahara might even be deemed analogous cases.[25] The thrust of my argument here is that the self-awareness of an impressive imperial heritage is a powerful psychological/cultural asset, one that can readily be translated into military prowess. I realize that it is currently fashionable to celebrate the soi-disant nation-state as the normative political-military actor in the international arena and to devalue the old multinational, polyethnic empires as supposedly obsolete and withering. But I suggest that we adopt this fashion to our intellectual and political peril. The land empires have impressive staying power. And if you think that my attempt to rehabilitate their repute is quixotic, I urge you to read a remarkable essay by the dean of contemporary American philosophers of history, William McNeill, in which he argues that most of mankind's great cultural achievements, on a global scale, are the creations either of multinational empires or of subnational city-states, and only rarely of the political unit now known as the nation-state.[26]

We turn next to another recent Middle Eastern conflict that suggests some lessons about the nexus between culture and war, to wit: W. Seth Carus's survey of the confrontation between Israel and Syria fought in Lebanon in 1982.[27] As so much of the literature on the several Arab-Israel wars is rhetorically and emotionally self-indulgent, Carus's restrained professional analysis is most welcome, even though this very austerity entails, for me, the cost of not providing much "meat" for speculation about the role of culture in this most recent of those wars. Nevertheless, though it may not have been his intention, Carus leaves me with the impression that the two belligerents in his scenario committed a pair of culture-informed, even if not culture-determined, miscalculations about each other.

The Israelis once again underestimated Syrian political will, specifically the willingness to accept painful military losses and yet refuse to concede anything politically—including even the formal legitimacy of the Israeli belligerent as a state. I believe that this persistent Israeli tendency to underrate the political will and the political resilience of their Arab foes—a tendency that (mis)leads the Israelis into seeking quick military "fixes" to this quarrel—stems in substantial part from a psychological reluctance to accept the fact that for the Arabs the quarrel is not basically a military or even a political one, but *au fond* a historic and even metaphysical one. To acknowledge the recalcitrant reality of this Arab perspective is too painful for the Israelis, as it promises only endless conflict and warfare, and hence they shrink from it and reach for alternative scenarios that will, supposedly, force the Arabs to "acknowledge the facts," such as Israel's existence, statehood, permanence, and legitimacy. The Syrians, in turn, once again as so often before, underestimated Israeli technical-military competence. There appears to be operative here a deep Arab need to cleave to a set of cultural stereotypes that prohibits conceding warrior status and martial prowess to Jews. Hence the everlasting search for scapegoats and betrayers to explain away the series of Arab defeats at Israel's hands—supposed British perfidy in 1948 and 1956, purported U.S. collusion in 1967 and 1973, and now, in 1982, allegedly shoddy Soviet ordnance and matériel.

This brings us neatly, albeit through verbal artifice, to the theme of the Soviet armed forces and the role of culture in their combat effectiveness as suggested by their recent performance in Afghanistan.

Of the eight recent wars that I have been instructed to regard as my data base for this chapter, the current Soviet-Afghan one would appear to present, prima facie, the most highly differentiated cultural profiles of the antagonists. It pits the standing, professional, armed forces of a global, industrial superpower against the irregular guerrillas of a premodern, peripheral, mountaineer society. If Col. Joseph Collins's statements about the low combat morale, the unreliability, and the high rate of defection of the Moslem Central Asian troops in the invading Soviet army are factual, then this war tells us quite a bit about the political culture of the Soviet armed forces and, indeed, of Soviet society in general.[28] The Collins data suggest that a system claiming that its culture is (in its own classic formulation) "national in form and socialist in content," in practice turns this formula inside out and manifests a cultural repertoire that may be socialist in form, but is very much ethnonational in content. The social fabric of the Soviet Union is suffused with ethnic salience and interethnic estrangement.[29] And demographic trends are likely to aggravate the resultant tensions within the society and—what is of particular importance in this book—within its armed forces, whose professional officer cadre will for several decades remain Russian and Slavic, while its recruitment levies become ever more non-Russian and non-Slavic—specifically Turko-Tatar and Moslem. The Collins chapter in volume 1 hints at the extent to which linguistic incompetence in Russian (the armed forces' language of instruction and of command) on the part of many recruits is already perceived as an operational problem by the high command.[30] It behooves us to pause for a minute and speculate about what this portends for the interplay among culture, political system, and military effectiveness in and for the Soviet Union.

I begin by suggesting that the historic Leninist-Stalinist synthesis is disintegrating—and perhaps has already disintegrated. That synthesis consisted of course of many components. The two components that are particularly relevant to this chapter's topic are:

1. The synthesis of the traditional Westernizer versus Slavophile/Populist controversy in the form of industrializing, modernizing, but also inward-facing, xenophobic, etatist Bolshevism

2. The synthesis between Russian hegemonial centralism and non-Russian ethnonational centrifugal propensities in the form of Soviet federalism

Let me immediately interpolate here the cautionary note that when I allude to the incipient disintegration of this synthesis, I mean this in the sense of an increasing precariousness of declared Soviet normative values and ideological culture. I am not now claiming the imminent political or institutional disintegration of the Soviet Union, still less the structural-administrative destabilization of its armed forces. (The Soviet Union is, after all, one of those great land empires whose tenacity I have acknowledged earlier.) Even in as tightly coordinated a society as the Soviet one there exists a substantial degree of buffering between and among the ideological-normative, the cultural, the political, the economic (and so on) niches and orders of society and hence a certain time-lag in the metastasis of pathological, malignant symptoms from one to another of these niches. Furthermore, let me also interpolate here the grudgingly respectful judgment that the Soviet ruling elite works very hard and very conscientiously to immunize the political and military niches and orders from contamination by subversive and disorderly symptoms originating in one of the other niches or orders, be they ideological, or cultural, or economic-administrative.

And the elite has so far been impressively successful in this endeavor, for despite ideological fatigue, normative-value disintegration, intellectual dissent, economic malaise, and ethnocultural frictions, the Soviet political system has remained stable and the military structure orderly.

Nevertheless, since in the long run all niches and structural orders of a society are interdependent and interconnected, it is appropriate to speculate about the eventual systemic implications of what I perceive as the incipient disintegration of the Leninist-Stalinist normative-ideological synthesis in the two identified dimensions of the Westernizer/Slavophile axis and the Russian centripetal/non-Russian centrifugal axis. Such speculation may enable us to be judicious rather than sensationalist or dismissive in our assessment of the significance of the comportment of the Soviet army's Central Asian contingents in Afghanistan.

When two binary, linked variables that are not direct causal functions one of the other disintegrate, break up, and recombine, four possible combinations may then emerge in the realm of logically feasible, theoretical possibilities, though of course they are not all equally probable in the real world of historical and political contingencies. I leave it to the historians and the Sovietologists to inform us which of the four hypothetically possible recombinations in figure 4–1 are most likely and least likely to emerge from the current travails and creeping disintegration of the Leninist-Stalinist synthesis in the Soviet Union.

Solution A appears to be the one that the Reagan administration expects to emerge from the current travails of the Soviet system. It is a "worst-case" scenario, combining the reflexive traits of Russian xenophobia, autocracy, and hegemonialism vis-à-vis the non-Russian peoples of the Soviet Union with repressiveness toward all dissent.

Solution B suggests an even sharper inward-turning of Russian xenophobia, this time so radical as to write off and release at least some non-Russian

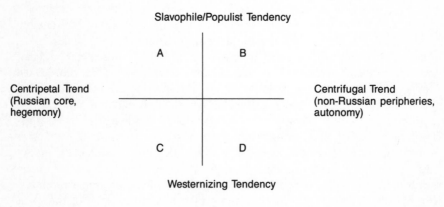

Figure 4–1

peoples of the Soviet Union—who would then become the beneficiaries of the resultant green light to their centrifugal aspirations. Occasional passages in Alexander Solzhenitsyn's writings indicate that he is reconciled to such a scenario. Within the Soviet Union, too, there are occasional Russian suggestions that many of the other nations in the system are but burdensome parasites whom it would be better to jettison. In Lev Tolstoy's *War and Peace*, Gen. Mikhail I. Kutuzov is deemed a great—and specifically Russian—moral sage precisely because he is depicted as also endorsing this prescription—despising, as he does in Tolstoy's pages, the tsar's acquisition of Finland, Poland, and other nations that will only seduce and deflect Russia away from her proper heritage and destiny and her own true culture. I will let the historians judge whether Tolstoy's literary Kutuzov replicates or distorts the real Kutuzov.

Solution C is a Russian version of the classic "white man's burden" defense of imperialism. It predicts a Westernized, modern, liberal Russia nevertheless retaining her non-Russian territorial acquisitions, partly for strategic reasons and partly to bring to these "younger brothers" the supposed benefits of an allegedly superior civilization—on the assumption that all except the Baltic peoples lag behind the Russians in their several levels of modernity.

Solution D stipulates a logical correspondence between the hypothetical selection of a Westernizing, cosmopolitan option by Russia and the recognition by such a Russia that the system's other peoples must, at a minimum, be granted greater pluralistic autonomy for their own ethnonational aspirations, and possibly even political independence.

The Soviet ruling elite seeks to deny, to smother, and to counteract the disintegration of the Leninist-Stalinist synthesis at the normative-ideological level—and thus to foreclose all four of the scenarios just sketched—with the rhetoric and the pseudoideology of a Soviet rather than a Russian *narodnost* (nationalism). It thereby seeks to straddle and to link both supraethnic Soviet and specifically Russian cultural symbols—and may be falling between two stools in its efforts. On the one hand, the regime's wish to sit partly on the Soviet stool affronts the nationalists of the dominant Russian ethnonation, who feel that it profanes their holy Russia on behalf of a cold, abstract, nonemotive, and unsatisfying formula; simultaneously it fails to attenuate or to satisfy the grievances, aspirations, and pride of the country's other ethnonations. On the other hand, ideological as well as political imperatives forbid a decision to sit fully on the Russian stool and abandon the supraethnic Soviet-Marxist one. The regime's relations with its several ethnic constituencies have thus come to resemble the predicament of the proverbial rider on a tiger, who can neither stay on nor get off without incurring prohibitive risks. Russian nationalism cannot be spurned lest the Russians disown the regime and the non-Russians perceive such a gesture as more a signal of ideological and political desperation than of integrative confidence. But neither can Russian nationalism be openly and explicitly adopted, or be permitted an uncontrolled life of its own, lest the other ethnonations be repelled and the Russians themselves perceive such developments as symptomatic of weakness and retreat on the part of the regime. Nor, finally, can the ruling elite realistically hope to revitalize the rhetoric and the apparatus of Sovietism as an authentic conferrer of symbolic legitimation and integration upon the state. The attempted resolution of this dilemma is the language of supraethnic Soviet *narodnost* and the real policy of flattering the Russians as the supposedly most progressive, productive, and leading ethnodemographic component ("the elder brother") of the Soviet state. But this hybrid stance only irritates the non-Russians without fully satisfying the Russians and fails to extract the regime from its degenerative symbolic-legitimation vortex.

The ethnonational problem is currently being managed and contained in the Soviet Union at a level below that of a crisis, thanks largely to an upward mobility escalator for most nonpolitical ethnic elites and professionals, as well as to the regime's toleration of ethnic aspirations that are marginal to the system's essential core and structure. Yet the interaction of this ethnonational problem with still other structural problems, policy dilemmas, socioeconomic constraints, and ideological impasses may yet render it incendiary in the coming decade and/or insoluble within the prevailing political system. Or, to state this point more analytically and more dialectically, the ethnonational problem complicates the many other problems—political, economic, administrative, cultural—that the Soviet elite faces and tends to stifle innovative and rational approaches to their possible solution. All such approaches point to greater decentralization—but this is precisely what the central elite fears as entailing the risk of centrifugal particularism and jeopardizing its own control over the entire Soviet system. Yet without such innovations the system drifts toward both stagnation and possible combustion. Meanwhile, the unresolved ethnonational problem, even at its current subcritical level, aggravates the tensions between the Russians and the other ethnonations—and between all of them seriatim and the regime. It thus poses a serious liability—substantive and symbolic—to the normative legitimacy of the Soviet system and to the integration and continuing stability of Soviet society and army.

If one probes a bit beneath the fastidiously clinical language and quantitative global data of the chapter in volume 1 by Harvey Starr and Benjamin A. Most on Third World wars in general,[31] one may learn or rather reconfirm an important lesson about a politicized cultural component that has energized most recent wars—and not only those in the Third World. Such Starr-Most terms as "internal wars" and "wars between actors of unequal legal status" screen the fact that they are really discussing ethnosecessionist wars and ethnically propelled civil wars and ethnically motivated irredentist incursions into target states. Of course, it was not Starr's and Most's responsibility to analyze how the basic cultural and psychological dimensions of ethnicity and of ethnofidelic bonding are translated into political space and into the military arena. Though unacknowledged, the product of these processes is the subject that their chapter really deals with. Their aggregative data and their extrapolated trends confirm that no type of society or political system is today immune from the growing pressure of politicized ethnic assertiveness, with its possible legitimating or delegitimating effects. Communist and non-Communist, old and new, advanced and developing, centralistic and federalistic states all must respond to the pressures of this ascendant culture-based ideology, which can propel relatively prosperous (for example, Basque, Croatian, Ibo, Sikh) and relatively poor (Québécois, Welsh, Anyanya, Assamese) ethnic groups into a sense of political grievance and possible militancy. The conventional academic wisdom used to claim that modernization and development would defuse and dissolve this allegedly primordial cultural/psychological sentiment of ethnicity or, at a minimum, would relegate it to a species of folkloristic trivia. But today we must acknowledge that it is rather this conventional academic wisdom that has been reduced to triviality by the power of the ubiquitous and growing phenomenon of ethnic assertiveness—a cultural/psychological value translated into political demands and military expressions.

A Fourth Definition of Culture

We have so far entertained three alternative notions of culture for the purpose of assessing the relationship of culture and war: (1) culture as stipulated, naturalistic, ethnonational character; (2) culture as civic commitment and social bonding; (3) culture as a community's historically developed philosophical-anthropological values. At this point, it is appropriate to introduce yet a fourth sense in which the term culture might appropriately be used in this chapter, and that is the specific strategic, operational, and logistical cultures of specific armed forces that are the expressions of sustained institutional histories. The bearer of the imputed culture in the first three definitions or uses of the term was the membership of the entire society; in this new, fourth sense the bearer is the professional military apparatus.

This fourth understanding of the term *culture* entails some refinement (not repudiation) of the point made earlier, that war imposes a logic of imitation on those who engage in it, and that therefore armies tend to resemble each other. That is true *en gros*, and it is especially true as regards weaponry, ordnance, and other hardware. Yet discrete armed forces also have discrete institutional pedigrees as well as overall rationalities. They have specific, historically transmitted styles of strategic assessments, of operational approaches, of organizational and logistical solutions to generic problems. And they maintain and sustain them not merely in reflexive cultivation of unquestioned tradition, but also in the belief that the fighting spirit and combat value of any armed force is significantly a function of its own specific institutional character. Armed forces, therefore, do not approach military problems in the spirit of some purely rational game theory. Their members, and especially their officers, are socialized into institutionally patterned beliefs, styles, attitudes, perceptions, approaches, and ideologies that are so strongly interwoven, inculcated, and embedded that they ought to be assigned to the plane of "culture" rather than of mere "policy."[32]

Examples illustrating this point come most readily to mind from World Wars I and II, but it is surely also valid for at least some of the eight recent wars on which we focus. There is the German military establishment's infatuation with the *Kesselschlacht* and its cultivation of *operativ* talent as the most prized of a commander's skills. There is also its organizational insistence that morale and esprit de corps require that its regiments and divisions be composed of men from the same district or locality, that replacements for casualties also come from there, and that the recovered wounded be returned to their original units.[33] Other armed forces cultivate analogous, albeit different and even contrasting, doctrines and commitments, expressing and embodying their particular institutional cultures.

Though the descriptive nomenclature of distinctiveness, particularity, and tradition that is required to describe this notion of military culture (our fourth) is quite similar to the terminology of the national character school of culture (our first), the two notions are in a real sense opposites. Military culture is shaped, honed, and nursed—indeed, created—by the military institution as a deliberately willed process, whereas so-called national character tends to be postulated as though it were something given, as a supposedly intractable biological-genetic constraint of nature. This distinction is neatly caught by a citation in Robert Harkavy's introductory chapter to volume 1: Moshe Dayan, as Israeli chief of staff and later as minister of defense, insisted that the selection, training, and indoctrination of Israeli officers be such as to "exorcise Jewish cleverness from the Israeli army" and inculcate it with a spirit of readiness for bloody combat.[34]

The Ethnic Composition of Armed Forces

So far, this chapter has been written as though the primary—indeed, the exclusive—function of armed forces is to engage in (or to prepare themselves to engage in) external warfare on behalf of their respective states. But this is of course a rather limited view of their real functions in real political life. Many governments of many states view their armed forces also as essential instruments of domestic security and regime support. And here—given the fact that the populations of most extant states are polyethnic—the ethnic composition of these armed forces becomes a very important datum indeed—far more salient and demonstrable than the supposed nexus between ethnonational culture and combat prowess that we assessed and found wanting earlier. Yet this new theme of ethnically conscious selection of the personnel of armed forces viewed as regime guardians does return us perforce to this chapter's earlier definitions of culture.

In Weberian ideal-type theory, of course, impersonal standards of functional competence and formal constitutional allegiance are alone supposed to govern the recruitment and promotion of personnel in the state apparatus and to assure the loyalty of the state's agencies to the political authorities. In practice, however, these political authorities often judge exclusive reliance on such purely rational-legal, institutional, impersonal standards of competence, obedience, and loyalty to be risky—especially in the case of army and police forces, which inevitably command equipment that could be diverted from their assigned missions to an attack or an ultimatum against the central government itself. Hence the frequent tendency of governments, in their endless quest for political loyalty and reliability on the part of the state's armed forces, to supplement (occasionally even to replace) the impersonal Weberian criteria of functional competence with ethnic criteria in the recruitment and promotion of personnel.

(Though rulers' bodyguards are not, *stricto sensu*, parts of a state's armed forces, it is nevertheless appropriate to indicate here that they too are often selected with an eye to their presumed ethnocultural reliability. Where rulers ignore or flout this criterion, as in the late Prime Minister Indira Gandhi's deliberate retention of her Sikh bodyguards as a demonstration of her "Weberian" confidence in their supposed nonethnic professionalism, the results can be dire.)

The preferred ethnic group is often, but not always, the political and governmental elite's own. The first variant is exemplified by President Hafez al-Assad's reliance on his fraternal 'Alawi officers to hold Syria's armed forces loyal to himself and by ex-president Idi Amin's utilization of his Moslem Nubian coethnics to achieve the same effect in Uganda. The alternative variant, in which the favored ethnic group is not the political elite's own, is illustrated by the quasi-praetorian role played by the Latvian Riflemen in the defense of Soviet Russia's infant Bolshevik regime on the morrow of its seizure of power and during its initial civil war ordeal, and by the prolonged favoritism shown by Morocco's King Hassan toward socially underprivileged and therefore supposedly faithful Berber officers. Particular "ethnic attention" may be devoted to recruitment for those subbranches of the armed forces that the government regards as especially sensitive for its own security, such as the intelligence branches of the defense and interior ministries, the riot-suppression gendarmerie, the counterinsurgency units of the army, and the like. Here, even a professedly transethnic and supraethnic regime may engage in deliberate ethnic "skewing" in its recruitment policies. One recalls the disproportionate former concentration of Jews and Poles in the Cheka and its successor emanations of the political police apparatus in the Soviet Union, and an analogous favoritism toward Serbs in Titoist Yugoslavia's equivalent institution, the UDBa.

All in all, therefore, the functional professionalization and the relatively high technological profiles that may characterize the armed forces and other security agencies do not contradict the possibility—indeed, the likelihood—that their personnel may be selected, promoted, and deployed on the basis of ethnic criteria so as to optimize the central political elite's sense of control.

Nemesis may, however, eventually exact a price for such deliberate ethnicization in the staffing of the agencies of state. First of all, the original reliability rationale may backfire against the governments as favored ethnic groups come to take a proprietary view of their traditional overrepresentation, or even monopoly position, in "their" particular branches of the armed forces and security agencies, and come to regard them as their ethnic groups' reserved and privileged fiefdoms. Second, they may go further and act out this perception through resistance and challenge to a central government seeking to reassert its control over them and/or seeking to diversify its ethnic recruitment policy. Third, when such ethnically skewed military, police, or administrative agencies are deployed by the central government to help it cope with a serious domestic interethnic conflict (or indeed any kind of domestic crisis), they will not be accepted by the contending ethnic groups as the neutral instruments of some supraethnic *raison d'état*, but will be perceived as ethnic participants, reflecting prevailing ethnopolitical stratification, with an ethnic stake of their own in the mode and shape of the conflict's prosecution and resolution. Indeed, in the Lebanese civil war of the mid-1970s the ethnically skewed (that is, overly Christian) army was ironically rendered useless to the government at the moment of its greatest need precisely because of this universal perception of that army as being already ethnically committed and biased. An analogous situation and perception has stigmatized the overly Protestant Royal Ulster Constabulary in the interethnic violence that has plagued Northern Ireland since the late 1960s. In other words, the overethnicization of the armed forces may compromise their legitimacy and discredit their acceptability as supposedly impartial executors of the state's transcendant regulative rules and values.

However, short of such extreme and hence limiting situations as interethnic civil war, selective and judicious ethnicization in the staffing of the armed forces and other security agencies often serves governments as a useful tool. They have found that it becomes a politically salient and controversial issue only at relatively infrequent intervals. Particularly in the case of armies, governments have learned that controlled and undemonstrative ethnic skewing in recruitment will generally be accepted by the polyethnic society as a whole—and will prove to be a resource and an asset to the government—provided that these armies be seen as professionally competent and not blatantly overpoliticized, and as not so expensive as to drastically deplete allocations for social, educational, and various ameliorative programs. Indeed, the issue may be partially defused if the favored ethnic group for military personnel recruitment is also the one that might be expected to be most insistent in demanding such compensatory socioeconomic programs—as with the Malays of multiethnic Malaysia—for this ethnic group is then less likely to regard funds allocated to the military and police as being diverted from its own needs in order to subsidize a rival ethnic group's fiefdoms.[35] In Lebanon and Ulster, alas, this happy equation was missing. There, the army's and the constabulary's highly visible and long-standing ethnic salience and interethnic controversiality arose in part from the fact that the poorer Moslem (Lebanon) and Catholic (Ulster) communities most in need of social programs had traditionally—even before the respective civil wars—resented expenditures on the "Christian" and "Protestant" security apparatuses, staffed, as these were, by their more prosperous ethnic rivals with lesser claims for publicly financed socioeconomic, ameliorative programs. The civil violence then aggravated and accelerated these polarizations in the ethnocommunal reputations of the military and the constabulary. In Lebanon, the polarization ultimately resulted in the neutralization and disintegration of the army.

Because the perimeters of the spectrum within which the ethnic skewing of personnel recruitment will be accepted as politically tolerable are imprecise and occasionally volatile perimeters, most governments are reluctant to concede openly that they engage in such skewing as a deliberate recruitment policy. Rather, they pretend that it accrues from allegedly unplanned and natural contingencies, such as the tendency of ethnic groups with a "martial tradition" and/or those characterized by economic marginality to take up soldiering and state service as careers promising esteem and upward mobility. While such sociohistorical tropisms undoubtedly do exist, they supplement but do not really contradict the observation that governments of polyethnic states, their disclaimers to the contrary notwithstanding, have traditionally and frequently found the deliberate exploitation of ethnicity as a recruitment policy in the staffing of the armed forces to be a useful *arcanum dominationis*.

Conclusion

The purpose of this chapter has been to formalize for its readers a number of propositions that they have long known (or at any rate have suspected) at a more diffuse level of cognition, to wit: The manner in which states fight wars and configure their armed forces is informed and constrained by cultural values and patterns. The political leaders of states and the high commands of armed forces do not approach the problems of war and of security in some purely game-theoretical, cost-effectiveness-assessing manner—although such rational appraisals also enter into their calculations and interact there with deep cultural values and patterns. But though all this may indeed be obvious, it nevertheless needs saying because of late the balance in American literature on war has tilted excessively and (I submit) dangerously toward overemphasis on putatively rational factors. Dismissing or failing to understand one's own, or one's foes', or one's allies' cultures (in all three useful meanings of the term *culture* as used here) can be dangerous for both the maintenance of peace and the successful prosecution of war. And we have indeed become dangerously insensitive to the cultural complexes that inform and shape various states' and regimes' modes of military planning and martial behavior.[36]

However, in correcting such insensitivity, we should also guard against tilting excessively in the opposite direction, of becoming intellectually mesmerized by culture and thus failing to appreciate that the patterns and traits of many societies and of their military establishments are probably quite rational for them, given their historical experiences and demographic-geographic situations. Thus we must not become overly analytical in the sense of abstractly disaggregating factors that are organically compounded. Conservatively, we must learn to appreciate that the power of culture derives from its deep roots, to understand that in the military dimension it leads to patterns of thought, planning, and behavior that are perceived to be historically validated and hence are likely to change only slowly (if at all)—and then only in response to deeply unsettling new historical experiences, and not in response to mere technological "fixes" or cerebral lessons in "rational" opportunity-cost programming.[37]

Notes

1. This term appears to have been coined by Gaston Bouthoul, *Les Guerres: Eléments de Polémologie* (Paris: Payot, 1951).

2. Joseph Rothschild, *Ethnopolitics: A Conceptual Framework* (New York: Columbia University Press, 1981).

3. Robert E. Harkavy, "The Lessons of Recent Wars: Toward Comparative Analysis," in *The Lessons of Recent Wars in the Third World,* vol. 1, eds. Robert E. Harkavy and Stephanie G. Neuman (Lexington, Mass.: Lexington Books, 1985), 16–18, note 46.

4. John Keegan, *The Face of Battle* (New York: Vintage, 1977), chap. 4.

5. Cf. Carl von Clausewitz, *On War,* eds. and trans. Michael Howard and Peter Paret (Princeton: Princeton University Press, 1976), 186, 479.

6. Letter commenting on an earlier draft of this essay from Warner Schilling, dated August 13, 1984.

7. Christie Davies, "Itali Sunt Imbelles," *The Journal of Strategic Studies* 5, no. 2 (June 1982): 266–69; B.H. Liddell Hart, "French Military Ideas Before the First World War," in *A Century of Conflict, 1850–1950,* ed. Martin Gilbert (London: Hamish Hamilton, 1966), 137, 141; William L. Shirer, *The Collapse of the Third Republic* (New York: Simon and Schuster, Pocket Books, 1971), 61; Stanislav Andreski, *Military Organization and Society,* 2d ed. (Berkeley: University of California Press, 1968), 82; John U. Nef, *War and Human Progress* (Cambridge: Harvard University Press, 1952), 252.

8. Niccolò Machiavelli, *The Art of War* (Indianapolis, Ind.: Bobbs-Merrill, 1965), 25, 61, 169, 202.

9. Niccolò Machiavelli, *Discourses on the First Ten Books of Titus Livius* (New York: Random House, 1950), book 2; *The Prince* (New York: Random House, 1950), chaps. 12, 13, 24.

10. Conversation with Warner Schilling, June 6, 1984. See also Ray S. Cline, *The United States Army in World War II. The War Department. Washington Command Post: The Operations Division* (Washington, D.C.: Office of the Chief of Military History, Department of the Army, 1951), 336–39, 343.

11. Adda Bozeman, *Politics and Culture in International History* (Princeton: Princeton University Press, 1960), 320–40.

12. John E. Mueller, "The Search for the 'Breaking Point' in Vietnam: The Statistics of a Deadly Quarrel," Richard A. Betts, "Comment on Mueller," Frederick Z. Brown, "Comment on Mueller," John E. Mueller, "Rejoinder," *International Studies Quarterly* 24, no. 4 (December 1980): 497–531.

13. Michael C.C. Adams, *Our Masters the Rebels: A Speculation on Union Military Failure in the East, 1861–1865* (Cambridge: Harvard University Press, 1978), passim. I thank my colleague Prof. Robert Jervis for drawing my attention to this book.

14. John K. Fairbank, "Introduction: Varieties of the Chinese Military Experience," in *Chinese Ways in Warfare,* eds. Frank A. Kierman, Jr., and John K. Fairbank (Cambridge: Harvard University Press, 1974), 8.

15. Harlan W. Jencks, "Lessons of a 'Lesson': China-Vietnam, 1979," in *Lessons of Recent Wars in the Third World,* vol. 1, eds. Robert E. Harkavy and Stephanie G. Neuman (Lexington, Mass.: Lexington Books, 1985), 157.

16. Ibid., 152.

17. Fairbank, "Introduction," 9, 25, and Edward S. Boylan, "The Chinese Cultural Style of Warfare," *Comparative Strategy* 3, no. 4 (1982): 345, 351–52, 359.

18. Harlan K. Ullman, "Profound or Perfunctory: Observations on the South Atlantic Conflict," in *The Lessons of Recent Wars in the Third World,* vol. 1, eds. Robert E. Harkavy and Stephanie G. Neuman (Lexington, Mass.: Lexington Books, 1985), 248. Also Richard Ned Lebow, "Miscalculation in the South Atlantic: The Origins of the Falkland War," *The Journal of Strategic Studies* 6, no. 1 (March 1983): 5–35.

19. Compare Ullman, "Profound or Perfunctory," 255, with Harkavy, "The Lessons of Recent Wars," 16–18.

20. William O. Staudenmaier, "Iran-Iraq (1980–)," in *The Lessons of Recent Wars in the Third World,* vol. 1, eds. Robert E. Harkavy and Stephanie G. Neuman (Lexington, Mass.: Lexington Books, 1985), 212, 215–17, 220, 226–27.

21. Cf. E. Shouby, "The Influence of the Arabic Language on the Psychology of the Arabs," *The Middle East Journal* 5, no. 3 (Summer 1951): 284–302. I find nothing implausible in the notion that the structure of a language has organizational and behavioral consequences for the societies and individuals that use it. Much of the anthropological oeuvre of Bronislaw Malinowski is devoted to this proposition.

22. Staudenmaier, "Iran-Iraq," 218–19, 224–25.

23. Steven David, "Realignment in the Horn: The Soviet Advantage," *International Security* 4, no. 2 (Fall 1979): 69–90.

24. Joseph Rothschild, *Pilsudski's Coup D'Etat* (New York: Columbia University Press, 1966), 3–7.

25. Ullman, "Profound or Perfunctory," and William H. Lewis, "War in the Western Sahara," in *Lessons of Recent Wars in the Third World,* vol. 1, eds. Robert E. Harkavy and Stephanie G. Neuman (Lexington, Mass.: Lexington Books, 1985).

26. William H. McNeill, "On National Frontiers: Ethnic Homogeneity and Pluralism," in *Small Comforts for Hard Times: Humanists on Public Policy,* eds. Michael Mooney and Florian Stuber (New York: Columbia University Press, 1977), 207–19.

27. W. Seth Carus, "Military Lessons of the 1982 Israel–Syria Conflict," in *The Lessons of Recent Wars in the Third World,* vol. 1, eds. Robert E. Harkavy and Stephanie G. Neuman (Lexington, Mass.: Lexington Books, 1985).

28. Joseph J. Collins, "The Soviet-Afghan War," in *The Lessons of Recent Wars in the Third World,* vol. 1, eds. Robert E. Harkavy and Stephanie G. Neuman (Lexington, Mass.: Lexington Books, 1985), 193, 198–99. For contrasting observations, see Ellen Jones, "Minorities in the Soviet Armed Forces," *Comparative Strategy* 3, no. 4 (1982): 300, 315–16.

29. Thus, the dissident Soviet mathematician Igor Shafarevich warns, "Of all the urgent problems that have accumulated in our life, the most painful seems to be that concerning relations beween the various nationalities of the U.S.S.R. No other question arouses such explosions of resentment, malice, and pain—neither material inequality, nor lack of spiritual freedom, nor even the persecution of religion." Igor Shafarevich, "Separation or Reconciliation? The Nationalities Question in the USSR," in *From under the Rubble,* ed. Alexander Solzhenitsyn, et al. (Boston: Little, Brown, 1975), 88.

30. Collins, "The Soviet-Afghan War," note 63. See also Ellen Jones, "Manning the Soviet Military," *International Security* 7, no. 1 (Summer 1982): 105–31.

31. Harvey Starr and Benjamin A. Most, "Patterns of Conflict: Quantitative Analysis and the Comparative Lessons of Third World Wars," in *The Lessons of Recent Wars in the Third World,* vol. 1 eds. Robert E. Harkavy and Stephanie G. Neuman (Lexington, Mass.: Lexington Books, 1985).

32. Jack L. Snyder, *The Soviet Strategic Culture: Implications for Limited Nuclear Operations* (Santa Monica, Calif.: Rand R-2154-AF, 1977), v, 38–40.

33. John Keegan, *Six Armies in Normandy* (London: Jonathan Cape, 1982), 243, 320.

34. Harkavy, "The Lessons of Recent Wars," note 51.

35. Cynthia Enloe, "The Issue Saliency of the Military-Ethnic Connection," *Comparative Politics* 10, no. 2 (January 1978): 275–76, 282.

36. Colin S. Gray, "Comparative Strategic Culture," *Parameters* 14, no. 4 (Winter 1984): 26–33.

37. Cf. Rebecca V. Strode, "Soviet Strategic Style," *Comparative Strategy* 3, no. 4 (1982): 319–39.

5

The Human Dimension
of Modern War

Martin van Creveld

Looking back at warfare as conducted during the last decade and a half, can one identify any important changes that have taken place in regard to the way in which it relates to the people who participate in it, the nature of the demands that it makes on them, and the way that they function in it? And, turning the problem around, what do these changes signify in relation to the nature of modern man in his capacity as a fighting animal? These are indeed very fundamental questions, and ones that the present chapter will try to provide with some answers, however partial and incomplete. To do this, it is proposed to proceed in two stages. In part one we shall examine the changes in military organization and manpower policies that have resulted from modern technology as applied to the field of warfare. In part two we shall discuss some phenomena that affect the modern soldier as he engages in campaigning. While making an occasional glancing reference to the technological systems that are needed for the conduct of nuclear war, the chapter does not deal with nuclear conflict as such; for, since there have not yet been any nuclear wars, no lessons from them can realistically be drawn.

The Age of Complexity

One basic fact about modern warfare that few if any observers would be inclined to dispute—if only because their livelihood depends on its being not only true but widely accepted—is its growing complexity. That complexity, in turn, is usually seen as being primarily the result of rapidly developing military technology. To illustrate the problem, the following represents a—necessarily very incomplete—list of the new technologies added to conventional arsenals since the 1973 Arab-Israeli war, in its own time probably the most modern air/land battle ever fought and also the first to witness the full-scale employment of guided missiles at sea;[1] second- and third-generation antitank missiles, constructed around sophisticated electronics that did not even exist twelve years ago; laser target acquisition and fire control systems for tanks;

artillery radar with all its ancilliary apparatus; attack helicopters carrying guided missiles; remotely piloted vehicles (RPVs) whose role in reconnaissance, surveillance, and damage assessment is growing all the time; a wide variety of C^3 (command, control, and communications) devices designed to enable units to determine their positions at all times and commanders to acquire a real-time capability for reading the battlefield; cluster bombs; air- and missile-deliverable mines; fly-by-wire aircraft with their sophisticated look-down radars, as well as HUD (head up display) and FLIR (forward-looking infrared) electronics; and EAW (electronic airborne warfare) aircraft, the importance of which in helping the Israelis defeat the Syrian Air Force during the 1982 campaign in Lebanon is said to have been very great.[2]

At sea, the greatest advances are probably represented by air-to-surface missiles which were absent from the 1973 war but which dramatically demonstrated their potential during the Falkland conflict and were also used in the war between Iran and Iraq. No less important were developments in the field of antimissile defenses, taking the form of missiles and of radar-linked, computer-directed automatic cannon capable of spewing out shells at very high rates. In the future, hostilities at sea will no doubt have to reckon with submarine-launched antishipping and cruise missiles now in the arsenals of several countries; but these are weapons that have not yet been used in the wars fought since 1973.

The above weapons and items of equipment for the most part represent additions to the TOEs (tables of organization and equipment) rather than simple substitutes; however, even when this has not been the case no mere list can take adequate account of the fact that most of the more recent technologies are themselves much more complex than their predecessors, consisting of so many more parts, making use of so many more advanced (often synthetic) materials and methods of manufacture, demanding so much more skill for maintenance and repair, and permitting only much smaller tolerances. For example, the fuel control system of the J-79 engine used to power the F-4 Phantom fighter-bomber that carried much of the combat burden in Vietnam had approximately 1,000 parts; its successor, the F-100 engine installed in both the F-15 and F-16 fighters, requires no fewer than 4,500 to do the same job. Not surprisingly man-hours per repair average 47.8 for the former engine, 328, or over six times as many for the latter.[3] Table 5–1, which has been reprinted so many times as to become something of a stock-in-trade among publications on the subject, tells its own story.[4]

To explain what such technological complexity can do to the personnel involved in military organization and warfare, let us take the case of the Israel Defense Forces (IDF), which at one time were famous for their lean structure and no-nonsense approach of focusing everything upon the central task of combat.[5] However, since 1967 and particularly after 1973 the IDF made a conscious decision that, in order to offset Arab numerical superiority, it would

Table 5-1
FY 1979 Material Readiness Indicators

	Complexity	Inventory	NMC(%)[a]	Available Aircraft	Unavailable Aircraft at Any Given Time	MFHBF[b]	MMH/S[c]	Cann-WR/100 Sorties[d]
Air Force								
A-10	Low	243	32.6	164	79	1.2	18	16.7
A-7D	Medium	376	38.6	231	145	0.9	24	9.3
F-4E	Medium	610	34.1	402	208	0.4	38	13.3
F-15	High	428	44.3	239	189	0.5	34	29.3
F-111F	High	95	36.9	60	35	0.3	75	44.9
F-111D	High	86	65.6	30	56	0.2	98	58.5
Totals		1,838		1,126	712			
Navy								
Marine Corps								
A-4M	Low	129	27.7	94	35	0.7	28	12.0
AV-8A	Low	92	39.7	56	36	0.4	44	13.4
A-7E	Medium	386	36.7	245	141	0.4	53	27.1
F-4J	Medium	342	34.2	226	116	0.3	83	22.2
A-6E	High	297	39.3	180	117	0.3	71	39.4
F-14A	High	292	47.1	115	137	0.3	98	69.6
Totals		1,538		956	582			

[a]NMC(%) = This factor measures the average percentage of aircraft that were "not mission capable" during FY 1979; for example, an F-111D was not capable of performing one of its primary missions. (For that fraction of time it may still have been flyable or capable of flying its missions in a degraded mode). The NMC data indicates a rough relationship between complexity and NMC: as planes get more complex, they tend to break more often, for there are more things that can go wrong.

[b]MFHBF = Mean Flying Hours between Maintenance Events. It is a measure of reliability. The number represents an average for a year. (For example, an F-14 may fly for a long time with no maintenance events, then suddenly several can occur.) Again, there is an inverse relationship between complexity and reliability. Simple planes tend to have a greater overall reliability than complex planes.

[c]MMF/S = Maintenance Manhour Per Sortie. This factor represents the total workload required to prepare the airplane for the next flight after it has landed.

[d]Cann-WR/100 Sorties = Cannibalization and War Reserve Withdrawals per 100 Sorties. This factor measures relative shortages of spare parts. If operating stocks are short, maintenance personnel have the option of temporarily obtaining the spare parts from the War Reserve spares kit, or of taking parts off aircraft that are temporarily grounded.

have to stake everything on modern technology.[6] Consequently it has turned into one of the most heavily armed, if not actually the most heavily armed, forces in history. As might be expected, no such massive infusion of more and more sophisticated technology, both imported and locally manufactured, was possible without a matching increase in human skills. As a result, the ratio of professional soldiers to the mobilized strength of the army, which used to stand at 1:24 in 1973, has since increased to over 1:10.[7] In other words, so complex is modern military technology that it is making the maintenance of forces consisting mainly of reservists and of conscripts more and more questionable, and this even in a country that, for perfectly good strategic, social, and economic reasons, is strongly committed to the idea of the nation in arms.

Not only is advanced technology compelling soldiers to become more professional; since there are clear limits to the number of skills that each individual can acquire during his or her useful military life, it is also forcing them to become more and more specialized. Each major new weapon system usually requires that a new arm, or branch, or department of the service be set up and be coordinated with all others. Each also requires that so many troops specialize in its operation, maintenance, and repair, with the result that the number of military occupation specialties (MOSs) in the ordnance corps of the Israeli Army is said to have more than doubled over the last decade. Since the number of specialties grows much faster than the size of the military establishment as a whole, there is a tendency for fewer and fewer men to share the same training or to attend the same courses and the same schools, with the result that the difficulties of coordinating, of creating cohesive units out of this mass of human atoms, grow larger all the time. The net effect of technological advance, as seen from the point of view of the individual soldier, is thus to prevent or at least render more difficult the maintenance of informal communications. These must accordingly be replaced by more and more formal procedures, often at no mean risk to the creativity of commanders and troops and to their capacity for improvisation, for finding original and appropriate solutions to military problems in the field. It is suggested that the Israeli performance in Lebanon, uncharacteristically heavy-handed and unimaginative as it was (there was, for example, no attempt to use light infantry for deep penetration, outflanking movements, ambushes, and surprise, even though the terrain was obviously ideal for that purpose), was partly conditioned by these circumstances; and the same is probably true in regard both to the U.S. conduct of the war in Vietnam and the clumsy, hammer-like manner of operation said to characterize much of the Soviet military presence in Afghanistan.

None of this should be construed to mean that, as opposed to their predecessors, modern armies consist exclusively of highly trained supermen; while it is true that some modern weapon systems such as the F-15 push human performance to its very limit (even to the point that the number of men capable of making adequate pilots is said to limit the size of an air force that a country can set up and maintain)[8] in other cases modern weapons and equipment actually make fewer and lesser demands on their operators than did their predecessors. For example, lasers and computers have made the job of a tank gunner considerably easier to learn, with intuition and experience being replaced by exact (and automatically performed) calculations as regards range and the effect of atmospheric conditions. Second- and third-generation antitank guided missiles are likewise easier to use than their first-generation predecessors, while fourth-generation equipment now entering the testing stage will offer a "fire and forget" capability and thus be simpler still. Where ammunition is cheap and may be fired off in practically unlimited quantities, training in marksmanship—that centuries-old stock-in-trade of the infantryman—may safely be curtailed or even discontinued. Where men live encased by machines—many of which are actually air-conditioned so as to improve crew performance and protect delicate equipment—and are supported by enormous logistic tails, fieldcraft and survival skills diminish in importance and are indeed threatening to disappear altogether from the most advanced armies. Thus, the point that needs making is not that the skills demanded of each individual soldier are necessarily becoming higher or more complicated or more difficult to acquire; only that the forces as a whole are becoming more skilled, with the result that they require more and more specialization and more and more elaborate organization, procedures, and equipment to keep track of all these specialties.

One special case that has to be considered in this context is the dilemma with which the process of specialization is facing those responsible for the organization and management of officers' careers. For reasons that are perfectly sound, it has traditionally been the policy of armed forces everywhere to eschew specialists in favor of all-round commanders when it comes to filling top-level posts, in other words to make sure that senior commanders know at least something about everything. Since there is nowadays so much more to know, however, tours of duty in numerous modern armies, including the West German, U.S., and Israeli ones, are showing a disturbing but typical tendency to become shorter and shorter.[9] This of course raises serious questions concerning the ability of such "limited liability" commanders on their way to the top to get to know their men, establish communications with them, and mold them into the sort of cohesive units that have always constituted the indispensable basis for successful military operations. The failure of the U.S. Army to deal with these problems effectively during the Vietnam War has been well documented;[10] and it is suggested that some aspects of the more recent Israeli performance in Lebanon—particularly the surprisingly high incidence of psychiatric casualties in a war that was by no means very intensive, or prolonged, or of a doubtful outcome—should be seen against the same background.[11]

This brief discussion of the way modern military technology affects military organization and the troops that make up that organization is not intended to be anywhere near exhaustive. Other aspects that could have been explored but were not include the growth of armies' technical, logistic, and administrative "tails" at the expense of the fighting "teeth" even to the point where, in some of the most up-to-date armed forces, troops who actually "carry fire" to the enemy number less than 10 percent of the total; the way, very noticeable in the West German Army among others, in which the same phenomenon is apt to drain the fighting units of top-quality manpower, taking away men who in previous ages would have become combat commanders and putting them to man (or plan) computers in the rear; the disruption of traditional hierarchical patterns of military command and their replacement by immense networks of communications extending in all directions; the related danger of the military ethos being ousted in favor of a managerial, bureaucratic, and technological one; and the way in which technological progress has caused the proportion of "command troops" (that is, personnel whose primary occupation it is to process information so as to control and coordinate the performance of others) to grow by a factor of five over the last three decades.[12] To the extent that specialization drives C^3 and C^3 itself has turned into a specialty (or rather, into an immense complex of related specialties) the process has become self-sustaining; nor is it easy to imagine any developments, short of a massive loss of technology such as is sometimes said to have accompanied the transition from the ancient world into the Middle Ages, which could slow it down or bring it to an end.

While even the above list probably falls short of covering all the problems confronting those whose job it is to manage man in modern war, it is not the intent of this chapter to suggest that any of them are necessarily insuperable. All I wish to point out is that they are inherent in modern military technology, and that, if they are to be understood and overcome, they must be seen in these terms. Also, it is suggested that armies that for one reason or another are unable to do this will have to rest content, if that is the proper expression, with a much lower level of performance. This is already the case in the war that Iran and Iraq are waging, where both sides seem to have nothing in common so much as the glaring inability to make the best use of the up-to-date military equipment in their possession, and which has consequently degenerated into a slugging match closely resembling the trench warfare of World War I. Also at the Falklands, it is reported that the Argentines failed to make the best possible use of the sophisticated missiles at their disposal, or else British losses might well have been heavier than they were.

The Face of Combat

Given these effects of modern military technology upon military manpower and the way in which it is organized, what can be said about the impact of modern combat on the same? Regarded from the point of view of manpower, of soldiers as individuals or in groups, does modern combat differ from its predecessors in essential ways, or does it remain basically the same phenomenon? To answer this question it is proposed to dissolve it into several constituent ones that, though necessarily far from exhaustive, are at any rate sufficiently interrelated and overlapping to provide a picture of sorts. In doing this, we are conscious of the limitations of analysis, for no analysis, being of necessity sequential, can fully capture living, changing, interacting human reality, particularly in regard to a phenomenon so complex and so multifaceted, so kaleidoscopic as combat.

The Age of Dispersion

One fact on which all observers seem to be agreed and which has been more carefully documented than most,[13] is that modern armed forces fight dispersed—that is, that each individual soldier on the average takes up far more room than he used to. This fact has been used as a basis for making all kinds of wild conjectures concerning the "emptiness of the battlefield" and the allegedly all but intolerable psychological burden that this puts on the individual soldier.[14] Moreover, this increased burden is said by some to come on top of the much longer duration of battles,[15] a combination that leaves one wondering whether all modern soldiers are supermen or else how, supposing this not to be the case, battles still continue to be fought at all.

By way of groping our way toward an answer, we might note that there is involved in the above presentation a fundamental misunderstanding that tends to be masked rather than brought out by the statistical methods of analysis employed. Certainly modern combat, taking place with the aid of modern technology, has very greatly extended the overall spaces that armed forces occupy and therefore (other things being equal) also the average room taken up by each individual soldier; however, this only increased the isolation of the latter *so long as the nature of the weapons with which he fought did not change.* However, it has been one of the outstanding characteristics of warfare during the last century or so that weapons did change, and none of these changes has been more pronounced or more important than the shift that has taken place from individual weapons to crew-operated ones. Consequent of this shift, the vast majority of today's soldiers no longer go to war as individuals, wielding their muskets or sabres and either riding their horses or walking on their own feet. Rather they tend to be cooped up inside steel shells, as in the case of tankmen, or else to cluster very closely around heavy weapons such as machine guns, mortars, cannon, and the like, the majority of which are either mounted on vehicles or tracted by them, thus making necessary close cooperation with additional soldiers. Even the infantryman with his rifle and bayonet, long the epitome of the individual fighting on his own, nowadays frequently rides into battle inside an armored vehicle, thus forming part of a team that, if it is to function or indeed to exist amidst the complexities of the machinery by which it is encased, must be extremely close-knit and well "played in." The long and the short of it is, modern combat in many if not most cases does just the opposite from what so much of the literature suggests; far from increasing the isolation of the individual, it has made him more dependent on his fellow troops than ever before.

One result of this trend, which would be completely inexplicable if it were true that modern war consists of isolated individuals huddling down amidst the spaces of an empty battlefield, is the increase in the role of junior leadership at the level of platoon, squad, and even below. Where the effective use of sophisticated technology depends on well-rehearsed teams of men usually numbering from four to ten achieving smooth and frictionless cooperation, no position in the entire army is more important than that of the tank commander or that of the person whose responsibility it is to ensure that his self-propelled cannon actually delivers the ten rounds a minute of which it is theoretically capable. Where operations are too spread out and proceed at too fast a pace to be capable of being effectively monitored by higher headquarters (as has often been the case during recent armored offensives) it falls to very junior commanders to make decisions on the spot.[16] Thus it is scarcely surprising that, where the general social structure of the nation and its system of military manpower organization have been conducive to the emergence of high-quality junior leadership, the results have generally been excellent, as in the case of the British in the Falklands and the Israelis in 1973 (less so, it is sometimes said, in 1982); where this is not the case, as in the Soviet Army and in the forces fighting each other along the Iraqi-Iranian border, performance has been mediocre at best.[17]

The Lethality of Combat

Closely related to this discussion is the claim, which may be found in much of the literature, that modern combat, owing to the greater power of the weapons that it employs, is more lethal than its predecessors; indeed that the story of warfare is that of a growth in lethality, which once again leaves one wondering whence came those modern supermen so much better able to withstand terror than their ancestors; or does the allegedly lesser lethality of previous wars mean that those who fought in them were not really stretched to their psychological limits? Furthermore, modern battles are often said to be not only more lethal than their predecessors but also to last longer; which combination makes it rather surprising that, at the end of the affair, there should sometimes be any troops left on the near side of the lunatic asylum's walls.

To put these matters into perspective, a little digression into history is necessary. Certainly until the time of Napoleon, and frequently even thereafter (one need only think of the leisurely *tour de France* that the Germans made in 1870–71 after beating the Emperor Napoleon at Sedan and Bazaine at Metz), most campaigns were nothing but extended hiking trips punctuated here and there by often well-regulated tournaments known as battles. The range of the weapons in the hands of both sides being limited to rather less than a mile, for most of the time they were not even in contact with each other; and while certainly suffering losses from sickness and possibly also from desertion, bloody casualties would be few, limited to skirmishes that took place between opposing patrols. Battles were limited in place and time; mostly they only lasted for a matter of hours, although as armed forces grew larger after 1809 there was a tendency for them to become prolonged over one, or two, or possibly three whole days.

Since these earlier engagements saw entire armies clashing at very close quarters, casualties in them were often horrific. For example, at Cynoscephalae in 197 B.C. the Macedonians lost no fewer than 13,000 out of 20,000 men; Roman casualties are unknown. At Crécy in 1346 the French lost 11,000 out of 30,000. At Malplaquet in 1709, out of 190,000 who engaged, 36,000, or 18.9 percent, became casualties. The figures for Hochkirch (1758) were 65,000, 17,000, and 26 percent; for Borodino, 250,000, 70,000 and a shocking 28 percent.[18]

Beginning approximately at the time of the American Civil War, these things gradually underwent a change. June–July 1862 witnessed a series of very intensive actions around Richmond known as the Seven Days' Battle, in which both sides together threw 195,000 men into the fight and lost some 35,000 of them, or approximately 2.5 percent of strength per day. Even at Gettysburg, where overall casualties amounted to close to 30 percent of the forces engaged, the average daily loss was only about 9 percent. Thereafter the figures declined very sharply. Although subsequent wars were still punctuated by an occasional day of exceptional butchery (the British during the first day at the Somme gave a particularly telling example of how to do it), on the whole it has become quite rare for an army to lose more than say 2.5 percent of its strength during any single day of combat. These trends, which are now somewhat over a century old, appear to be confirmed by the most recent wars. Take the most intensive (and certainly the most "modern") among them all, namely, that fought between the Israelis and the Syrians in the Bekaa Valley from June 8–11, 1982; out of a total of 67,000 troops approximately 5,400 were killed or wounded, which works out at a daily average of 2 percent of strength.[19]

What is the explanation behind these figures? Clearly none can be found in the characteristics of weapons, the increasing lethality of which has been well documented.[20] Nor does the phenomenon have anything to do with the relationship between offense and defense because, as I have shown elsewhere,[21] technology in principle is unable to affect that relationship substantially. Supposing a third explanation, namely, that modern troops are somehow more reluctant to kill their enemies than were their ancestors, is also discounted (for lack of evidence, if nothing else), then it becomes necessary to take another look at the structure of modern armed forces. As we have noted, that structure is characterized by nothing so much as the fact that, as the fighting teeth shrink in relative size, more and more troops are spread over huge areas in the rear and are engaged in administration, supply, repair, maintenance, and a vast variety of tasks connected with C³I (command, control, communications, and intelligence).

While it would certainly be untrue to say that all these men are perfectly safe from enemy action—since many if not most of them are liable to be killed at any moment by an incoming bomber- or missile-delivered warhead—there is no question but that the likelihood of this happening is fairly small at most times and indeed that the routine of a great many of these men closely approximates that of civilians. Nor are the losses that do take place among this part of the forces necessarily linked to those at the front in any direct way; if anything the opposite is true, since means are always finite and weapons that are employed for butchery at the front will not be available for attacking the rear.

Thus, since modern weapons are sometimes so powerful as to be capable of wiping out entire units (and also because, as we have noted, in many cases modern troops are very closely bunched together), losses on the modern battlefield can still be horrific; but unless the fighting is accompanied by severe and sustained bombardment in the rear, or else forms part of an encircling movement, these casualties for the most part will affect only a small and diminishing fraction of the forces. To cite an extreme example, the Israeli Air Force during the first two days of the 1973 war lost approximately a fifth of its aircraft, but when one compares the number of pilots killed, wounded, or captured to the number of personnel in the force as a whole, they are perceived to constitute a very small fraction. Similarly during the four days of the Bekaa Valley battle in 1982, tanks were lost at a rate that exceeded that of overall casualties by a factor of four to one. These facts tend to confirm our interpretation that the lethality of warfare has not so much declined as it has changed its locus.

Since modern armies, unlike their predecessors, almost invariably see their fighting teeth attrited away much faster than their logistic and administrative tails, an imbalance between the two is often created, one that, unless it is somehow corrected, will lead (and in recent wars often has led) to waste as a huge shaft supports a smaller and smaller blade. Basically, two methods suggest themselves for dealing with this problem. One is to fill up casualties on a current basis as they occur, the other to let units bleed white and then reconstitute them periodically and en bloc. As I have explained in detail elsewhere,[22] the former solution is the more efficient one from a purely administrative and technological point of view, whereas the latter is more likely to help preserve the cohesion of formations and their fighting spirit. Whatever the solution actually adopted, it will have no small effect on the willingness of the soldier to fight and die, as the Americans found out in Vietnam and others are still finding out.

The Role of Man on the Battlefield

For several decades now, there have been predictions that the day would come when, given the advance of technology, machines would replace men on the battlefield, which would consequently become entirely "automated."[23] In one version of this vision, if one may call it by that name, more and more sensors, computers, and weapons will be directly linked to each other, thus increasingly taking men out of the decision loop. In another more extreme version, the battlefield itself will actually be populated by machines, each possessed of its own sensors, weapons, and computerized brains, which will then proceed to fight each other without shedding human blood. Clearly none of these scenarios has as yet been completely realized; in the light of recent wars, however, to what extent may they be said to be on their way to realization?

In attempting to obtain an insight into this problem, one does well to consider war not as a single whole, but rather as differentiated according to the type of environment in which it takes place. Other things being equal, the simpler that environment the easier it is for machines to take the place of man, and the greater also the dependence of man upon machines not only for fighting itself but also for sheer survival. Regarded from this point of view, outer space by definition presents the simplest environment of all. In ascending order of complexity it is followed by the atmosphere, next by the hydrosphere (otherwise known as seas and oceans), and finally by terra firma. The latter in turn differs very greatly in regard to the complexity of the environments that it offers. These range from the simplest of all, namely, flat, open desert, all the way to the most complicated, which is provided by human beings: their fields, factories, habitations, and arteries of communication.

Although to date no wars have taken place in outer space, it certainly seems as if the vision outlined above, that of the automated battlefield run entirely by machines, is well on its way to realization in that environment. The numerous types of military hardware that, even at the present moment, are circling the earth while engaged in a variety of tasks—surveillance, the relay of information, serving as navigational aids, and so forth—do not require the presence of humans for their operation. Nor does it look as if the so-called Star Wars program for laser- or particle-beam-based antimissile defense now under active development in the United States (and probably in the Soviet Union as well)[24] will require that man be present in the battle stations. On the contrary, such are the psychological and physiological demands of man, and so hopelessly slow and inaccurate and inconsistent his reactions, that his presence at almost any point in the decision-making loops that these systems involve will almost certainly be looked upon as an intolerable encumbrance. The computers of course will have to be programmed by people, though it is entirely conceivable that even part of that job may one day be done by other computers. Once the system is in place, the role of humans will be limited to maintenance, repair, monitoring, and testing. Given a threat, the system will presumably have to be activated by releasing a series of built-in safety catches, a process that itself will tend to remove any human operators who are left. From that point on everything will happen by itself with human interference minimal or zero.

Since the earth's atmosphere represents the next simplest environment that we have listed, it is not surprising that here too we find extensive attempts to replace at least some of the men—read, pilots—involved by machines. There is indeed nothing new in these attempts; already during the First World War experiments aimed at replacing manned aircraft by radio-controlled ones for some kind of missions, and in World War II this was actually done on selected occasions.[25] Since then a variety of missiles, guided and unguided, have steadily replaced aircraft on some types of missions (particularly those that require no very high accuracy in hitting pinpoint targets or moving ones). At the other end of the scale the most recent wars have witnessed remotely piloted vehicles taking some types of reconnaissance away from manned aircraft (incidentally, reconnaissance was the first mission with which the latter were entrusted) and also playing a growing role in such rules as fire control, damage assessment, and combating antiaircraft defenses. So far air-to-air combat as well as tactical strike missions and interdiction (besides of course a variety of logistic and support missions carried out by aircraft and helicopters) have been left in the hands of human pilots; but for how long? As the Israeli campaign in Lebanon demonstrated, already more and more of the pilot's functions are being taken away from him and entrusted either to on-board computers and sensors or else to ground control. One would perhaps hesitate to forecast that these trends may reach their logical conclusion any time soon; their direction, however, is clear enough.

A special case to be considered in the present context is that of antiaircraft and antimissile defense. On the one hand, this kind of warfare takes place against a background—the atmosphere—that is relatively simple; on the other, it requires very high speed, very great accuracy, and very rapid calculation. It would be hard to think of any kind of environment more suited to machine warfare, and a move toward machine warfare there accordingly has been, what with radars, computers, and transponders acquiring targets, tracking them, making them out for friendly or hostile, deciding in which order they are to be engaged, and actually firing and guiding the weapons.

As in antiaircraft warfare, so at sea; to the extent that war in this environment also is becoming increasingly dominated by missiles and by a variety of electronic countermeasures, the role of human operators in it has been diminishing. As a result small missile boats with miniscule crews now pack firepower equal to or greater than that deliverable by the battleships of old. On board these boats, as indeed in many of the more sophisticated naval vessels that are used by today's navies, the task of operating the equipment has become almost trivial compared to that of maintaining and repairing it.[26]

On land, however, the situation is fundamentally different. No sensors yet devised are capable of reliably distinguishing enemy targets from their environments, particularly under conditions of darkness, smoke, and dust so often encountered on the battlefield. While aircraft may carry IFF (identification friend/foe) transponders, a way has yet to be found to implant such gadgets in the breast of every individual foot soldier. In some parts of the world, notably the very important Western European theater, climatic conditions (frequently rain and fog) further complicate the problem of target acquisition and tracking, whereas other areas present exceptionally difficult environments in the form of mountains, jungles, or, perhaps worst of all, connurbations (the conjoining of several urban areas). In view of these circumstances land warfare has remained a comparatively primitive affair technologically, which is tantamount to saying that it is still very manpower intensive. In the Falklands and Lebanon, let alone Afghanistan and along the Iraqi-Iranian border, the vast majority of those who were actually engaged in fighting did so in land operations, often in humble tasks such as loading shells, driving vehicles, defending strongholds, and participating in search and destroy missions that differed little—if at all—from those of their predecessors in World War II or even before. Once again, the breakneck speed of technological progress and the unexpected directions that it often takes make one hesitate to venture predictions as to the future direction of things; for the present, however, it seems clear that, on the ground at any rate, the automated battlefield is nowhere near.

To sum up, there is a sense in which recent wars have caused the role of man on the modern battlefield to diminish as more and more of his functions are taken over by sensors, radars, and self-guiding, self-acting weapons. As a rule, the simpler the environment in which the battle takes place the more true this proposition, and vice versa; which helps explain why modern armies such as those of the Israelis in Lebanon and the Soviets in Afghanistan, not to mention that of the Americans in Vietnam, have not found the sophisticated military technology in their hands of much use in dealing with low-intensity guerrilla warfare waged in what is by definition the most complex of all environments, namely, that made up of civilian populations. Although the prevailing trend toward automation may be expected to continue in the future, the day when there is no room left for man in battle is not likely to come about anytime soon, if at all. Furthermore, to say that many forms of modern warfare are less manpower intensive than were those of their predecessors is not necessarily the same as saying that the role of those humans who are left is becoming less critical. Insofar as no technological system however sophisticated can ever be programmed to foresee all possible eventualities (not least those arising from its own breakdowns and malfunctions), it is clear that there will always be room in such systems for well-trained human operators to seize the initiative, communicate informally with each other, and improvise.[27] When everything is said and done, no technological system can be better than the people who operate it; nor is it possible for technology to become completely automated, that is, independent of man, without at the same time ceasing to do anything useful for him.

Conclusions

To conclude, the reader will have noticed that this chapter has focused on changes in the way war is waged and has carefully avoided saying anything about human nature itself. Specifically, no attempt has been made to explain anything in terms of "modern man" (by which we usually mean the inhabitants of a few economically highly developed countries around the globe) being more, or less, suitable for warfare than his ancestors; that he is more (or less) inclined toward military service, more (or less) bellicose, more (or less) cruel in his warlike behavior. Since such claims have often been made in the literature,[28] however, it is proposed to end the chapter by saying at least a few words on these problems.

To begin with the question of suitability, it may be true that "modern man" is less exposed to physical violence in his day-to-day life than were his predecessors in most historical societies, and that the physical and psychological adjustment involved in the shift from peace to war is accordingly more difficult for him than it was for them. Whatever the truth in this argument (and nobody has yet proved or even attempted to prove that the inhabitants of high-violence areas such as inner cities make better soldiers than anybody else), it has been one of the cardinal points of this chapter that, in modern warfare, the number of troops actually engaged in fighting is declining all the time, whereas those engaged in a variety of other tasks are becoming more and more numerous. To put it in another way, there definitely is a sense in which warfare itself is becoming less violent, and often less lethal as well, for those who take part in it; so this is an argument that is not easily sustained.

Nor does the present author see much merit in the opposite argument, namely, that modern man is more suitable for warfare than his predecessors owing to his more intimate familiarity with machines and the working habits that they dictate. As the historical record shows, war has always made use of the best available technological means, and one would be hard put to prove that the weapons of one period were more (or less) suitable to "the nature of man" than those of any other. There have been times when technology dictated that war consist largely of a multitude of single combats, and man adapted to that. At other times it demanded that he operate in huge compact blocks, and he adapted to that also. There have been periods and places when fighting was done face to face, others in which the combatants never even saw each other but merely pushed buttons from miles away or thousands of feet up. Thus, whatever the nature of military technology at any particular time and place, man on the whole has adapted to it well enough.

Those who argue—whether in approbation or with disapproval—that modern societies are too effete, permissive, and materialistic to wage war effectively will do well to recall that ours is by no means the first historical age to express such beliefs; and that, in the past, periods in which the disinclination to military service was strong and widespread have always been overtaken by others much more militaristic. The civilized eighteenth century—civilized in relative terms, since the point was by no means always obvious to contemporaries, as is witnessed by some famous passages in Swift's *Gulliver's Travels* and Voltaire's *Candide*—was succeeded by the immense brutalities of the French Revolution. The idea of soldiers as the scum of the earth was replaced by that of armies as the school of the nation. Historically peoples long considered "soft" have not seldom turned extremely bellicose, and the reverse has also been known to happen. Looking back, one suspects that the view that "modern youth" is soft has its origin in the last treeman's forlornly decrying his sons' unfortunate move into the comparative luxury of caves. It has not prevented any number of wars' taking place since, and it surely will not prevent many more from taking place in the future.

Not to belabor the point unnecessarily, the present author does not share the belief—regardless of whether it is shored up by sociology, psychology, biology, or any odd hybrid of those—that the difference between ourselves and our ancestors in regard to war is more than skin deep. Quite on the contrary, the ease with which many people, including those who are ostensibly most highly civilized and express the noblest pacifist sentiments, not infrequently cast off all restraints at a moment's notice and then proceed to commit enormities and brutalities that would have put Attila to shame must be counted as one of the most terrifying phenomena of the modern world. When everything is said and done, nothing that has happened in recent years gives the slightest indication that modern man's attitude to and suitability for warfare differs appreciably from that of previous generations. An unpleasant reflection, no doubt; but one that mankind will have to live with if its assessment of itself and of the world in which it lives is not to be entirely unrealistic.

Notes

1. Short, useful surveys of the state of the art of military technology may be found in S.J. Deitchman, *Military Power and the Advance of Technology* (Boulder, Colo.: Westview Press, 1983), and RUSI (Royal United Services Institute) and Brassey, *Defence Yearbook* (Oxford: Oxford University Press, 1984), 237–342.

2. See W. Seth Carus, "Military Lessons of the 1982 Israel-Syria Conflict," in *The Lessons of Recent Wars in the Third World,* vol. 1, eds. Robert E. Harkavy and Stephanie G. Neuman (Lexington, Mass.: Lexington Books, 1985).

3. Figures from J. Fallows, *National Defense* (New York: Vintage Books, 1981), 39.

4. Table originally prepared by F. Spinney for *Defense Facts of Life* (Boulder, Colorado: Westview, 1985), 52.

5. The best general work on the IDF remains E.N. Luttwak and D. Horowitz, *The Israeli Army* (London: Allen Lane, 1975), which emphasizes precisely these qualities. However, the book is now in urgent need of updating.

6. For a good discussion of the rationale behind the drive towards advanced technology see several articles in Z. Ofer and A. Kover, eds., *Quality versus Quantity* (Hebrew) (Tel Aviv: Ma'arachot, 1985).

7. Figures from International Institute of Strategic Studies (IISS), *The Military Balance 1973–74,* (London, 1974), 33, and *The Military Balance 1983–84* (London: IISS, 1984), 56.

8. Ofer and Kover, *Quality versus Quantity,* 296. Here it is suggested that the size of Israel's population limits that of its air force.

9. In Vietnam, American company and battalion commanders held their posts for less than six months on the average; see W.C. Westmoreland, *A Soldier Reports* (Garden City, N.Y.: Doubleday, 1967), 296–97. Information in my hands suggests that in the IDF, the average tour of duty has been reduced by about 40 percent since 1967.

10. See R.A. Gabriel and P.L. Savage, *Crisis in Command, Mismanagement in the Army* (New York: Hill and Wang, 1976).

11. See G.L. Belenky, C.F. Tymer, and F.J. Sodetz, *Israeli Battle Shock Casualties; 1973 and 1982* (Washington, D.C.: Walter Reed Army Institute of Research, 1982), for data on this issue. For a discussion see also M. van Creveld, "Not Exactly a Triumph," *Jerusalem Post Magazine,* December 10, 1982, pp. 6–7.

12. It was around 3 percent in World War II, but had risen to 15 percent in 1975; see M. van Creveld, "Bundeswehr Manpower Management," RUSI and Brassey, *Defence Yearbook* (Oxford: Oxford University Press, 1983), 51.

13. By far the most detailed figures are provided by T.N. Dupuy in *Numbers, Predictions and War; Using History to Evaluate Combat Factors and Predict the Outcome of Battles* (Indianapolis, Ind.: Bobbs-Merrill, 1979), 28.

14. See for example R.F. Bigler, *Der Einsame Soldat* (Frauenfeld: Huber, 1963), whose title speaks for itself.

15. J. Keegan, *The Face of Battle* (London: Jonathan Cape, 1976), 302–4.

16. For an analysis of command in armored battle and the role of junior leadership in it, see "The Strategy of the Tank," in *Strategy and Politics,* ed. E.N. Luttwak (New Brunswick, N.J.: Transaction Books, 1980), especially pp. 299–302.

17. The Syrians too are said to have suffered from a shortage of qualified junior officers in 1982, mainly owing to President Assad's determination to recruit them as far as possible among his fellow 'Alawites, who form only 11 percent of the population. See J.S. Bermudez, "The Syrian Tank Battalion," *Armor* (November–December 1984): 18.

18. All figures from Harbottle's *Dictionary of Battles,* 3d ed., rev. G. Bruce (New York: Van Nostrand Reinhold, 1981).

19. Data from T.N. Dupuy, "Measuring Combat Effectiveness; Historical-Qualitative Analysis," in *The Lessons of Recent Wars in the Third World,* vol. 1, eds. Robert E. Harkavy and Stephanie G. Neuman (Lexington, Mass.: Lexington Books, 1985).

20. See T.N. Dupuy, *Numbers, Predictions and War* (New York: Bobbs Merrill, 1977), p. 26, for a table showing the theoretical relative lethality of various weapons.

21. "Technology, Attack and Defense"; an unpublished paper. Briefly, this paper argues that any technology that can be used for the defense necessarily can be used by the offense also. Had technology favored either the offense or the defense to any great extent and for any length of time war itself would have become impossible, and indeed this is precisely what may already be happening in the case of nuclear-armed missiles directed against value targets.

22. See *Fighting Power; German and U.S. Military Performance, 1939–1945* (Westport, Conn.: Greenwood Press, 1982).

23. For a good outline of the entire problem see P. Dickinson, *The Electronic Battlefield* (London: Boyar, 1976).

24. The most balanced account of the possibilities of Star Wars is in A.B. Carter and D.N. Schwartz, eds., *Ballistic Missile Defense* (Washington, D.C.: Brookings, 1984).

25. The Germans in particular used radio-controlled glider bombs against shipping in the Mediterranean, and also had a contraption known as "Beethoven," consisting of a fighter that, after first riding a bomber piggyback toward its target, released it and exercised guidance by radio control.

26. See B.D. Cole, "Train the Warrior—Educate the Officer," *Proceedings of the Naval Institute,* January 1985, pp. 45–47.

27. For some sagacious remarks on the place of humans in very large and complex military-technological systems, see P. Bracken, *The Command and Control of Nuclear Forces* (New Haven: Yale University Press, 1983), 11ff.

28. See above all Keegan, *The Face of Battle,* chap. 5; K. Lorenz, *On Aggression* (London: Methuen), chap. 13; and D. Morris, whose views on the problem are conveniently summed up in *Manwatching, A Field Guide to Human Behavior* (New York: Abrams, 1977), 158–59.

6
War Economics

Gavin Kennedy

Introduction

A popular catchphrase among economists—of the kind that evocatively sum-marizes the main thrust of the discipline—is the assertion that "There ain't no such thing as a free lunch," or TANSTAAFL for short. The gist of TANSTAAFL is that somebody somewhere pays for whatever we consume, "free" lunches included. If we engage our scarce resources in one activity, we cannot perforce engage them in another. Behind this basic though oft forgot-ten notion lies the concept of opportunity cost: the real cost of doing anything is what we have to give up to do it.

The TANSTAAFL principle is applicable to war: "There ain't no such thing as a free war: somebody somewhere pays for it" (TANSTAAFW?).

Wars cost economic resources as well as human lives and suffering. In an attempt to avoid the costs of war, *all* countries have defense expenditures, though some (for example, Costa Rica) disguise them as well-armed internal security forces, and others (for example, Iceland in NATO) free-ride on powerful allies.

The option of avoiding defense expenditures—in order to use the resources for some other preferred purpose, such as welfare—is not taken, for if it were the country would risk being absorbed by a neighbor or being riven by inter-nal subversion. Because of the fatal weakness of pacifism—pacifists have no defense against nonpacifists—policies of avoiding defense expenditures on the grounds that defense provision promotes war, or because attractive alternative uses of defense resources exist, are not likely to be implemented in the near future.

Defense Budgets and Deterrence

Whereas wars may be avoided (states can choose not to contest even an impor-tant issue by force of arms), the consumption of resources to deter wars can-not be, for the evidence shows that a failure to deter aggression, particularly where there is scope for hostilities, almost always invites it. Defense, therefore, is a regrettable necessity and a lower cost alternative to the expense of war.

A classic example of the false economy of nondeterrence can be seen in the immediate run-up to the Falklands invasion by Argentina in 1982. Britain, up to 1982, had only a nominal defense force on the islands, consisting of a detachment of marines (twenty-two lightly armed men in all). The British government, prompted by concerns at the costs of U.K. defense, conducted a defense review and issued a White Paper, *The Way Forward* (Ministry of Defense (MOD) 1981), which announced, inter alia, the imminent withdrawal from the South Atlantic of the patrol ship, HMS *Endurance,* and a reduction in the Royal Navy's surface fleet, including its troop-landing craft. These policies appeared to signal an unwillingness to contest by force of arms claims to sovereignty over the Falkland islands. From this misread signal, an Argentine invasion looked winnable (Ullman 1985).

Hence, whatever the arguments about the morality of defense preparations, there is a universal consensus among states that defense is a prudent and proper provision for governments to undertake and an economy to resource.

The case for prudent provision has a long pedigree among economists. Adam Smith in *The Wealth of Nations* (1776) specifically charged as the *first duty* of the state, "that of protecting the society from the violence and invasion of other independent societies." If there was any doubt as to how the first duty should be discharged, Smith added that it "can be performed only by means of a military force" (Smith 1776, book v, s. 1).

Moreover, Smith considered that if there had to be a choice between expenditures on defense and opulence, he came down firmly on the side of defense, for without defense a nation would soon cease to enjoy its opulence. This thought is probably not too far away from the minds of defense planners in the Gulf States, given the narrow margin they have between their present oil-based affluence, and their strategic vulnerability to external aggression (see Cordesman 1984, 541–67).

Shares of Defense in State Budgets

The case for prudent provision has certainly been mirrored in the practice of all states in the allocation of their revenues. Defense, which takes the lion's share of public expenditures in the early stages of the evolution of a modern state, gradually gives up its status as the major consumer of state revenues as the state matures. The proportion of the state budget spent on defense falls relatively (though it rises absolutely). This has been the experience of all modern states since the early nineteenth century.

In the advanced, richer economies, defense takes up less than 7 percent of GNP (with norms of around 4 percent) and under 20 percent of public expenditures (with norms of around 12 percent). Those countries with relatively high proportions (that is, in excess of 20 percent) of public expenditures allocated to defense tend also to be countries with relatively low GNPs per capita (an indicator of a less-developed economy). They also tend to be countries facing or believing that they face serious threats to their security. Which factor is most predominant in accounting for a high D/GE (defense/government expenditure) ratio—the relatively low level of economic development or perceptions of the threat environment—is an empirical question best addressed by studies of each case.

The countries discussed in this book that appear in table 6-1 (in italics) conform to the experience of most Third World countries in that they have high D/GE ratios. Iran, Israel, and Somalia have D/GE ratios at or above 40 percent. Iran is engaged in military activities that divert considerable amounts of government revenue; Israel is able to maintain such a high ratio by virtue of the external financial support it receives from the United States; and Somalia has such a high ratio because it is desperately poor and maintains a defense presence because of the threat it perceives from Soviet-backed Ethiopia (whose D/GE ratio is 34 percent). Morocco (20.3 percent), Argentina (23.1 percent— though falling to 13 percent in 1984), and Syria (29.1 percent) all have high D/GE ratios in excess of 20 percent.

The ratios for Vietnam and Afghanistan are not available. Both countries are heavily socialized and have comparatively large government budgets relative to a standard GNP calculation. Both are also engaged in counterinsurgency warfare, Vietnam in Kampuchea and Afghanistan within its own territory. It is a safe assumption that their actual D/GE ratios, if known, would place them in table 6–1.

This general relationship has provoked some rather naive disarmament literature (typically, U.N. sponsored research, for example Thee [ed.] 1981, United Nations 1978) that allude to a causal relationship running from high defense spending to low per capita income. The alleged relationship is spurious. The high D/GE countries are, in the main, newer states going through the transition from high to low proportions of public expenditure on defense as they develop economically and take on wider economic and social roles.

Developing countries are not poor *because* they have relatively high defense expenditures as proportions of their available resources for development; they have relatively high D/GE and D/GNP ratios because they are poor and face hostile environments.

A failure to understand this relationship, even for the best of motives, leads to the recommendation that poor countries spend less on defense and thereby expose themselves to high security risks, which can have the most appalling even if unintended consequences for those who live in poor countries (see Leontief and Duchin 1983 who neglect the political reality that countries do not risk reducing defense expenditures even for more economic growth).

Table 6–1

Defense Expenditures as a Proportion of Government Spending (D/GE) and as a Proportion of GNP (D/GNP), 1982

Country	D/GE	D/GNP	Defense Expenditure ($ billion)
South Yemen	48.3[a]	n.a.[b]	0.12[c]
UAE	47.4	9.8	2.4
Iran	46.9	14.2	15.3
Pakistan	45.6	7.1	1.8
Israel	44.6	35.7	6.8
Oman	43.4	23.8	1.7[a]
Taiwan	42.4	7.8	3.5
Somalia[f]	40.0	n.a.	n.a.
South Korea	36.0	6.0	4.3
Burma	35.0	3.5	0.18
Ethiopia	34.0[a]	n.a.	0.36[c]
Saudi Arabia	29.6	17.7	27.0
Syria	29.1	13.4	2.4
Peru	28.1	8.2	0.39[a]
North Yemen	27.6	16.4	0.33[c]
India	27.6	3.3	5.5
Greece	25.7	7.0	2.6
Thailand	25.3	5.0	1.3[a]
Jordan	24.8	12.1	0.42[a]
Paraguay	24.7	1.9	0.08[a]
Argentina	23.1[a]	n.a.	10.0
Singapore	22.9	n.a.	0.7[a]
Zambia	22.2[a]	n.a.	0.6[d]
Turkey	21.6	5.2	2.7
Morocco	20.3	9.0	1.1[a]
China[e]	20.1[a]	n.a.	11.8[a]

Source: IISS, *The Military Balance: 1984–85*, table 4; extracted and rearranged.
[a]1981.
[b]n.a. = not available.
[c]1980.
[d]1979.
[e]Not comparable; see source: 1982–83, pp. 78–79.
[f]From *Africa Guide*, 1984.

Most wars since 1945 have taken place in the Third World, at a human cost approaching 20 million dead, and investment in deterring war is an appropriate and unavoidable use of their scarce resources.

Comparative Defense Budgets

Too much ought not to be read into any series of comparative defense expenditures. Not only are measures of defense expenditures subject to considerable variation between countries, because of differing definitions as to what should or should not be included, and the suspicion that some countries "massage" their published defense statistics (Ball 1983, 1984a), but the volatility of exchange rates precludes any precise meanings being attached to comparative measures (Neuman 1978; Kennedy, chapter 3, 1983). There is apprehension about the status of national income accounts and the analyses that they spawn, in many Third World countries, and about sources of defense statistics from developed countries—see Ball (1983) for criticism of data from the International Institute for Strategic Studies (IISS), London; the Stockholm International Peace Research Institute (SIPRI), Stockholm; and the Arms Control and Disarmament Agency (ACDA), Washington, D.C.

Despite the inadequacy (which runs from unintentional inaccuracy to outright falsification) of national income accounts and defense budgets, there is, however, some value in *ordinal* comparisons of data where the magnitudes of the differences are less important than the rank order of the magnitudes, but I acknowledge the caveats of many writers about making use of GNP measures (see Neuman 1978, Kennedy 1983, Blackaby 1983). In column four of table 6–1, total defense expenditures are shown using comparative data.

The range of annual defense expenditures is extremely wide, running from about $200 billion by the superpowers to $2 billion (with many more countries, including some of those discussed in this book, having defense budgets under $500 million). The big spenders, that is, those spending over $6 billion in 1982, from the cases in this book—Iran, Iraq, Argentina, China, and Israel—have defense budgets comparable to those of some middle-ranking NATO members.

From the perspective of defense economics, the relative scale of the defense budget is an indicator not just of the "burden" of defense in respect to the economy (D/GNP), but also of the military resources that are available if a country has to go to war (roughly, the kind of data presented in the annual *Military Balance,* IISS, 1983, and in national intelligence assessments).

Defense resources consist of personnel, consumables, and equipment. The proportion of the defense budget allocated to each element during peacetime depends on the military doctrine of the defense planners, which is, of course, influenced by geography, politico-economic, and historical factors unique to the countries concerned, or rather, on how these factors are perceived by those who decide on defense planning (Neuman 1984, 1–28).

A peacetime defense budget of $20 billion a year suggests a sophisticated inventory of military equipment; a budget of under $400 million suggests a lightly armed infantry model, perhaps with an inventory of a few (very few) helicopters and armored personnel carriers (many of which can be nonoperational through shortages of spares and poor maintenance performance).

War of course causes a substantial increase in expenditures going to consumables (gasoline, ammunition, and so forth). The surge in spending on consumables can be substantial and can require a country to get immediate assistance from external suppliers. Both Israel and Britain sought (and received from the United States) replenishment supplies of consumables during their conflicts in 1982.

Prevalent as war is on a global scale, it is an infrequent experience for the majority of countries. This makes decisions about the size and composition of the budget a less than accurate science. Defense planners prepare for contingencies that are likely but which might never occur (the rationale, in fact, for defense spending is to deter contingencies by preparing to face them; though the planners must still prepare for the "right" rather than the "wrong" contingencies, otherwise a country becomes vulnerable to military "surprises" for which it is not prepared).

Because the preparations that they make are not tested, defense planners have no means of evaluating the efficiency of their preparations—are they preparing for the right contingencies? Only in war is a defense force and its doctrine tested, and though valuable lessons are available from other peoples' wars (including the "surprises" for which they did not prepare), they never carry quite the same authority as lessons from one's own wars.

Entry Costs of War

It is always easier to get into a war than to end one. Faced with a national emergency, the modern state does not start without military resources, for it already has a defense force available for use as needs, circumstances, and opportunities present themselves. At any given moment there is a defense inventory of men, consumables, and equipment in stock, available for use in an emergency. This force has been paid for by previous years' defense budgets. It takes time, perhaps more than is available, and substantial resources to augment a defense force to cope with unforeseen contingencies. While mobilization of military reserves is a feature of the defense plans of many countries, most rely on existing standing forces to "hold the line" in an emergency, if only temporarily, and none relies exclusively on mobilizing untrained civilian resources *after* it is attacked.

The quality of the personnel (including their training, leadership, commitment, adaptability, and readiness); the quantities of the consumables (including their deployment and accessibility, their logistical support, and reserves); and the quality and quantities of defense assets (including their availability and their technology) constitute the effective force that will be tested against the actual as opposed to the theoretical contingencies that occur if deterrence fails and war occurs.

Thus, governments have at their disposal a military force with a larger capital inventory—tanks, aircraft, ships, missiles, small arms, communications, and so on—than they could purchase from a single year's procurement expenditures.

Ball (1984b, 7) reports that in twenty developing countries, operating costs (personnel and consumables) accounted for between 70 percent and 90 percent of security spending, leaving very little, both proportionately and absolutely, for the procurement of weapons systems each year.

The existence of defense resources (personnel, consumables, and equipment), which the economy has already forgone the use of in other roles, makes for a relatively *low entry cost* to war. The reason for having defense forces in being is so that the state has the option of defending perceived national interests.

With standing military forces the resources allocated to defense have already been sacrificed economically, except where, as in Israel, the bulk of the personnel resource consists of part-time (but well-trained and motivated) soldiers mobilized quickly from the economy. Here, the withdrawal of personnel has an immediate effect economically (which leads Israeli military doctrine to favor short blitzkrieg-type wars, like that in Syria in 1982, Lebanon being a costly exception), but in most cases where there are standing armies, mobilization does not have an immediate economic effect.

If a war depletes available military inventories, war costs will rise, sometimes substantially, as evidenced in Israel's expenditure of a year's GNP during the 1973 Yom Kippur war.

The economic costs of starting a war, because they can be low, are less influential in the initial stages of decision making about war than are the purely military and political judgments of the government and its advisers. Optimists, who predict a short, sharp march to victory, are more likely to influence decisions than are pessimists, who worry about the costs if things go wrong.

This might explain why the judgments made by Iraq in 1980, prior to its invasion of Iran, did not include an assessment of the long-term economic costs if their military expectations of a quick victory were not met (a lesson for defense planners?—"What will it cost if our military capabilities fall short of what turns out to be required?"). The Iraqi military believed that the war would not last long—given their perceptions of pending Iranian disintegration—and that they could fight with the forces they had at their disposal. The economic costs of continuing the war, while by no means totally unbearable, are now very apparent to both sides.

Iraq in 1980 was blessed with $35 billion of foreign exchange reserves from the output of its oilfields (3.2 million barrels a day prior to the war, now down to 650,000). Not only has its reserves been run down to about $4 billion, but Iraq has required to be supported by aid worth $30 billion from friendly Gulf States (mainly Saudi Arabia, which has both "lent" foreign exchange and credited revenues from additional output of its own oil—in a slight fudging of OPEC rules—to an Iraqi account) (Lloyd's Bank 1984).

At the time when the Iraqi government decided on war, the Iraqis were able to contemplate a low-cost war—using up the stock of consumables already purchased in the defense budget, with minor depletions of hardware and personnel in a speedy victory—followed by a glowing economic future based on the development plans already underway before the war started. The fact that these expectations were frustrated and that the war has dragged on at an economic cost of $1 billion a month (National Westminster Bank [NWB], June 1984) indicates the economic consequences of a wrong politico-military judgment.

In the case of Argentina, the entry costs of the Falklands war were effectively close to zero in 1982. Most of the war materiel had been assembled—and paid for—by 1979 for a proposed war with Chile over the contentious issue of the Beagle Channel (*Financial Times,* July 22, 1982). This meant that the bulk of the military inventory required for use in the Falklands operation had zero cost to the decision makers in March 1982.

The Argentine economy had already paid for its war materiel, and in economics a bygone is a bygone. This is true even where Argentina's defense inventory was paid for by borrowing—once the debt is incurred, the interest payments, because they cannot be avoided, become a fixed cost and had to be borne whether Argentina went to war with Chile in 1979, or with Britain in 1982, or remained at peace. Only where a decision can be made in respect of future uses of resources is it relevant to consider their costs. Hence, such borrowings, once they were undertaken in 1977–78, had no relevance to the war or peace decisions of the Argentine government.

When we consider the state of the Argentine economy at that time (GNP falling, foreign debt rising, inflation accelerating, unemployment growing), it is surprising that they risked the additional economic burden of a war with the United Kingdom. There is no doubt that the relatively low entry costs, combined with the belief that victory would be swift because it would be uncontested, removed fears of additional costs from a prolonged war and made the economic aspects of the decision supportive of its politics.

Hence, in both Iraq's and Argentina's cases, when we consider that a valued prize (the Shatt-al-Arab; the Falklands) appears to have a near zero *economic* cost to acquire, we can understand why a look at the arithmetic was a temptation to be hawkish.

The decision of the U.K. government to go to war was also based exclusively on the immediate availability of the necessary resources, out of the defense inventory Britain had committed to NATO, for the Task Force, and not from any consideration of the economic consequences of a prolonged war, or, in the light of events, the consequences of an early victory.

Once the ground forces of each country came into contact, the military issue was settled fairly quickly. At no time during March to May 1982 was the U.K. economy affected (at least not negatively) by a diversion of resources to the Falklands war. As with Argentina, most of the materiel had already been paid for in previous defense budgets, and therefore U.K. entry costs to the war were low too. Some immediate additional costs (to convert merchant ships for the Task Force and for consumables for the air-bridge to Ascension Island) came out of the government's contingency funds and did not require any additional taxation or borrowing.

The materiel losses on each side (mainly aircraft, small arms, and munitions from Argentina, and ships from the United Kingdom) could have no economic effect on either economy, for the resources used in these military assets had already been sacrificed from other uses at the time that the assets were constructed. A ship that has been paid for in a previous budget cannot be an *additional* cost to the current economy when it is sunk in combat—this would be double-counting economic costs. Its replacement, *if undertaken,* will be a cost on a future defense budget, and because all military assets have a finite life, war losses merely accelerate replacement programs.

Since 1982, however, the economic costs of retaining the Falklands have grown considerably and these have become a distinct burden on the U.K. economy. Whereas the Falklands war had little effect on the general economic situation of Argentina (and defeat for Argentina terminated its war costs, except for the costs of economic sanctions imposed during the war), the situation for the United Kingdom is altogether different. The United Kingdom is making a substantial investment of military resources in the Falklands, of which the new airport (at £215 million) is the most visible, and has undertaken to replace lost assets costing £1,040 million and to meet garrison costs of about £400 million a year up to 1986 (MOD 1984). The consequential costs of the Falklands war for the United Kingdom, because of its victory, are burdensome by any standards, and were almost certainly avoidable if expenditures on deterrence had been undertaken prior to 1982.

Benefits of Losing Quickly

Mercifully, Somalia and Argentina were saved from prolonged war costs by defeat. In Somalia's case, the failure of its attempt to annex the Ogaden deepened its alienation from the Soviet Union which had brought beneficial economic changes with the ending of Soviet-style economic controls. The main consequence of the loss of the Ogaden war was to flood western Somalia with refugees.

The Ogaden war indicates the fragility of an opportunist strategy of using a standing military force for a quick "grab and keep" operation. Somalia invaded the Ogaden in the belief that the disintegration of the Ethiopian regime under internal stresses (separatist wars, civil resistance, and so forth) made reaction to a fait accompli either unlikely or, if attempted, unsustainable.

The entry costs for Somalia were low. But using forces that are narrowly balanced with an adversary exposes the parties to any shift in the balance caused by one of them acquiring additional military resources at short notice. Normally, it requires time and also a well-managed state to divert civilian resources into a defense effort. It is the absence of both that entices the adversary in the first place. If a defender can bring additional forces to bear on the contest more quickly than its opponent can respond, it will achieve a military advantage unforeseen by the attacker.

The attacker can gain an early advantage by exploiting a weakness, but once it commits its forces it has, by virtue of its quick-result strategy, few reserves of military materiel or economic resources to cope with "surprises." The fact that the military in Third World countries is often grossly inefficient by NATO standards, either in fighting capability or logistical support, and often cannot field their declared inventories, enhances the vulnerability of those who go for a "quick" war.

In the Horn war, Ethiopia acquired the Soviet Union as a new ally and in consequence received additional fighting forces from Cuba and a massive injection of military materiel. Once these forces were deployed at the head of a superior logistical system, the war turned in Ethiopia's favor, and Somalia was routed. The forces Somalia had in being for a short opportunist adventure were not sufficient to sustain a longer (and larger) war. Poor countries can start cheap wars but cannot always sustain expensive versions of them.

The defeat of Somalia and its inability to continue its war might be regarded as a blessing rather than as a disaster. Four years later Somalia is looking stronger economically than is Ethiopia (which is still racked by secessionist wars and economic chaos).

Somali inflation in 1980 stood at 80 percent, but following the adoption of policies to meet IMF (International Monetary Fund) targets, inflation fell to 24 percent in 1983. Somalia's foreign trade expanded (exports up by 66 percent to $120 million; imports up by 58 percent). The Ethiopians have encouraged some guerrilla groups to harass the Somalis, but they are nowhere near the scale of threat that the antigovernment separatists represent within Ethiopia. Somalia allocates nearly 40 percent of its budget to "political and security matters" (the rest to "economic and social development") (Africa Guide, pp. 296–308) but on the whole is pursuing a liberal economic policy, supported by foreign aid from Western sources.

Argentina's failure in the Falklands discredited an already weak military system that gave way to a civilian government in 1984. This has strengthened Argentina politically and, in due course, might do so economically.

The economic situation in Argentina in mid-1982 was described as "very grave" by the government. Pastore, the minister for the economy said, "The Argentinian economy is in a state of unprecedented collapse, which can only really be classified as a national emergency" (*Financial Times,* July 22, 1982). But we must be clear that the economic situation was not a product of the war with the United Kingdom because this was deteriorating before the possibility of an invasion of the Falklands occurred to anybody in the Argentine government.

Argentina's foreign currency reserves fell from $10 billion in 1979 toward $3 billion in 1982; foreign debt climbed from $13 billion in 1978 toward $38 billion in 1982; the GNP fell 6 percent in 1981, and inflation rose from 165 percent to 400 percent between 1981 and 1982. Without the Falklands war the Argentine economy, except in specific details, would have been in no less of a mess than it was as a result of it. The war's main effect was political. It also resulted in a cut in the defense budget from 17 percent of government expenditure in 1982 to 13 percent (ABICOR Report, Sept. 1983), with additional reductions in personnel in 1984–85 (Jane's Defence Weekly [JDW], Dec. 15, 1984). According to IISS in 1982, Argentina's D/GE ratio reached 64 percent in 1981 prior to the Falklands war (IISS 1983, 125).

In 1984 Argentina's GNP was still below the level it reached in 1974. Per capita income has fallen 13.5 percent in ten years. Inflation has been accelerating (600 percent in late 1983, according to NWB, Oct. 1984), unemployment is increasing. The Falklands war altered the political context in which these problems must be tackled—even victory in Port Stanley would not have done much to assist this process, except negatively by keeping in power the military who had signally failed to cope with Argentina's economic problems during their tenure.

China appears to have taken the advice that was given to the United States by some critics of its Vietnam War: declare a victory and withdraw. According to sources quoted in Jencks (1985), China's "lesson" to Vietnam cost it $1.31 billion (in 1979 U.S. Dollars), presumably in additional consumables. The higher "conservative" costs of between $3.2 and $6.4 billion, quoted in Jencks, appear to refer to replacement of lost assets.

The war also taught some lessons to China, for it exposed many deficiencies in the PLA (People's Liberation Army) (particularly in doctrines and weapons inventory) and demonstrated the need for modernization and rethinking in military matters. The remedial policies for dealing with these deficiencies can be regarded as the results of a beneficial lesson to China. In addition, a general modernization program for the PLA, arising out of the experiences of the war but going beyond a mere replacement program for lost assets (which constitute only a tiny proportion of the PLA's inventory), may produce further benefits to China, well worth, in the longer run, the strict costs of a short war and well below what a prolonged Vietnam war might cost.

Vietnam's war costs arise from the continuing counterinsurgency in Cambodia rather than from its short war with China. For this war it has received considerable economic assistance from the Soviet Union and has granted extensive, and expanding, base facilities to the Soviet Union in both Vietnam and Kampuchea.

Paying for One's Own War

The fortuitous benefits of losing (or terminating) a war quickly, even one that a country started, are missed by those who find themselves in a war without prospects of an early decision. Wars are prolonged because the adversaries have substantial resources at their disposal (as in Iran and Iraq), or because they are low intensity in nature (as in Morocco, Nicaragua, and El Salvador), or because of the intervention of powerful outsiders (in Afghanistan).

The question of who pays for a war (TANSTAAFW) is of crucial significance because who pays for it may determine how long it lasts, who actually fights it, and at what level of intensity it is fought. Conceptually, the costs of war are met along a continuum running from entirely self-financed at one end to totally externally financed at the other. Wars can also be conceived as being fought entirely by one's own military forces or by a mixture of one's own and an ally's forces. In figure 6–1, some recent wars have been allocated to a matrix representing the various combinations of the source of finance and the national composition of forces.

Of the wars that have continued for some years, rather than a few days or weeks, we can see the effect of varying the source of finance and the force composition. Morocco has financed and fought its war with the Western Sahara separatists *Polisario* largely out of its own national resources. It has received military aid from the United States, but this is paid for in annual interest payments (thus reducing U.S. influence), and other aid it has received—for example, from France—has been on a scale insufficient to permit external influence to bear on Morocco's war policies (compare U.S. influence on Israel, for example, in the limited objectives of the Suez crossing in 1973).

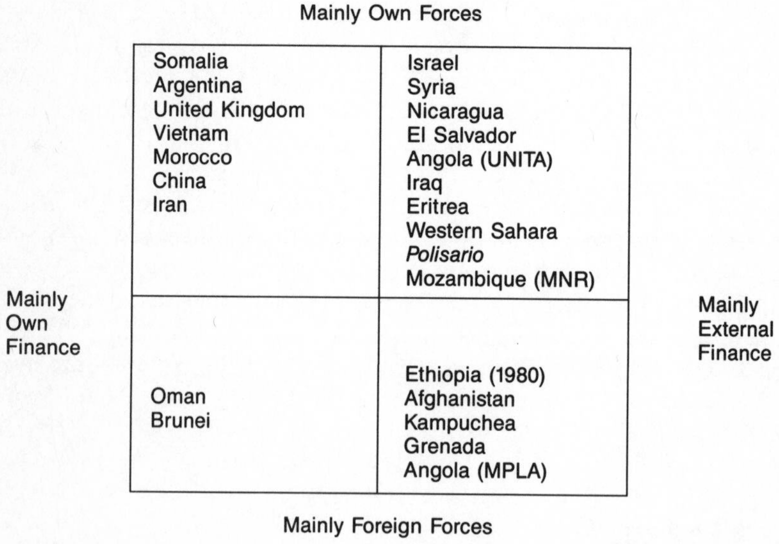

Mainly Own Forces

Somalia Argentina United Kingdom Vietnam Morocco China Iran	Israel Syria Nicaragua El Salvador Angola (UNITA) Iraq Eritrea Western Sahara *Polisario* Mozambique (MNR)
Oman Brunei	Ethiopia (1980) Afghanistan Kampuchea Grenada Angola (MPLA)

Mainly Own Finance   Mainly External Finance

Mainly Foreign Forces

Figure 6–1. **Source of Finance and Force Composition**

The *Polisario* forces are numerically smaller (Lewis, 1985), yet they have held down Moroccan forces for ten years over the Western Sahara. They have managed to continue the struggle for two reasons.

First, guerrilla warfare is a low-cost activity for insurgents—a few lightly armed men do not require long logistical chains to keep them operating and can choose when and where to operate and when to rest; conversely, fighting a guerrilla war is a high-cost activity for the state—thousands of troops in prolonged antiinsurgency operations are extremely expensive. Whereas guerrillas can walk (or ride the bus: consider El Salvador!) to an action of their choosing, government troops require highly protected convoys or expensive helicopter sorties just to move about the territory whether they are attacked or not, and they must remain in a state of constant readiness that is both wearisome and demoralizing (see Clarke 1983 on the strains of counterinsurgency in Northern Ireland).

Second, the *Polisario* has been logistically supported by both Algeria and Libya. *Polisario* forces can retire for rest and recuperation across safe borders, they can train and be trained in security, and they can adapt their strategy and tactics to the changing political and economic circumstances of their enemy.

Guerrillas, however, who are too dependent on outside assistance are vulnerable to the shifting interests of their sponsors (for example, the Kurds "betrayed" by Iran in 1975; the *Polisario* and the "merger" of Morocco with Libya in 1984, and shifts in allegiance in Mauritania; the Mozambique National Resistance and South Africa's rapprochement with Mozambique in 1984; the threat to UNITA in Angola if South Africa "settles" the Namibia question, and so forth).

External assistance to *Polisario* and the failure of Morocco to defeat them (indeed, Moroccan forces have been badly mauled in several encounters), have kept the war going. The economic costs to Morocco have been severe.

Morocco depends on mining as the main source of its foreign earnings (part of the attraction of the Western Sahara—apart from "historic" claims, and so on—is its vast mineral reserves), and these have been hit badly by world recession. Output of minerals generally fell 6.2 percent in 1982, and prices of phosphates, of which Morocco is the world's third largest producer, have been sliding for some years ($65 a ton in 1970 to $30 in 1983).

The government imposed a national security tax (NST) in 1982 to pay for the "war effort in the Western Sahara," and in 1983 the NST could be the equivalent of a month's income for those upon whom it is levied (*Africa Guide* 1984, 214–18). The value added tax was raised from 17 percent to 19 percent on certain consumer goods; travel taxes were also imposed, and import controls introduced. These are attempts to curb the current account deficit and slow down the growth in foreign debt ($11 billion in 1983).

The scissors effect of falling foreign earnings and rising public expenditures to maintain a military presence in the Western Sahara add to domestic stresses.

Austerity is a wearying pressure on political stability, every bit as serious as the absence of a military solution to the *Polisario* challenge. There were reports of an attempted coup in 1982.

The United States provided military aid, but Morocco ran into repayment problems. In March 1983, further aid was jeopardized when Morocco almost defaulted on a $10 million interest payment for earlier military aid. In summary, the burden of the indecisive war is felt more severely by Morocco than by the *Polisario,* hence, perhaps, the intriguing maneuvers of Morocco with Libya in 1984.

On the positive side of the war, Morocco's ability mainly to self-finance its military operations has enabled it to embark on an investment program in communications, particularly roads, which both assist its military operations and consolidate its economic absorption of the disputed territory. It has established, at least for the moment, a four hundred-mile "wall" behind which most of the habitable territory is secure. A program to build 1000 miles of roads is underway, integrating Morocco more closely with the Western Sahara, and airports in the territory are to be improved. Other infrastructure investment is being undertaken in housing, schools, and utilities. These important investments, in the long term, add to Moroccan capacity to create GNP and afford its war.

In 1986 the Iran-Iraq war appears to have stalemated. Neither side has achieved a decisive military victory in six years of war. But the economic effects have been muted or made more palatable by the unique nature of the oil-based economies of each country. Iraq intended to capture Iranian oil installations in the Abadan area in a lightning strike against a weakened if not disintegrating Iran (Cordesman 1984, 645–48) in order to boost Iraqi oil earnings and, perforce, impoverish Iran at a stroke. The war would have resulted in a massive knockout economic blow to a long-standing rival. In any event Iraq failed militarily and in doing so failed in its overall ambitions. It is now fighting a war of attrition, partly military (on the southern front) and partly economic (attacking Kharg Island oil tankers). It is reported (*New Scientist,* Jan. 17, 1985, 10–11) to have spent $1 billion in hydrological construction near Basra to alter the flood plain on the border to its military advantage (which will have beneficial ecological consequences when the war is over).

From the prospect of adding Iranian oil earnings to its own income (or ransoming them for territorial gains), Iraq saw its huge cash surplus of $35 billion (a sum slightly higher than its annual GNP) bleed away. It also suffered its own oil-loading facilities at Mina al-Bakr and al-Fao being put out of commission by Iran on November 29, 1980. From earnings of $26 billion in 1980, Iraqi oil earnings fell to under $10 billion in 1982. This forced Iraq into a dependent position on allies, the Arab oil states, who were dragged into subsidizing Iraq's adventure if only because of their own fears of the consequences of an Iranian victory. A decision to end the war—assuming Iran agreed—is no longer a purely unilateral decision for Iraq; it must take account of its vulnerable paymasters.

Iran was already in economic turmoil following the revolution against the shah in 1978–79. Oil output was between 5 and 6 million barrels a day during 1972–78, but was seriously disrupted by antishah strikes in late 1978 (ceasing altogether for a while in 1979). When output resumed in mid-1979, it did not reach above 4 million barrels and even that was not sold easily (due to the U.S. hostage crisis sanctions and its unilaterally high prices). The war severely curtailed oil output, falling to under 2 million barrels a day during 1980–82 (2.4 million barrels a day in 1983; Lloyd's Bank 1983). This has forced Iran to invest in alternative fields, including offshore, and in pipelines to deliver oil to ships outside the range of Iraqi air strikes, but it has not yet forced it to rely on external assistance.

With Iranian export earnings down from $21 billion in 1977–78 to $12 billion in 1980–81, the economy has been severely strained both by the revolutionary turmoil and by the Iraqi war. The countryside was denuded of 1.5 million people in 1979 (mainly going to Tehran) as a result of the economic disruption. Conscription into the armed forces and the "revolutionary guards" mopped up much surplus manpower (unemployment was between 2 and 4 million in 1981). The demands of preparing for large offensives boosted the domestic economy in 1981–82, but still left nonwar economic activity with substantial surplus capacity.

The economic situation four years into the war, however, is not entirely unpromising for Iran and strengthens its resolve to dictate terms for the end of the war. Oil export earnings are projected to climb toward $20 billion in 1984, with imports under $18 billion (mainly food and military equipment). Some major industrial developments are nearing completion (in steel, petrochemicals, copper refining, port capacity, and a new airport).

Iran needs military assets, which are expensive to acquire and costly to maintain. The political isolation of Iran, a product of its conduct, has forced it into "back-door," largely hard cash deals on an inadequate scale (hence the will-it-won't-it launch an offensive stance of 1984–1986). To meet its war aims—Iraq's unconditional surrender—Iran needs a thriving and growing GNP, which means rising incomes from oil exports. Iraq, in contrast, dependent on allies for funds, needs a decisive economic blow at Iran's GNP and a continuing ability to break Iranian offensives.

Getting Someone Else to Pay for One's Wars

The cases of Israel and Syria are similar to but operate on a different level from those of El Salvador and Nicaragua. All four countries are financially dependent for their military operations and general defense upon the superpowers, and all four countries deploy their own national military forces, in the main, when issues are contested by force.

Syria has an economy styled on Soviet planning norms. It is dependent on economic grants from abroad. In 1977 these grants were equivalent to 7.5 percent of total government revenues, rising to 42 percent in 1979. In 1982 they stood at 25 percent (Lloyd's Bank 1984). Bearing in mind the high D/GE ratio of 29.1 percent (table 6–1), the ability of Syria to sustain a large armed force of 21,000 men in Lebanon in 1982 (IISS 1982–83, 62), as well as 203,000 men at home, is largely a function of the external, mainly Soviet financial aid that it receives. Its dependence on the Soviet Union for military materiel is almost complete: its air force, navy, and ground forces are almost entirely Soviet supplied; it can also rely on being totally replenished with inventories lost in combat with Israel, not least following the 1982 war (Carus 1985).

Being totally dependent on external sources for defense and war expenditures, Syria is able to continue its economic development unhindered by severe budgetary strains, though it is subject to the usual inefficiencies associated with Third World economies, compounded by the drawbacks of Soviet-style planning. The military situation actually helps unemployment—conscription keeps down jobless totals, and so does emigration to avoid conscription. The émigrés are a major source of repatriated foreign currency for Syria.

To fund its development goals, Syria exports phosphate (Syria has been hit like Morocco by the world recession, with only 755,000 tons out of an output of 1.4 million tons being sold in 1983) and also pipes oil to its Mediterranean ports. Syria took Iran's side in the Gulf war and confiscated Iraqi oil in transit through its territory. It accepted a gift of $200 million of oil from Iran in 1983 and buys Iranian oil at a discounted price.

The economy grew at over 6 percent (allowing for massaged statistics), and income per head grew at about half that rate (GNP per capita was $1,911 in 1982). While development plans are regularly curbed as unrealistic—a feature of Soviet-style planning in the Third World—the overall economic picture is by no means disastrous. Syrian inflation at 20 percent (1984) compares favorably to that of Israel's. In short, Syria, with continued Soviet military aid and Iranian financial support, can comfortably sustain its relatively poor but improving economic position and continue to be a major threat to the security of Israel.

Israel is a richer country than Syria. Their GNPs are not that far apart—Israel's is $22 billion, Syria's is $18 billion (1982)—but Israel is numerically smaller in population, which pushes its per capita GNP to over $5,000 (all caveats about comparative GNPs applying!). Israel, like Syria, is dependent on external funding to ensure its security. Unlike Syria, a political dictatorship of ruthless inclinations, Israel is a democracy, and its citizens can only be exhorted to behave responsibly.

Economic growth in Israel is slowing down. The economy, which trebled in size between 1953 and 1961, only doubled between 1961 and 1982. In fact it only grew 8 percent in real terms between 1972 and 1982, and actually declined by 1 percent during 1982–83.

Partly, Israel's economic problem is its very dependence on external finance. It has an endemic import deficit (it exports 41 percent of GNP and imports 61 percent), caused in the main by its heavy investment in defense, which accounts for the high government share in GNP (33.6 percent) and the high D/GNP ratio (24 percent).

Israel finances its imports partly by government-backed credits and partly by funds from the Jewish Agency. The bulk of imports are financed by the U.S. government (see table 6–2), which committed itself to $2.6 billion of "military and economic aid" for 1985.

Foreign dept at $23 billion is larger than Israel's GNP, and the economy is characterized by Argentine-scale hyperinflation at 400 percent, and by "heavy and increasing indebtedness" (NWB, October 1984). The major cause of this situation is the "persistently large budget deficit—stemming from massive defence expenditures—which has been financed by excessive monetary expansion" (NWB, Oct. 1984).

W. Seth Carus's chapter (in volume 1) on the Syrian-Israeli war of 1982, with its emphasis on technological sophistication, particularly in electronic warfare, indicates the inescapable reality facing Israeli defense planners. Without investment in high-technology warfare, Israel would fare less well against its opponents. Technology is expensive and while some of it can be developed indigenously, all of it can only be paid for by help from the United States. The access of opponents to highly sophisticated military technology, either paid for by loans from the Soviet Union or by aid from the Arab oil states, forces Israel into the semidependent position of relying on the United States. But its inability to manage the massive transfers into its economy—which require the austerity of a permanent war economy—causes the endemic economic strains in its society.

The coalition government faces serious economic problems, none of which, it can be argued, were avoidable, given the nature of the Israeli security situation. Unlike Argentina, which indulged in a war to divert domestic attention from the military government's failings, Israel has had to divert its economic strength into strong defenses and regular warfare out of dire necessity.

Table 6–2
U.S.-funded Support for Israeli Public Sector Purchases Abroad
(billion Israeli shekels)

	1979	1980	1981	1982
Israeli public purchases abroad	3.4	10.2	28.1	41.3
Israeli public purchases financed by U.S. grants	3.1	7.3	16.2	30.5

Source: Lloyd's Bank, *Group Economic Report*, 1984.

As long as the parties to conflict are sustained by outside finance, there is no doubt that conflict can continue. As long as nationals in each country are prepared to undertake the fighting, the willingness of outsiders to sustain their economies must ensure them against the full burden of their wars and the consequences of their attachment to the issues at stake.

Israel, Iraq, and Syria are sustained economically while engaged in wars of varying intensity; this support has enabled their economies to develop, though with varying degrees of success. Iran and Morocco have largely financed their own wars and have continued their development, albeit on a scale below their potential. In the absence of war, Iran and Morocco are assured of a higher growth rate—the opportunity cost of their wars—but in the absence of war, and the threat of war, in countries financed externally, such as Syria and Israel, the opportunity cost of war may not be very high; they only get aid because of their wars, and how much aid would they attract if they did not pose a threat to each other? Iraq would not require external financial support in the absence of war with Iran, for its own oil resources, presently blocked by the Iranian war, would supply funds sufficient to raise its growth rate.

War may be destructive, but it can also inject growth into economies (for example, militarily related infrastructure investment and expansion of consumables production), and as long as destruction is confined to military assets (tanks, aircraft, ships) and not to the economies (except of third parties such as the Lebanon), we cannot assume that war inevitably causes economic decline.

Economic Destruction of War

War is destructive of people; it can also be destructive of productive capacity. The loss of the latter reduces the ability of an economy to meet the needs of war. By reducing economic activity—the production and distribution of goods and services—it also lowers living standards (the consumption of goods and services). These economic costs are not inconsiderable. In the extreme they can promote the wholesale destruction of an entire people (genocide). Indeed, the tactic of deliberately destroying the economic base of a population has been a feature of warfare since Roman times (Carthage). It has appeared in modern times in Nigeria-Biafra, 1967–70; Kampuchea, 1974; Ethiopia-Eritrea, 1983–85; and Afghanistan, 1983–85. To the destruction of armies is added genocide by famine and disease (seen dramatically in 1984 in Eritrea and Tigre provinces of Ethiopia and southern Sudan, 1986).

The ethos of insurgency is to avoid contact with the state's armed forces. In low-intensity warfare, in order to wrest control of the population for its "alternative" state, the economy is the target. The armed forces, unable in the main to make contact with the insurgents, also attack the economy; food stocks that are or might be available for guerrilla consumption are a prime target, as are logistical routes that supply and sustain them.

In Afghanistan, the Soviet Union is undertaking the overwhelming bulk of the fighting with an armed force estimated to be about 105,000 strong in 1983 (though compare Urban [1985] who quotes much lower numbers and much lesser involvement by Soviet troops in actual combat). The Afghanistan government's Army has ceased to function effectively; its force size came down from 80,000 in 1980 to 30,000 in 1983 (*Far Eastern Review* 1984, 118–21; Urban [1985] reports that the Afghan army is 10,000 stronger in 1984 than in 1980). Press reports suggest that Afghan troops do not carry side arms except when pressed into battle—a sure sign of total distrust of their "hosts" by the Soviet commanders.

The cost of fighting the war, that is, the cost of military materiel and consumables, is met by the Soviet Union, which regards Afghanistan, militarily, as an adjunct of the Soviet district of Turkestan. Hence Afghanistan appears in figure 6–1 in the bottom right box. Afghan exports to the Soviet Union doubled from 31 percent of its total foreign trade in 1976 to 61 percent in 1981, and these exports help to compensate for imports of military power.

The considerable destruction of the war, however, is borne by the Afghan economy. The population of Kabul doubled from 600,000 in 1979 to 1.2 million in 1983, indicating rural devastation. The destruction of rebel villages aims to turn dissidents into refugees and deprive guerrilla forces of an economic base. If the rebels cannot rely on local food, they have to carry what they eat with them, which imposes a porterage burden and reduces the amount of war materiel they can carry and therefore their military effectiveness.

Half the schools and the hospitals, 14 percent of state transport, 75 percent of all communications, and several hydroelectric links have been damaged by the war. The destruction is equivalent to half the value of the economic investment made over the past twenty years and is estimated at 25 billion afghanis ($1 = 50.6 afs; *Far Eastern Review* 1984).

With the guerrilla war affecting the suburbs of Kabul (1984), there is little doubt that the destruction will continue. As long as the guerrillas cannot compel a Soviet withdrawal, the Soviet policy of destroying the economy outside the territory that they control, thereby ensuring that those who remain loyal to Kabul will eat and the rest will not, is a war-winning if long-term strategy.

The economies of El Salvador and Nicaragua are considerably more developed than Afghanistan's. They too are experiencing wars of insurgency across parts of their territories but on nothing like the scale of destruction in Afghanistan. El Salvador's GNP fell 25 percent between 1980 and 1982 (declining a further 1 percent in 1983), and Nicaragua's fell 25 percent in 1979 alone, growing from this lower base by 10 percent in 1980, 7 percent in 1981, and between minus 3 percent and plus 2 percent in 1983 (Bank of London and South America [BOLSA 1983, 17).

Both countries rely on foreign aid to sustain their economies in the face of insurgency activity. To date there is no destruction of economic life in either country on the scale of Soviet activity in Afghanistan, but insurgency does have a mutilating economic effect, particularly in the rural districts where the wars are fought.

In El Salvador, per capita GNP at $560 is comparable to levels it had attained in the 1960s. Coffee yields have been hit by coffee rust disease, which is almost wholly attributable to the insecure situation in the countryside—farmers are inhibited from attending to their crops when they fear murder, abduction, and intimidation. This has pushed the harvest down below 3 million sacks (1980) to 2 million sacks in 1983. Likewise with the cotton crop, which fell 45 percent in volume from the prewar 1978 yield. Land allocated to cotton production fell 50 percent in 1983, and a further drop of 25 percent is predicted (ABICOR, May 1984). Export earnings fell from $1.1 billion in 1979 to $700 million in 1982, pushing the country's balance of trade into deficit (−$183 million in 1982).

Without financial aid from the United States and elsewhere, El Salvador could decline rapidly and the war turn in favor of the insurgents. The government acknowledged this danger in its dramatic attempt in 1984 to entice some of the insurgents into peace talks.

The Nicaraguan government came to power through a successful insurgency, which severely disrupted the economy. To this burden the Sandinistas added their own version of "socialism." The slowdown in economic growth—now probably negative—is partly caused by domestic economic policies and partly by the outbreak of new insurgency. Output is still (1984) to be reestablished at its 1978 level. That the economy is not performing well is not as serious a burden as it might be elsewhere. Radical left governments always operate at a low level of consumer expectation, if only because political goals are regarded as more important than GNP, and dissenting opinion is more easily isolated—where they are not turned into refugees (as in Vietnam and Afghanistan), they are intimidated into silence.

Soviet aid to Nicaragua and the government's control of the bulk of the economy could mean a long haul for the insurgents, particularly if the war is "Sovietized." The United States is minimally aiding them, and, given their narrow economic base, they do little more than disrupt the Sandinista's control of the country (which explains their efforts at economic sabotage).

Conclusions

There is no such thing as a free war; somebody pays for it. Wars can cost substantial economic resources, and avoiding them by investing a proportion of the GNP in defense expenditures is by far the cheaper option.

The relatively high costs of defense and the much higher costs of actual war explain why poorer countries seek military aid and financial assistance. War creates its own urgencies, not the least of them being the prospect of defeat, and these add to the pressures to seek external assistance. The exact circumstances that lead one or other of the superpowers to support a country that faces the prospect or the reality of war could bear further research, as could the relative influence on events of the donor and the recipient once such support is undertaken.

The wars discussed in this book represent a mixture of military, financial, and direct intervention (see figure 6–1). The impact of the types of support on the conduct and political objectives of the war, including its termination, need further investigation. A country purchasing arms for cash might be expected to have a greater degree of independence in its war objectives and behavior than one that is receiving such aid as an emergency grant. The donor might see arms sales as an objective of its own foreign policy ("a cost effective way of providing support for pro-Western regimes," HC 1981, 37) or feel compelled to assist because of perceptions of the threats to itself if it did not do so (for example, Saudi Arabia's support for Iraq).

The Soviet Union is directly engaged in one war (in Afghanistan) and indirectly engaged in three others (in Vietnam, Ethiopia, and Angola). This intervention is in contrast to that of the United States, which, apart from Grenada, and its low-key involvement in Central America, has refrained, largely for domestic reasons, from matching recent Soviet proclivities for intervention. Arms transfers, training, and other assistance to El Salvador and to the insurgents in Nicaragua is on a very muted scale compared with Soviet actions in Asia and Africa. Why this is so is mainly a political question, but there may also be economic lessons present too.

Wars of insurgency are relatively cheap to mount, and, for the payoffs to a superpower, they are relatively cheap to sustain externally. U.S. experience in Vietnam showed the heavy military, economic, and political costs of directly intervening. The Soviet Union faces high economic and political costs from its intervention in Afghanistan and from its material support for Vietnam in Cambodia.

To keep a pro-Soviet regime off balance and to give time for an internal opposition to develop, it may be cheaper for the United States to provide material assistance for a low-intensity war than it would be (assuming the agreement of Congress) for the United States to intervene directly. There might be a lesson in how South Africa is dealing with cross-border insurgency—it does not intervene directly but puts counterpressure on its neighbors by supporting insurgency against them (for example, Angola and Mozambique).

The military doctrines in Mao's theory of "the protracted war" (1954) can be applied by both pro-Soviet and pro-Western insurgents. Protracted war is peculiarly suitable to Third World countries, and in its economic aspects it is a question worthy of further study.

Those countries that have internal sources of funds (phosphate, oil, and so on) can sustain high-level responses to either insurgency (as in Morocco) or conventional warfare (as in Iran). This need not be at the expense of infrastructure investment, nor need the opportunity cost in forgone growth be regarded by them as unacceptable (choice is a value judgment!). For some countries (for example, Israel), the prospect of defeat is so unacceptable that it engages in defense expenditures greatly in excess of what is good for it economically. Something similar drives Saudi Arabia to support Iraq, and other Arab countries facing serious security problems.

In summary, who pays for the war is a useful place to start an analysis of the nature of a war, its duration, and its economic consequences for GNP, growth, and development. War costs can be avoided by persuading somebody else to pay for them. For a superpower, high (conventional) war costs can also be avoided by paying somebody else to fight them. For a Third World country wishing to avoid either circumstance, war costs can be avoided by a suitable investment of scarce resources in defensive deterrence.

References

ABICOR Reports, London (various dates, country identified in the text).

Africa Guide. London, 1984.

Ball, Nicole. *Third World Security Expenditures: A Statistical Compendium.* Stockholm: National Defence Research Institute, 1983.

Ball, Nicole. "Measuring Third World Security Expenditures: A Research Note." *World Development* 12, no. 2 (1984): 157–64.

Ball, Nicole. "Security Expenditure and Economic Growth in Developing Countries." Swedish Institute of International Affairs, Stockholm, October 1984 (unpublished).

Blackaby, Frank. "Introduction: the military sector and the economy." in *The Structure of the Defence Industry: An International Survey,* edited by Nicole Ball and Milton Leitenberg, 6–20, London: Macmillan, 1983.

BOLSA (Bank of London and South America). *Review* (date in text).

Carus, Seth W. "Military Lessons of the 1982 Israel-Syria Conflict." in *The Lessons of Recent Wars in the Third World,* vol. 1, edited by Robert E. Harkavy and Stephanie G. Neuman. Lexington, Mass.: Lexington Books, 1985.

Clarke, A.F.N. *Contact.* London: Secker & Warburg, 1983.

Cordesman, Anthony H. *The Gulf and the Search for Strategic Stability: Saudi Arabia, the Military Balance in the Gulf, and Trends in the Arab-Israeli Military Balance.* Boulder, Colo.: Westview Press, 1984.

Far Eastern Review, Asia Yearbook, 1984.

Financial Times (London).

HC (House of Commons). "Overseas Arms Sales: Foreign Policy Aspects." Minutes of Evidence, Foreign Affairs Committee, Session 1980–81. London: HMSO, 1981.

International Institute of Strategic Studies (IISS). *The Military Balance 1983–1984, 1984–1985. London: IISS (annual),* 1983.

JDW *(Jane's Defence Weekly).* London (weekly).

Jencks, Harlan W. "Lessons of a Lesson: China-Vietnam, 1979." In *The Lessons of Recent Wars in the Third World,* vol. 1, edited by Robert E. Harkavy and Stephanie G. Neuman. Lexington, Mass.: Lexington Books, 1985.

Leontief, Wassily, and Faye Duchin. *Military Spending: Facts and Figures, World wide Implications and Future Outlook.* New York: Oxford University Press, 1983.

Lewis, William H. "War in the Western Sahara." In *The Lessons of Recent Wars in the Third World,* vol. 1, edited by Robert E. Harkavy and Stephanie G. Neuman. Lexington, Mass.: Lexington Books, 1985.

Kennedy, Gavin. *Defense Economics.* New York: St. Martin's Press, 1983.

Lloyd's Bank. *Group Economic Reports* (country and date in text), London.

Mao Tse-tung. *On the Protracted War.* 1938. Peking: Foreign Languages Press, 1954.

MOD (Ministry of Defence). *The United Kingdom Defence Programme: The Way Forward.* Cmnd. 8288. 1981.

MOD. Memorandum to the House of Commons Defence Committee. HCDC 166, 1984 (unpublished), Public Record Office.

NWB (National Westminister Bank). *Economic Report* (country and date in text).

Neuman, Stephanie. "Security, Military Expenditures and Socioeconomic Development: Reflections on Iran." *Orbis* 22, no. 3 (Fall 1978): 569–94.

Neuman, Stephanie. *Defense Planning in Less-Industrialized States.* Lexington, Mass.: Lexington Books, 1984.

Smith, Adam. *An Inquiry into the Nature and Causes of the Wealth of Nations.* London, 1776.

Staudenmaier, William O. "Iran-Iraq (1980–)." In *The Lessons of Recent Wars in the Third World,* vol. 1, edited by Robert E. Harkavy and Stephanie G. Neuman. Lexington, Mass.: Lexington Books, 1985.

Thee, Marek, ed. *Armaments, Arms Control and Disarmament.* Paris: UNESCO, 1981.

Ullman, Harlan K. "Profound or Perfunctory: Observations on the South Atlantic Conflict." In *The Lessons of Recent Wars in the Third World,* vol. 1, edited by Robert E. Harkavy and Stephanie G. Neuman. Lexington, Mass.: Lexington Books, 1985.

United Nations. *Economic and Social Consequences of the Arms Race and of Military Expenditures.* New York: United Nations, 1978.

Urban, Mark L. "The Limited Contingent of Soviet Forces in Afghanistan." *Jane's Defence Weekly,* Jan. 12, 1985, 71–73.

7
The Role of Military Assistance in Recent Wars

Stephanie G. Neuman

Introduction

A Question of Focus

Armed conflict has become endemic in the Third World. Some believe that the mere incidence of recent wars indicates a decline in the power of the major states because of their inability to prevent the outbreak of violence or limit its intensity.[1] For these observers, the rising number of weapons suppliers is noted with special concern and alarm. In their view, the general availability of military equipment not only promotes armed conflict, but also indicates that the major powers have suffered a relative "loss of control" over the international system.[2] Thus the availability of weapons from diverse suppliers, particularly during wartime, is thought to have negative implications for the position of the superpowers in the global balance of power.[3]

This chapter attempts to test these assumptions by examining the role security assistance has played in recent wars.[4] It focuses on the activities of the combatants and their suppliers in an effort to assess how the global arms trade actually functions during wartime. Two general questions are addressed: What kind of military assistance did the combatants receive from whom? And what are the implications for the structure of the international system and the role of the superpowers in it?

A Sample of Wars

The sample of eight wars chosen for this project, five conventional interstate wars and three involving insurgencies, compose the data base for this chapter:

This chapter is adapted from a longer work, *Military Assistance in Recent Wars: The Dominance of the Superpowers,* The Washington Papers, no. 122 (Washington, D.C.: Center for Strategic and International Studies, Georgetown University, with Praeger Publishers, 1986).

1. *Conventional Wars*

   Ethiopia/Somalia (the Horn)
   Vietnam/People's Republic of China (PRC)
   Iran/Iraq (the Gulf)
   Argentina/Britain (the Falklands)
   Israel/Syria/Palestine Liberation Organization (PLO) (Lebanon)

2. *Insurgencies*

   Morocco/*Polisario* (Western Sahara)
   El Salvador/Honduras/Nicaragua/Contras (Central America)
   Afghanistan/Soviet Union/Afghan rebels (Afghanistan)

The duration of these armed conflicts varies widely. Spanning the time period 1977 to the present, some are still in progress, while other short engagements were terminated in less than a month (see table 7–1). The differential impact of these wars on patterns of military assistance and the consequences for recipients and donors are the central themes discussed below.

A Model of Arms Supply Relationships[5]

Four basic arms supply patterns characterize supplier-recipient relationships during recent wars. Table 7–2 depicts their frequency and distribution.

Internal Transfers. Countries with extensive indigenous defense industries that are only moderately dependent upon external sources of supply fall into this category. For the most part, their suppliers are their own defense industries. Only one less-developed country (LDC) combatant, China, falls neatly into this category, although Israel produces some of its own military equipment and other countries such as Argentina have varying levels of military production capability.

Bilateral, Government-to-Government Agreements. References to the arms trade in the general literature are usually made in this context. These agreements include all legally binding understandings between the governments of sovereign states for the sale or gift of military equipment and/or related services. Recipients may choose to obtain arms principally from one major supplier, or they may decide to procure weapons from a number of government sources. Ten of the combatants in this study obtained their resupply primarily through bilateral agreements with another government. Eight of these states dealt principally with one of the superpowers: Ethiopia, Afghanistan, Vietnam, Syria, and Nicaragua procured weapons from the Soviet Union, while Israel, Honduras, and El Salvador obtained supplies from the United States. Iraq and Morocco have received a large proportion of their military equipment through bilateral arrangements with other governments as well. (See table 7–2.)

Table 7–1
The Sequence and Duration of Recent Wars

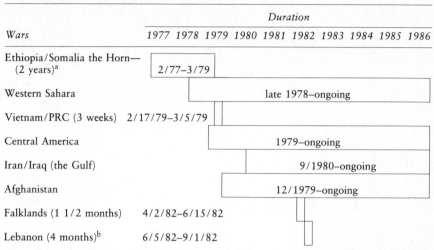

	Duration									
Wars	*1977*	*1978*	*1979*	*1980*	*1981*	*1982*	*1983*	*1984*	*1985*	*1986*
Ethiopia/Somalia the Horn— (2 years)[a]	2/77–3/79									
Western Sahara			late 1978–ongoing							
Vietnam/PRC (3 weeks)	2/17/79–3/5/79									
Central America			1979–ongoing							
Iran/Iraq (the Gulf)				9/1980–ongoing						
Afghanistan			12/1979–ongoing							
Falklands (1 1/2 months)		4/2/82–6/15/82								
Lebanon (4 months)[b]		6/5/82–9/1/82								

[a]Because of the ongoing nature of conflict in the Third World, it is often difficult to establish exactly when recent wars began and when they ended. For example, three different dates are commonly used to mark the onset of the Horn war: February 1977—the first independent report of fighting in the Ogaden; June 1977—the first official Ethiopian accusation that Somalian regular troops were involved; and July 1977—the first confirmation by Somalian officials that "volunteer Somalian troops" were fighting in the Ogaden. For the purposes of this study, February 1977, when the first tank skirmishes were reported, is used to designate the beginning of the war.

[b]The war termination date used here is the day the PLO withdrew its forces from Lebanon. That date would not be acceptable to the PLO, which claims that its war against Israel continues; however, because the major military transfers involved Syria and Israel, the Lebanon conflict is treated here as an interstate war and the unofficial cessation of armed hostilities between Syria and Israel as the war termination date.

Indirect Transfers. Third party sales, whereby equipment or services provided by one government to another government are transferred by the latter to a third government or insurgent force, are included in this category along with other nongovernment sources of military equipment (such as the private arms trade). Iran, Argentina, Somalia, and insurgent forces, all subject to embargoes during wartime, have resorted mainly to indirect sources, while Iraq, Morocco, Nicaragua, Honduras, and El Salvador have received assistance from indirect sources as well as principal government suppliers.

Another form of indirect transfer occurs when one country acts as a surrogate or proxy supplier for another. It is often difficult, however, to distinguish between this type of indirect transfer and direct bilateral, government-to-government agreements. Given the sensitivities of the parties involved, particularly during wartime, both suppliers and recipients often have a stake in concealing whether a donor government is acting independently or in cooperation with

Table 7–2
Patterns of Resupply During War

Type of War	Internal	Bilateral/ Government to Government	Indirect	Restricted Transfers
Conventional	PRC	Vietnam Syria		Argentina
	Israel		Iraq	Iran
		Ethiopia		Somalia
Insurgencies		Afghanistan		Afghan rebels
		Morocco		Polisario
		Honduras		Contras
		El Salvador		
		Nicaragua		

another power. Throughout this study, the distinction between direct and indirect bilateral assistance has been made wherever possible.

Restricted Transfers. This category covers what one might call "negative transfers." It includes embargoes, political restrictions, and the inability or unwillingness of a supplier to provide certain military technologies or services to a combatant. Just as the availability of supplies has proved critical to a war's prosecution and outcome, so too has the inaccessibility of assistance. Because indirect transfers are generally a product of and associated with transfer restrictions instituted by one of the superpowers, they are discussed in tandem in this chapter.

A Methodological Note

The term *security assistance* is used here synonymously with *military assistance* and *military aid* to describe the transfer of military equipment and/or training and other related services to another country, whether this is in the form of a sale, offset arrangement, or grant. Following the U.S. Arms Control and Disarmament Agency's usage, *military equipment* is defined as conventional "weapons of war, parts thereof, ammunition, support equipment, and other commodities considered primarily military in nature. . . . Also included are transfers of equipment for defense industries."[6] Unfortunately, in the following analysis the definition of *security assistance* may be more rigorous than the data supporting it. The dollar values used below are obtained from arms trade statistics compiled by the U.S. Departments of Defense and State through 1983, and some of the 1983 figures were only estimates at the time of data collection. Furthermore, with the exception of security assistance figures for the United States, data for all other countries are only approximations and must, therefore, be regarded with some caution.[7]

Pre-War and Wartime Patterns of Weapons Procurement and Supply: The Role of the Superpowers

Since the end of World War II, bilateral agreements between governments have been the most common means of procuring arms and services for industrializing countries, and most have relied on one principal donor for them.[8] The superpowers have traditionally dominated this market. Although their combined share dropped from 81 percent in 1963 to 60 percent in 1983, the United States and the Soviet Union remain the largest single suppliers of military assistance to the LDCs, and they continue to dominate the world's arms trade.[9]

These general trends are reflected in the prewar procurement patterns of the combatant countries analyzed in this study.[10] Based on the dollar value of military goods and services transferred to them, out of the fourteen states involved in the eight wars, nine, or 64 percent, obtained their arms during prewar periods directly from one major supplier;[11] of these, seven (50 percent) were largely dependent upon the Soviet Union or the U.S. for military assistance.[12]

During periods of armed conflict, the picture changes dramatically, even though the proportion of countries dependent upon the superpowers for military assistance remains about constant. Of the nine countries fighting wars long enough to receive significant resupplies, five (56 percent) have relied primarily upon the United States or the Soviet Union for support. However, this statistic conceals the sharp decline in the total dollar value of superpower aid during wars, and the differential effect various types of conflict have upon the procurement behavior of combatants.

As a rule, long wars have had a disruptive impact upon prewar bilateral supplier-recipient relationships.[13] Here change is the norm rather than the exception (see table 7–3). For example, of the four LDCs that have waged conventional battles lasting two years or more all have altered their pattern of procurement because of superpower resupply restrictions. Somalia, which received its military assistance from the Soviet Union prior to the Horn war, turned to Western suppliers and established a diversified pattern of procurement after its onset. Ethiopia, on the other hand, which previously received materiel from a variety of Western states, became almost totally dependent upon the Soviet Union during and after the war. Iraq, principally reliant upon the Soviet Union before it invaded Iran, remained dependent but also further diversified its suppliers, purchasing more equipment from the West, East Europeans, and other Third World countries as the war progressed. Iran, originally a dedicated U.S. customer for military hardware and services (75 percent of its total procurement), was forced to purchase arms wherever they were available, even across blocs. Thus, although three of the four states engaged in long conventional wars had relied mainly upon one of the superpowers for military assistance before

Table 7–3
Patterns of Procurement in Long Conventional and Insurgent Wars:
A Comparison between Prewar and Wartime Periods [a]

	Change		No Change	
Type of War	*M/P to D/M* [c]	*D/M to M/P*	*M/P*	*D/M*
Conventional [b]	Somalia Iran Iraq	Ethiopia		
Insurgencies		Nicaragua El Salvador Morocco Honduras [d]	Afghanistan	

[a] Derived from appendix to this chapter.

[b] Short-war combatants—Syria, Israel, Argentina, the PRC, and Vietnam—are not included.

[c] M/P—Monopolistic or Principal supplier (one supplier provides 50 percent or more of all military assistance to a recipient). D/M—Diversified or Multiple suppliers (two suppliers each contribute 45 percent or more; three or more suppliers, none of which provide more than 49 percent of a recipient's military assistance).

[d] Honduras changed from Israel (prior to 1979) to the United States as its principal supplier.

hostilities began, only two continued to do so during wartime, and only one, Iraq, maintained a (reduced) supply relationship with its original donor (see tables 7–3 and 7–4. For all four, even Ethiopia, the dollar value of military assistance from diversified sources rose dramatically.

The pattern for unconventional wars has been somewhat different. Governments fighting insurgencies (five) have not changed bloc suppliers,[14] and whereas most governments fighting long conventional wars have received less direct assistance from the superpowers, governments involved in unconventional wars have grown more dependent upon them. (see table 7–4).

In general, levels of aid have risen dramatically during recent wars (see figure 7–1 and table 7–5),[15] and they have stimulated increased transfers from diversified sources as well. This is true for unconventional as well as conventional conflicts. Among governments facing insurgencies, aid from Western Europe rose 23 percent, from Eastern Europe almost 90 percent, and from the Third World more than 450 percent (see the appendix to this chapter).

Although the number of combatants principally dependent upon the superpowers for military assistance remained about constant (see tables 7–3 and 7–4) and the dependency of those fighting unconventional wars upon them deepened, the dollar value of U.S. and Soviet aid fell precipitously from a prewar yearly average of $6 billion to $2 billion. As a proportion of total aid to the combatants, their share declined from its prewar level of 75 percent to 38 percent. The U.S. contribution alone dropped from an annual prewar average of $2.5 billion to $156 million, or 2.7 percent of total wartime assistance to combatants. Deliveries from other sources have expanded proportionately, with

Table 7–4
Patterns of Procurement and Supply during Long Wars:
A Comparison of Prewar and War Periods[a]

Prewar		War	
Monopoly/ Principal (M/P)[b]	Diversified/ Multiple (D/M)[c]	Monopoly/ Principal (M/P)	Diversified/ Multiple (D/M)
Conventional Wars:			
Somalia[d] (USSR)	Ethiopia[e]	Ethiopia[d] (USSR)	Somalia[e]
Iran[e] (U.S.)			Iran[f]
Iraq[d] (USSR)			Iraq[f]
Insurgencies:			
Honduras[e] (Israel)	El Salvador[e] (U.S./Israel)	Honduras[e] (U.S.)	
Afghanistan[d] (USSR)	Nicaragua[e]	El Salvador[e] (U.S.)	
	Morocco[e]	Nicaragua[d] (USSR)	
		Afghanistan[d] (USSR)	
		Morocco[e]	

[a]Derived from appendix to this chapter.

[b]M/P—one supplier provides 50 percent or more of all military assistance to a recipient.

[c]D/M—two suppliers each contribute 45 percent or more; or three or more suppliers, none of which provide more than 49 percent of a recipient's military assistance.

[d]Eastern bloc

[e]Western bloc

[f]Mixed, cross-bloc

Third World suppliers showing the largest gain, growing from not quite 3 percent before war to 22 percent of total military assistance during periods of combat (see the appendix to this chapter).

Short wars, like long unconventional conflicts, have not negatively affected prewar procurement relationships. Those five countries involved in hostilities that lasted from a few weeks to a few months, Syria, Israel, Argentina, Vietnam, and the PRC, have all maintained their original prewar supply patterns. Israel and Syria continue to receive most of their equipment and services from the United States and the Soviet Union, respectively. Argentina has not changed its practice of obtaining weapons from a variety of largely Western sources, with of course the exception of direct purchases from Great Britain. Vietnam has remained dependent upon the Soviet Union for military assistance, and China continues to purchase defense technologies sparingly and selectively from a number of Western countries. One obvious reason for this continuity is the time factor. Finding alternate sources of compatible materiel and arranging for significant deliveries so quickly has been impracticable and sometimes

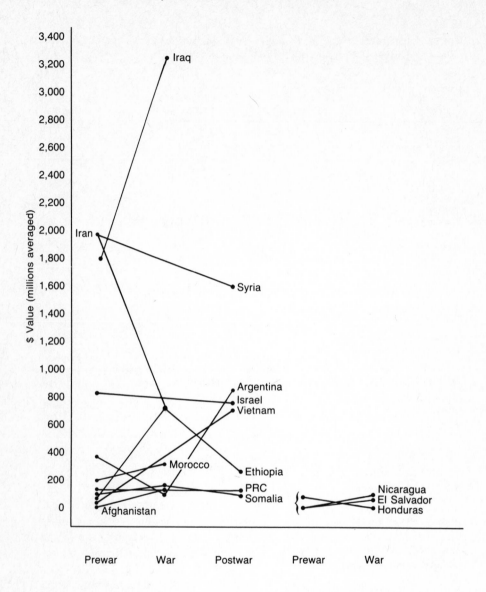

Source: Derived from table 7–5 and appendix to this chapter.

Figure 7–1. Dollar Value of Military Assistance to Combatants during Prewar, War, and Postwar Periods

Table 7–5

Dollar Value (Millions Averaged) and Percentage Change of Military Assistance to Combatants during Prewar, War, and Postwar Periods [a]

Combatants	Prewar	War	% Change	Post-war	% Change Prewar
Ethiopia	46.4	765.7	+1550.0	286.0	+516.4
Somalia	80.6	152.8	+89.6	105.7	+31.1
Afghanistan	28.3	132.5	+368.2	—	—
Morocco	207.2	358.8	+73.2	—	—
Nicaragua	8.5	46.4	+446.0	—	—
Honduras	15.5	7.7	−50.3	—	—
El Salvador	3.5	30.1	+760.0	—	—
Vietnam	40.5	—	—	691.4	+1607.2
PRC	112.5	—	—	121.5	+8.0
Iran	2029.9	784.2	−61.4	—	—
Iraq	1849.6	3291.8	+78.0	—	—
Argentina	373.6	100.2	−73.2	831.6	+122.6
Syria[b]	2203.2	—	—	1521.2	−31.0
Israel	885.0	—	—	790.4	−10.7

[a]Derived from appendix to this chapter.

[b]Total Soviet resupply to Syria in 1983 not included. Dollar values for Soviet resupply of Syria in 1983 are only conservative "best" estimates based on mid-1983 figures.

unnecessary given the short duration of hostilities. Therefore, unlike long wars, short wars have had only marginal impact upon established military assistance ties, but even among these combatants a rise in the number of suppliers and the dollar value of their deliveries is evident in the postwar period.

For most warring states, then, periods of armed conflict have forced changes in their style of procurement. Some have changed bloc orientation, some have become more dependent upon a principal supplier, while others have turned to diversified sources for their defense needs. In quantitative terms, while the dollar value of military aid to most combatants has escalated during conflict, the contribution of the superpowers, particularly the United States, has declined, and other suppliers have moved in to meet the demand.

Differences between Eastern and Western Styles of Military Assistance

Size, Speed, and Quality of U.S. and Soviet Arms Deliveries

Eastern and Western bloc military assistance programs generally differ in both content and pace of delivery. The Soviets, for example, tend to follow a "surge pattern," delivering large amounts of equipment relatively quickly. The U.S.

Central Intelligence Agency (CIA) estimates the average time lapse between contract and delivery of Soviet arms to be one-half to one-third that of the United States.[16] This delivery style stands in marked contrast to the West's, which is characterized by smaller numbers of arms delivered over a longer period of time.

An analysis of the dollar value of transfers to the combatants during prewar, war, and postwar periods illustrates these differences. Note in table 7–5 that with one exception the largest proportional increases in the dollar value of military assistance during wartime occur among Communist-supplied recipients. (Ethiopia, 1,550 percent; Nicaragua, 446 percent; Afghanistan, 368 percent). A similar resupply effort was launched for Vietnam after its border war with China (1,607 percent). Only El Salvador among the Western-supplied recipients has experienced a comparable rate of growth (760 percent) over prewar levels.

However, these large percentage increases in military transfers need to be kept in comparative perspective. As table 7–5 and figure 7–1 demonstrate, although the yearly average of $766 million in aid to Ethiopia represents a 1,550 percent increase over prewar assistance levels, a slightly larger procurement ($784 million yearly average) constitutes a decline of 61 percent for Iran. Thus in absolute terms the levels of military assistance vary considerably from one combatant to another, determined by the recipients' ability to pay, the existing regional balance, and the strategic importance of the area to its suppliers. Regardless of supplier, the largest resupply assistance per year has gone to the combatants in the Middle East (averaging between not quite $1 billion and $3 billion per year), followed by countries in Asia and Africa, which have all received less than $1 billion annually (from $100 million to $700 million averaged), and Central American countries that have received between 1 percent and 5 percent of the latter amount (ranging between $8 million and $46 million; see table 7–5). It is therefore erroneous to equate the "arms race" in the Middle East with the "arms walk" in other less-developed regions of the world even during wartime.[17] Although relative to U.S. programs Soviet equipment has arrived in larger numbers and more quickly, the quantity of materiel delivered by both superpowers to the Middle East cannot be equated with their resupply efforts in other less-developed regions of the world.

Qualitative differences characterize superpower styles of military assistance as well. The experience of Western-supplied states, for example, has differed from their Communist bloc counterparts in two major ways. First, their inventories tend to grow more slowly, reflecting in part traditional U.S. ambivalence toward arms transfers as a foreign policy tool, Europe's limited production and delivery capabilities, and Western tactical and strategic orientations toward war. Second, Western-supplied inventories are generally both smaller and more advanced than those supplied by Warsaw Pact countries.

In an effort to assess the relative sophistication of equipment in the LDC combatants' inventories, I used age as an indicator, taking as a base year the item's original production date and subtracting it from the inventory year. This method was based on the assumption that new generations of weapons incorporate modern innovations and are therefore more technologically advanced than older systems. This of course is not always the case, particularly for degraded export models or upgraded older technologies. However, I have tried to account for these variations wherever possible.

Table 7–6 presents the comparative age of items in the combatants' inventories. These inventories illustrate the qualitative differences between Eastern and Western military assistance programs, which are most pronounced in combat aircraft deliveries. Taking a comparison of Ethiopia and Somalia as an example, Table 7–7 shows that in 1976–77 Ethiopia's Western-supplied inventory was smaller and more modern across the board than Somalia's. By 1979–80 Ethiopia's change to Communist sources of supply was reflected in its comparatively larger and older force structure. Somalia, on the other hand, deprived of Soviet military assistance since the onset of the war, was now dependent upon Western donors. Although the size of its inventory diminished considerably due to general attrition and battle losses, the weapons Somalia did manage to acquire, particularly combat aircraft, were relatively modern, reducing the average age of Somalia's combat aircraft inventory by 5.4 years during the same time period (see table 7–6). In general, the supply patterns in recent wars suggest that the displacement of Eastern suppliers by Western donors increases inventory modernity and vice versa.

Here again, major regional differences exist. In the Middle East intense competition between the Eastern and Western blocs has produced comparatively larger inventories as well as relatively more modern equipment on both sides. Combat planes and helicopters number in the hundreds in Iraq, Iran, Syria, and Israel; tanks and armored vehicles in the thousands. The average age of the equipment is about seventeen years. In contrast, Central American inventories are smaller and older. During the early 1980s, in each major weapon system category, the number of items in inventory remained below thirty, and the average age was more than twenty years. The inventories of combatants in other regions range somewhere between in size and modernity (see table 7–6).[18]

*Training as a Component of Eastern
and Western Military Assistance*

Numbers of weapons and "other services" tell only part of the military assistance story. Training—the instruction of foreign personnel in military-related skills—often overlooked by analysts of the arms trade, is a vital component of military assistance programs. Without it weapons are of little use to the soldiers who bear them; indeed, training, or the lack of it, has more often than not determined the combatants' fortunes in war.[19]

As in the arms trade, the superpowers are the largest suppliers of military-related education. However, there are major differences in the proportion of

Table 7-6
Comparative Qualitative Force Structure:
Average Age of Weapon Systems in Inventory by Type of System[a]

Ethiopia/Somalia:

	1976–1977		1977–1978		1978–1979		1979–1980	
	Ethiopia	*Somalia*	*Ethiopia*	*Somalia*	*Somalia*	*Ethiopia*	*Ethiopia*	*Somalia*
Combat Aircraft	15.8	24.8	16.8	25.3	25.5	19.2	20.2	19.4
Helicopters	13.8	20.0	18.1	21.0	22.9	19.0	18.2	23.0
Tanks	23.2	34.4	20.2	32.6	32.1	24.7	25.8	32.1
Armored Personnel Carriers (APCs)	13.0	27.6	17.6	35.4	25.6	21.9	22.3	25.6
Missiles	—	—	—	18.5	12.8	8.0	20.0	15.0

Iran/Iraq:

	1979–1980		1980–1981		1981–1982		1982–1983	
	Iran	*Iraq*	*Iran*	*Iraq*	*Iran*	*Iraq*	*Iran*	*Iraq*
Combat Aircraft	7.9	16.0	7.9	13.2	7.9	15.4	7.1	16.1
Helicopters	10.2	16.8	10.8	16.6	12.9	17.1	12.9	15.6
Tanks	17.1	24.7	17.1	23.5	13.7	24.7	16.9	25.6
APCs	22.6	21.7	23.6	22.7	24.7	11.9	25.7	12.9
Missiles	11.0	13.2	12.0	14.2	13.0	15.2	14.0	13.8

Vietnam/PRC:

	1978–1979		1979–1980		1980–1981	
	Vietnam	*PRC*	*Vietnam*	*PRC*	*Vietnam*	*PRC*
Combat Aircraft	19.7	24.1	22.3	25.0	16.3	25.8
Helicopters	20.4	20.4	18.2	21.5	18.9	21.7
Tanks	32.0	25.0	25.9	26.0	28.1	29.0
APCs	24.0	12.0	20.3	12.0	21.6	22.0
Missiles	13.2	15.5	14.0	15.5	15.0	15.7

Morocco:

	1978–1979	1979–1980	1980–1981	1981–1982
	Morocco	*Morocco*	*Morocco*	*Morocco*
Combat Aircraft	16.6	15.2	15.1	16.6
Helicopters	9.9	11.1	12.5	3.8
Tanks	26.3	21.9	28.0	29.0
APCs	17.0	16.5	14.0	15.8
Missiles	7.2	8.2	9.2	10.2

Afghanistan:

	Afghanistan	Afghanistan	Afghanistan
Combat Aircraft	22.1	24.0	26.3
Helicopters	20.9	17.5	17.7
Tanks	26.0	27.3	27.9
APCs	23.5	24.5	25.5
Missiles	8.0	9.0	10.0

Israel/Syria[b]:

	Israel	Syria	Israel	Syria	Israel	Syria
Combat Aircraft	8.2	14.3	10.9	17.1	13.3	15.3
Helicopters	15.5	14.8	15.5	15.1	14.6	15.1
Tanks	27.2	26.7	28.4	23.5	26.8	23.7
APCs	28.1	23.6	30.7	24.6	29.8	25.6
Missiles	7.9	15.3	11.3	16.9	11.9	16.3

Argentina:

	Argentina	Argentina	Argentina
Combat Aircraft	13.7	15.3	13.6
Helicopters	15.1	15.2	16.2
Tanks	31.4	23.2	20.5
APCs	19.5	20.4	19.5
Missiles	13.9	16.3	16.1

El Salvador/Nicaragua:

	El Salvador	Nicaragua	El Salvador	Nicaragua	El Salvador	Nicaragua	El Salvador	Nicaragua
Combat Aircraft	27.8	19.0	27.3	20.0	27.7	23.0	24.6	24.5
Helicopters	12.6	23.2	13.6	15.7	19.9	16.8	21.1	17.0
Tanks	26.0	37.0	27.0	38.0	28.0	32.5	29.0	31.0
APCs	13.1	—	14.1	—	13.6	—	14.6	21.0
Missiles	—	—	—	—	—	—	—	—

Source: Derived from *The Military Balance 1976/77–1983/84* (London: IISS, 1976–1983).

[a] Average age of each weapon system type in inventory =

$$\frac{\left[\begin{array}{l}\text{Year in}\\\text{LDC inventory}\end{array} - \begin{array}{l}\text{Year of}\\\text{original}\\\text{production}\end{array}\right] \times \begin{array}{l}\text{no. in}\\\text{LDC}\\\text{inventory}\end{array} + \left[\begin{array}{l}\text{Year in}\\\text{LDC}\\\text{inventory}\end{array} - \begin{array}{l}\text{Year of}\\\text{original}\\\text{production}\end{array}\right] \times \begin{array}{l}\text{no. in}\\\text{LDC}\\\text{inventory}\end{array} + \cdots}{\text{Total no. of weapon system type in inventory}}$$

[b] Israel upgrades its old infantry equipment, therefore the date of original production may be unrelated to an item's capability.

Table 7–7
Size and Age of Ethiopia's and Somalia's Inventories:
A Comparison Between Western and Eastern Supply Patterns[a]

	Ethiopia[b] 1976–1977 (compared with Somalia)		Ethiopia[c] 1979–1980 (compared with Somalia)	
	Size	Age	Size	Age
Combat aircraft	− 30.0	+ 9.0	+ 78.0	− 0.8
Helicopters	00.0	+ 6.2	+ 38.0	+ 4.8
Tanks	− 172.0	+ 11.2	+ 600.0	+ 6.3
APCs	− 220.0	+ 14.6	+ 432.0	?

Source: Derived from table 7–6.

[a]Average age of each weapon system type in inventory =

$$\frac{\left(\left[\begin{array}{c}\text{Year in}\\ \text{LDC inventory}\end{array} - \begin{array}{c}\text{Year of}\\ \text{original}\\ \text{production}\end{array}\right] \times \begin{array}{c}\text{no. in}\\ \text{LDC}\\ \text{inventory}\end{array}\right) + \left(\left[\begin{array}{c}\text{Year in}\\ \text{LDC}\\ \text{inventory}\end{array} - \begin{array}{c}\text{Year of}\\ \text{original}\\ \text{production}\end{array}\right] \times \begin{array}{c}\text{no. in}\\ \text{LDC}\\ \text{inventory}\end{array}\right) + \ \cdots}{\text{Total no. of weapon system type in inventory}}$$

[b]Western supplied.
[c]Eastern bloc supplied.

training, services, and hardware each has delivered to LDCs. On average, weapons and ammunition make up only 38 percent of U.S. military assistance programs, with support equipment (18 percent),[20] spare parts and modifications (18 percent), and support services (training, construction, repairs, and so forth, 26 percent) composing the remaining 62 percent. Soviet deliveries are inversely structured (2/3 equipment; 1/3, support, spares, and services).[21] It is estimated that in recent years U.S. deliveries of military services have been four times greater than those of the Soviet Union.[22]

Listed in table 7–8 is the training component of U.S. military assistance programs to LDCs engaged in recent wars. It gives some idea of the proportion of training to other types of U.S. military-related transfers. Although the percentage of military training to other kinds of U.S. military-related transfers varies considerably from country to country, and in some instances is very small, the U.S. military education program is, when compared with that of other suppliers, the largest in the world. Counting only military personnel from combatant states, the United States alone has trained nine times more men than the Warsaw Pact countries.[23]

The Central American states have received proportionately more training aid than states in other regions. As table 7–9 indicates, military education programs in Central America are not just a function of the present regional conflict but characterize U.S. military assistance programs to these countries since 1955. Although the number of El Salvador's military trainees rose sharply in

Table 7–8

Military Training as a Percentage of Total Military Assistance Provided by the United States to the Combatants[a] (Dollar Value, 1950–1982)

Country	Percentage
Afghanistan	100.0
Argentina	7.0
China	0.0
El Salvador	17.8
Ethiopia	9.4 (1953–1977)[b]
Honduras	57.8
Iran	4.6 (1950–1979)
Iraq	2.5 (1955–1971)
Israel	0.5[c]
Morocco	3.7
Nicaragua	64.7
Somalia	3.3
Syria	98.2
Vietnam	?[d]

Source: Department of Defense Security Assistance Agency (DSAA). *Fiscal Year Series as of September 30, 1984* (Washington, D.C.: Data Management Division, Comptroller, DSAA, 1984). Data on the dollar value of Foreign Military Sales Program (FMS) training provided by DSAA, June 1985.

[a]International Military Education Training Program (IMET), a grant-aid program and training procured under the FMS. Included are training programs offered at U.S. facilities. The figures do not include military advisory or technical teams in the field.

[b]U.S. military assistance began in 1953 and ended with the onset of the Horn war.

[c]FMS only, no IMET.

[d]Training figures not disaggregated for Vietnam. Included with equipment in the Military Assistance Security Fund (MASF), a special fund set up by the Department of Defense during the Vietnam War.

1982 and 1983, and a similar rise is occurring for Honduras, the transfer of hardware and other services has also increased, so that the proportion of training to other military assistance in real terms has declined. Generally, however, training is a politically less sensitive issue than weapons transfers and therefore is more likely to be funded by the U.S. Congress.

Although most military-related instruction is provided by the superpowers directly to LDC recipients, during conflict both have enlisted the aid of allies and friends. In each of the wars examined here, others have supplemented the training efforts of the United States or the Soviet Union, and in politically delicate situations where a superpower chooses to keep its distance, they have served as indirect sources of this form of aid.

Table 7-9
Training of the LDC Military Personnel in Communist Countries and in the United States
(number of trainees and percent increase, 1955–1981)

	Soviet Union and Eastern Europe							United States							
	1955–1975 Total No.	1977 No.	1978 No.	1979 No.	1981 No.	1955–1981 Total No.	% < [a]	1955–1975 Total No.	1977 No.	1978 No.	1979 No.	1980 No.	1981 No.	1955–1981 Total No.	% < [a]
Ethiopia	—	—	—	—	2,095	2,095	+100.0	3,683	47	—	—	—	—	3,914	+6.3
Somalia	2,450[b]	100[b]	0	0	50	2,600	+6.1	—	—	—	—	—	21	21	+100.0
Morocco	150	0	0	0	0	145[c]	0.0	2,130	85	199	109	129[d]	150[e]	2,934	+37.7
Afghanistan	3,550	475	0	0	1,555	5,580	+57.2	419	14	20	—	—	—	487	+16.2
Iran	275	50	0	0	70	395	+43.6	10,601	—	—	—	—	—	10,601[f]	0.0
Iraq	3,200	875	275	50	10	4,410	+37.8	410	—	—	—	—	—	410	0.0
Syria	3,825	525	600	0	565	5,515	+44.2	20	—	—	—	—	—	20	0.0
Israel	—	—	—	—	—	—	—	—	—	—	—	—	—	—	—
Vietnam	—	—	—	—	—	—	—	47,935	—	—	—	—	—	47,935	0.0
Nicaragua	—	—	—	—	260	260	+100.0	4,976	234	275	6	—	—	5,737	+15.3
Honduras	—	—	—	—	—	—	—	2,619	116	219	226	166	261	3,863	+47.5
El Salvador	—	—	—	—	—	—	—	1,708	47	—	—	125	256[i]	2,369	+38.7
Argentina	—	—	—	—	—	—	—	3,803	140	—	—	—[h]	—	4,802	+7.3
Total Combatants:	13,450					21,000	+56.1	78,304						83,093	+6.1
Total All Third World:	41,200[g]					57,795	+40.3	354,287						380,253	+7.3

Source: For the Soviet Union and Eastern Europe, 1955–1975, 1977, 1978, and 1979: CIA, *Handbook of Economic Statistics, 1976; 1978; 1979; 1980* (Washington, D.C.: GPO); and for 1981 and 1955–1981, U.S. Department of State, *Soviet and East European Aid to the Third World, 1981,* Publication 9345 (Washington, D.C.: Bureau of Intelligence and Research, February 1983). For the United States: U.S. Department of Defense Security Assistance Agency, *Fiscal Year Series,* as of September 1982. Includes IMET (grant-aid training) program only. FMS and commercial training not included.

a% ∨ = percent increase.
bDoes not include 25 trained in China.
cUnexplained discrepancy; possibly corrected figure.
dSeven more Moroccans were trained under FMS.
eFive more Moroccans were trained under FMS.
fIn 1973, Iran stopped receiving IMET, paying for its own training through FMS. In 1979, there were 760 Iranians training under FMS. After 1979, all training programs ended.
gTotal for 1955–1975 does not include 3,000 trained in China. The number of LDC military personnel actually in training in 1975 was 3,775, not including 625 trained in China.
hSixteen Argentine military personnel were trained under FMS.
iIn 1982, the number rose to 747 military personnel trained by the United States.

The Impact on Recent Wars

There is some evidence to suggest that these variations in style of military assistance have had important consequences for the LDC combatants. For example, during recent conflicts, large prewar inventories appear to have been more destabilizing than smaller, more modern ones. In all of the conventional wars surveyed here, countries with numerical superiority were the aggressors, for example, Somalia, the PRC, Argentina, and Iraq. In the latter case, Iraq, which had agreed reluctantly to a diplomatic resolution of the Shatt-al-Arab dispute in 1975 when Iran had the military advantage, invaded Iran in 1980 after Iran's arsenal had diminished through attrition and its armed forces were weakened through revolutionary disarray.[24] Somalia, with three times the number of tanks and armored vehicles and twice the number of combat aircraft, attacked Ethiopia in February 1977. The situation in the Falklands was not very different. Although Argentina's force structure was only about one-third the size of Britain's, given the scanty deployment of British forces in the Falklands and the long logistical pipeline for resupply, the Argentine military calculated on its numerical (and psychological) advantage and acted upon it.[25] And in Asia, the PRC, with four times the number of men and a huge inventory, attacked to teach Vietnam a lesson.

In contrast, smaller inventories with better-trained and motivated soldiers and more modern equipment have not served the defenders badly. Iran, despite the disarray of its U.S.-trained and equipped military turned a rout into a stalemate, and Britain, despite the disadvantage of distance, defeated Argentina in eleven weeks. In Asia, the PRC withdrew its forces after seventeen days without achieving a decisive military victory. During recent wars fought in the Third World, although quantitative advantage has encouraged adventurism, the qualitative advantage of the defenders has determined the conflict's outcome.[26]

U.S. and Soviet Resupply Patterns: Restraints, Influence, and Global Competition

As the above discussion indicates, both superpowers have exhibited distinctive styles of military assistance. During wartime, however, the similarities between them may outweigh the differences. Public impressions to the contrary, both superpowers have shown concern about escalating Third World conflicts with arms exports and have exercised restraint, particularly during the early stages of war, or until some obvious political or strategic advantage has been perceived. Whatever the gain to be derived from immediate support, it has been weighed against both the cost of alienating the other combatant and driving it into the arms of the other camp, and the possibility of initiating a direct superpower confrontation in the region. Thus, during recent short wars, the United States and the Soviet Union refrained from resupply altogether and in other longer wars have also refused to do so, at least during the initial, confusing stages of the conflict. For example, at the beginning of the Ethiopian-Somalian hostilities both superpowers temporized,[27] and during the initial phase of the Iran–Iraq war, they stopped supplying both sides.[28] To date they continue to exercise moderation.[29]

In addition to denying immediate support to belligerents, both the Soviet Union and the United States have generally refrained from releasing state-of-the-art technology, particularly to LDC combatants. The ostensibly modern systems delivered are often degraded export models or they remain under superpower control. For example, although the Soviets have transferred large amounts of equipment to Syria, there is little evidence to suggest that the level of sophistication of Syria's inventory has been greatly raised as a result. The general assessment among intelligence analysts is that the Syrians have done little more than recoup their losses[30] and that the Soviets are interested in enhancing defensive not offensive capabilities. Furthermore, as of spring 1986, the Soviets have retained control over the more advanced systems, such as the C^3I system they are building for the two SA-5 air defense complexes sent to Syria.[31]

In Vietnam, the Soviet Union has been equally careful not to transfer its state-of-the-art equipment. To date the Soviets have allowed the Vietnamese only older technologies such as the SU-22 Fitter fighter-bomber, a downgraded version of a more advanced Soviet model, the KA-25 antisubmarine warfare helicopter (in production since 1966), and the MiG-21 (in production since the early 1960s).[32] The more modern Soviet equipment now in Vietnam is Soviet and remains under tight Soviet control.[33] Even in Afghanistan, the Soviets appear to have learned from the U.S. experience in Vietnam. According to one analyst, they decided from the beginning to limit their investment in Afghanistan and at present appear to have settled for controlling the principal towns and highways. As of 1983, the Soviet contribution to the Afghan military averaged less than $150 million a year, and their total investment in the war has remained low relative to total Soviet military expenditures.[34] In Central America, although powerful by regional standards, Soviet military assistance to Nicaragua has been limited in dollar value (on average $26 million yearly) and level of sophistication. It is noteworthy that even in the Middle East, where the quantity of arms transferred is highest, neither the Soviet Union nor the United States has been willing to transfer first-line equipment to either side in the Iran–Iraq war.

In general, Soviet transfers represent systems that have already been deployed in Soviet units for several years. Even when they are released for export, they are often modified versions that are not equipped with the most recent Soviet subsystems. Those that are not modified, as in the case of certain supplies to Syria, remain under Soviet control for extended periods of time.[35]

Although U.S. arms transfers to the LDCs have tended to be more modern than those of the Soviets, the United States also has been reluctant to part with state-of-the-art technology, or any equipment that might be destabilizing, particularly to countries in areas of conflict. The inventories of Communist-supplied countries are on average only eight to ten years older than those of U.S. recipients. In some regions such as Central America, the force structures of Honduras, El Salvador, and Nicaragua (originally Western-equipped) are older than those of some Communist clients in Africa and the Middle East. As one observer of the Central American war complained, "Most of the equipment from the U.S. is used; often it is very old and sometimes it is junk."[36] When new U.S. systems are transferred to Third World states, like their Soviet counterparts they are often downgraded models.

In addition to restraint, superpower resupply programs both during and after recent wars have been conditioned on significant political or military concessions from the combatants. This has been true for all types of wars—short wars, insurgencies, and longer conventional conflicts. U.S. arms transfer restrictions in 1982–83 implemented to induce Israeli compliance in Lebanon and the Soviet resupply of Vietnam in 1979 are two examples.

The latter agreement well illustrates the political costs to the recipient and the strategic benefits for the supplier that often accompany superpower resupply efforts. Until the arrival of Soviet aid in 1979, there was no evidence that the Vietnamese had allowed a significant Soviet presence inside their territory, nor were there significant arms transfers from the Soviet Union to Vietnam. After the Chinese invasion of and subsequent withdrawal from Vietnam, however, the Vietnamese government gave the Soviets permission to use Cam Ranh Bay and Da Nang bases as a quid pro quo for military and economic assistance. As a result the strategic character of East Asia has changed. Soviet surface ships and submarines now make regular visits to Cam Ranh Bay, which gives them improved, if still limited, naval capabilities in the South China seas. In addition, the new facilities have helped the Soviets expand their intelligence and communications capabilities in the region.[37]

Syrian-Russian relations in 1982 provide a third example of the same phenomenon. In 1977, despite its dependence upon the Soviet Union for military assistance, Syria apparently rejected a Soviet request for military "facilities" or bases. It is unknown whether this issue was related to the Soviets' delayed response to Syria's pleas for resupply in June 1982. In any case, tensions between the two countries rose to new heights at that time. Syria had lost almost one hundred planes and virtually all of its antiaircraft defenses. The Soviet decision to comply with Syria's request in late 1982 was probably motivated by a desire to recoup its international reputation as a reliable supplier but was evidently influenced by strategic considerations as well. Syria remains the only game in town for the Soviets, and although no formal base rights have been granted, five thousand to seven thousand military advisers and technicians accompanied the resupply package.[38] Moreover, the Soviets have obtained limited access to ports and facilities in Syria, and the large Soviet presence has facilitated their intelligence-gathering capabilities in the region. From the Soviet perspective the rewards of resupply have not been insignificant.

Clearly, political considerations have also determined the speed and dedication of the superpowers' commitment to governments fighting insurgent wars. Their concern to avoid any negative change within their spheres of influence has prompted them to respond more decidedly to countries such as Afghanistan (the Soviet Union) and to those in Central America (the United States) than they have to countries in more remote "fringe" regions of the world. The U.S. reaction to a Moroccan request for arms during its struggle with the *Polisario* guerrillas in the Western Sahara is a good example. As long as the United States did not see or agree upon a clear-cut strategic or political gain, it did not offer significant assistance. Throughout the Carter years the pros and cons of the Western Sahara issue were furiously debated,[39] paralyzing the policy-making process, and polarizing parts of the administration. Only after a constellation of external and domestic forces was in place,[40] and the political advantages perceived, was a clear military aid policy articulated. Up until that point, Morocco's sources of supply were limited and diversified.[41] In 1982, the Reagan administration, in exchange for U.S. access to Moroccan ports, bases, and communications stations, raised Morocco's Foreign Military Sales (FMS) credits from $34 million to $100 million for fiscal year 1983.[42]

On balance, U.S. and Soviet security interests have been well served by their restraints on arms transfers. In return for easing embargoes or restrictions and resuming military assistance relationships, both have realized significant strategic and political gains. From the perspective of the United States and the Soviet Union, when used adroitly, restrictions on arms transfers during war can have as many (if not more) advantages as government-to-government agreements during peacetime.

In short, the superpowers have used military assistance as a foreign policy tool, both to further their political interests and to prevent any loss of influence in regions of strategic importance. In an effort to avoid any escalation of local conflicts that might affect them adversely, they have been notably restrained in their resupply activities. Even in those instances where political advantage has been sought by keeping the war alive through arms transfers (for example, the U.S. assistance to the Afghan rebels and Soviet support of the Sandinistas), the responses of the United States and the Soviet Union have been moderated by their global concerns and responsibilities.

Diversification and Indirect Sources of Supply: The Response of the Combatants

To LDC combatants, especially those fighting long wars, when both superpowers desist from direct resupply or make unacceptable political demands, there is no option other than turning to other outlets for procurement. Constrained by the need to find equipment that can be integrated easily into existing inventories without time-consuming training in maintenance and operations, LDC combatants have turned increasingly to other European or LDC producers as well as to less orthodox means of resupply. Smuggling or illegal transfers often with the acquiescence of an interested foreign government; third party transfers whereby equipment sold to one government by another is delivered to a third, with or without the permission of the original seller; purchases from the private international arms market; weapons left in battle zones after a conflict—these are only some of the indirect methods of arms acquisition used in recent wars. Although bilateral agreements between the superpowers and the LDCs remain the main mode of trade, other sources of supply have become important channels of military aid during periods of armed hostilities for many combatants.

A combination of political and economic factors has served to reinforce this trend. First, there has been an increase in the number of governments able and willing to export a wide variety of Eastern and Western derived arms. A rising number of states produce military equipment, enlarging further the pool of available suppliers, particularly for the technologically less advanced implements of war, for example, small arms, ammunition, machine guns, light cannons, artillery, patrol boats, and light armor. Even states that do not manufacture arms have found the means, often clandestine, for sending equipment from their own inventories to the combatants. In this way, the world's growing arsenals and military production capabilities have served to make multiple direct, as well as indirect, sources of supply an attractive alternative for all sides in recent wars.

Second, the East-West ideological orientation of Third World buyers and their suppliers is in decline. As a result, combatants have had access to a larger, politically unrestricted population of donors. During the Horn war, as noted above, both Somalia and Ethiopia changed their principal source of military supply, turning from East to West and vice versa. After the Somali-Soviet relationship deteriorated, a mixed bag of suppliers began provisioning Ethiopia— the Soviet Union, Libya, South Yemen, Vietnam, Cuba, East Germany, Bulgaria, China, and Israel. This strange ideological conglomeration of suppliers—Israel aligned with virulently anti-Israel and Communist countries, and China allied with the Soviet Union—did not seem to concern the new "Marxist" Ethiopian regime, nor for that matter its supporters. Similarly, the Gulf war has seen an eclectic group of suppliers providing assistance to Iraq and Iran, and sometimes to both. Since the beginning of the war, out of forty suppliers, ten—Communist and non-Communist alike—have delivered military equipment to both sides.[43]

In combination, these trends have had an important impact on the arms trade during combat. In each of the wars examined here, other than the short three-week PRC-Vietnam confrontation, multiple and indirect sources of supply have played a significant role. This pattern is particularly pronounced during long wars, where diversified relationships have become the rule rather than the exception.[44]

Dependency, Power, and Influence: The Role of Military Assistance

It is these developments—an obvious increase in diversification and a growing number of suppliers—that prompt some observers to declare that superpower influence in the international system has been eroded. Fewer states, they argue, need to buy arms from the superpowers, thereby reducing the leverage of the latter and increasing the political and military independence of the former, especially during periods of regional conflict.

However, the extent to which the increased number of suppliers works against superpower interests is not patently clear. From the perspective of the United States and the Soviet Union, diversified procurement by combatants has not been without its political and strategic utility. Both perceive that the stakes of war have grown dangerously high and neither wants to become involved in a regional conflict that may lead to a wider, more destructive superpower confrontation. Consequently, the availability of friends and allies eager to sell compatible materiel and services to the combatants and the increasing number of states with indigenous production capabilities have provided the superpowers with the means to conduct their global competition less visibly. Each has had reason to permit, and in some cases promote, alternate sources of supply to armed forces during combat.[45]

Furthermore, there is some evidence to suggest that in spite of increased diversification, the superpowers have maintained considerable influence over the transfer of arms to combatants. In fact, a case might be made that the United States and the Soviet Union have been involved directly or indirectly in the resupply of one or both of the local forces during all recent wars, and that many of the "diverse" sources have acted with one or the other superpower's overt or tacit approval. The Soviets, for example, have used both Third World countries (such as Libya, Syria, South Yemen, Algeria, and Cuba) and certain Eastern bloc states to supplement or substitute for direct Soviet aid.[46] This was certainly the case at the onset of the Iran-Iraq war, when the Soviet Union was still temporizing over its policy but continuing to resupply Iraq through other Warsaw Pact countries while testing the waters in Iran.[47] And in Central America large numbers of Eastern bloc suppliers have provided military assistance to the Nicaraguan government. Cuban, East European, PLO, and Libyan personnel have supplemented Soviet efforts.[48]

Although the connections are less clear in the West, and U.S. friends are sensitive to the charge of "surrogate," "substitute," or "proxy," a similar indirect pattern of supply has emerged. Through a system of subtle persuasion, the prohibition of transfers to third parties, and the promise of future economic or political rewards, the United States has managed to exert considerable influence over the flow of arms and services to the combatants.

The complex Western network supplying the Afghan rebels is only one example. Here, modest U.S. assistance has been supplemented by Saudi Arabian financial aid, Egyptian training, and Egyptian and Chinese arms transfers. Pakistan has permitted the weapons to move across its borders and has tolerated training camps within its territory.[49]

In Central America the relationship is even clearer. Here the Reagan administration publicly discussed the role of substitute suppliers. Thus in the face of Congress's reluctance to support the Nicaraguan insurgents, and as a tactic to persuade it to do so, the administration announced its intention to bid friendly Asian countries to help channel aid to the Contras.[50] In August 1985, the Nicaraguan government claimed that South Korea had sent military experts to advise the Contras. Other countries, heavily dependent upon the United States for economic and military support, such as Honduras, El Salvador, and Israel, have also reportedly increased their aid to the rebels.[51] Brazil, Venezuela, and Argentina are said to be indirectly sending military equipment to the Contras as well. And Israel's role in the region has been referred to in the press as that of a "surrogate supplier."[52]

El Salvador has benefited from assistance proffered by an assortment of close allies too. In addition to indirect equipment transfers, supplementary support has been forthcoming from European allies and from Israel. Britain, Belgium, and Israel have each volunteered to train members of the Salvadoran army in their own countries, and West Germany lifted a five-year ban on aid to El Salvador in 1984 by providing technical and financial assistance.[53]

On the other hand, U.S. efforts to limit Nicaragua's access to Western equipment have also been quite effective. France, however reluctantly, acquiesced to the Reagan administration's request that it "slow down" delivery of an arms package it had sold to the Sandinista regime in Nicaragua. The French also agreed to "delay" delivery of the two Alouette III helicopters that the United States found most objectionable. Senior U.S. officials reportedly said that they thought any new French arms deals with Nicaragua "most unlikely."[54] Other European and Latin American countries have followed suit, so that Nicaragua, once the recipient of military assistance from multiple Western suppliers, now finds itself almost completely dependent upon Communist bloc states for its military assistance.[55]

The Horn war provides further examples. Although the United States refused to transfer weapons to Somalia, persistent rumors circulated in the American press that the United States had permitted Saudi Arabia to purchase new U.S. weapons for Egypt in exchange for the delivery of Egypt's older Soviet-built weapons to Somalia.[56] Ethiopia also accused the United States of secretly collaborating with Iran, Saudi Arabia, and Egypt to supply Somalia with other arms purchased in Western Europe and the United States and sent from West Germany and Iran. Since the war's end, Egypt has continued to help train Somali troops for their skirmishes against Ethiopia, and it is supplying them with armored vehicles, antitank rockets, and other weapons and ammunition.[57]

However, the extent of superpower control over the arms trade during wartime is perhaps least elusive in and best illustrated by the Iran-Iraq war. Because they share the goal of containing violence in the Middle East, the United States and the Soviet Union have moved to contain the flow of sophisticated weapons to both combatants.[58] On the Soviet side, although the Soviet Union has provided the bulk of Iraq's arms since the spring of 1982, it has refrained from delivering systems that might upset the Middle East status quo or the Gulf stalemate. Its relations with Iran have been equally careful. The Soviets have not supplied modern major weapons, and apparently they have successfully prevailed upon North Korea to keep its exports to Iran moderate. To date, North Korean transfers have consisted of older, less-advanced systems and large quantities of ammunition and quartermaster supplies—items Iran needs to carry on the war, but no major weapons that might change the balance. Warsaw Pact states have also been restrained by the Soviets from sending larger systems to Iran. As one State Department official observed, "The Warsaw Pact states are so dependent upon the U.S.S.R. for spares for their own military equipment, the Soviets have them over the barrel in situations like this."[59]

Until late 1983, the United States maintained a generally neutral posture on the Gulf war, refusing to assist either side with military goods. But a secret National Security Decision Directive was issued in November 1983 that led to a series of actions often described as a "tilt" toward Iraq. As one State Department official expressed it, "We want to keep Iraq in the field and get the war ended."[60] Since then the United States has provided some financial and other purportedly nonmilitary aid to Iraq, offered air protection to other Arab states against Iranian attacks on shipping, pressured Western and Asian nations to reduce their arms supplies to Iran, and encouraged moderate assistance to Iraq.

U.S. pressure on its allies regarding assistance to Iran has been discreet but not unsuccessful. The Europeans have agreed to stop deliveries to Iran, with the exception of prior prerevolution orders,[61] and although there is still a lively black market in spares, small arms, and ammunition, since 1983 even this, according to U.S. State Department officials, has slowed as U.S. containment efforts have become more focused.

America's LDC allies—often reluctantly—have also cooperated. South Korea reportedly has refrained from further shipments to Iran since mid-1984, and in late 1984 or early 1985 Israel revised its arms sales policy to the Gulf, stopping all military shipments to Iran as well.[62] As a result of pressure from the United States, China, too, apparently stopped transiting arms to Iran through North Korea in mid-1984 and broke off a proposed $1 billion sale of fighters and tanks to the government of Ayatollah Khomeini.[63] And in June 1984 the Brazilians banned arms sales to Iran. It was reported that Brazil had agreed to restrict its weapons sales "abroad" in return for "access to U.S. defense technology."[64] As a result, Iran has been unable to acquire any modern major weapons since the beginning of the war.

Supplies to Iraq from Western sources have also been influenced by U.S. interests. One analyst claims that the United States in mid-1982, concerned about a possible Iranian breakthrough but officially still neutral toward both Gulf belligerents, relied primarily upon France to prevent Iraq's collapse. Increased deliveries of French weapons began arriving in 1983 and 1984, which also may have served as a partial offset for France's cooperation vis-à-vis Iran. It is noteworthy, however, that despite the increases in the quality and quantity of French arms transferred to Iraq, they have not been sufficient to give Baghdad a decisive advantage, a testament, according to some observers, both to Iraq's unimpressive use of French equipment in combat and to the relative export restraint of the French.[65]

Thus, although there are still leakages in the system, when the political stakes are high, and the superpowers are united, they have been able to slow the flow of major systems and contain the level of sophistication of equipment entering the region of combat. The reliance of many if not most states in the international system, European as well as LDCs, upon one or the other of the superpowers for sophisticated military technologies and subsystems,[66] advanced military research and development,[67] and other forms of technical, economic, and military support has been a powerful incentive for compliance. Through a delicate system of tacit rewards for restraint and the threat of punishment for infractions, both superpowers have been able to "stanch the flow" and modify the level of armed hostilities in various regions of the world.

This discussion has not meant to suggest that superpower control has been or can be total. The participating countries have reasons of their own for cooperating and often pursue their own political and economic interests even when they promote those of one of the superpowers. And when the basic national interests of a superpower's allies or friends are at stake, they may not be compliant. Still, the United States and the Soviet Union retain the option of withdrawing support and wreaking economic punishment if sufficiently displeased—a price most smaller or less affluent states are frequently unwilling to bear.

In sum, there is some evidence to suggest that in recent wars both major powers have found the availability of diverse sources of military aid to be both politically manipulable and useful. This availability has served the multiple purpose of distancing them from direct involvement in regional conflicts, providing friends and allies with needed sales, and regulating the technological level at which regional conflicts are fought. Although diversification and indirect sources of supply have permitted Third World combatants to continue fighting, often at tremendous cost in lives, the type of weapons and training available to them have remained limited. In effect the superpowers have retained control over the quality if not the quantity of the arms trade and ultimately, therefore, over the level of sophistication at which wars can be fought in the Third World.

Judging from recent conflicts in the Third World, neither war nor the rising number of weapon suppliers has served to destabilize the global balance of power or reduce the influence of the United States and the Soviet Union in it. To date, the superpowers have not clashed with each other on the battlefield, and their military competition has been relegated to conventional proxy battles in local wars. Diversification rather than diminishing the influence of the superpowers in the international system apparently has worked to maintain it.

Notes

1. Although power has proved to be a difficult concept to define and measure, the field of international relations has come to associate it with the ability of one actor to influence the behavior of another. For example, Hans Morgenthau, a "Realist," writes that "power may comprise anything that establishes and maintains the control of man over man" (Hans Morgenthau, *Power among Nations*, 4th ed. [New York: Alfred A. Knopf, 1967], 9). And Nye and Keohane of the so-called Interdependence school define power as "the ability of an actor to get others to do something they otherwise would not do . . . Power can be conceived in terms of control over outcomes . . ." (Robert O. Keohane and Joseph S. Nye, Jr., *Power and Interdependence: World Politics in Transition* [Boston: Little, Brown, 1977], 11).

2. The term "loss of control" is used by Nye and Keohane to refer to the relative inability of states to control policy outcomes: "Small and middle powers, and even great powers within a balance-of-power system . . . have had to adjust to changes rather than to shape the forces of history. It may be that United States policymakers have less control now than in the 1950s, but it was the 1950s that were exceptional, not the present" (Joseph S. Nye, Jr., and Robert O. Keohane, "Transnational Relations and World Politics: An Introduction," in *Transnational Relations and World Politics*, ed. Joseph S. Nye, Jr., and Robert O. Keohane [Cambridge: Harvard University Press, 1972], xxiii).

3. For expressions of this view, see U.S. Arms Control and Disarmament Agency (ACDA), "Third World Arms Production," in *World Military Expenditures and Arms Transfers, 1969–1978* (Washington, D.C.: ACDA Dec. 1980), 21; Andrew J. Pierre, *The Global Politics of Arms Sales* (Princeton: Princeton University Press, 1982), 4.

4. For a definition of terms see the section in this chapter, "A Methodological Note."

5. The following framework owes much to earlier work by Amelia Leiss et al., *Arms Transfers to Less Developed Countries* (Cambridge: Center for International Studies, Massachusetts Institute of Technology, 1970). Ronald Slaughter, "The Politics and Nature of the Conventional Arms Transfer Process during a Military Engagement: The Falklands-Malvinas Case," *Arms Control* 4, no. 1 (May 1983): 16–30, has also contributed a useful typology of arms supply relationships.

6. U.S. Arms Control and Disarmament Agency (ACDA), *World Military Expenditures and Arms Transfers, 1972–1982*, (Washington, D.C.: ACDA, Apr. 1984), 106.

7. For a more detailed discussion of the arms trade data and its weaknesses see S. Neuman, *Military Assistance in Recent Wars: The Dominance of the Superpowers* (Washington, D.C.: Center for Strategic International Studies, 1986).

8. Leiss et al., *Arms Transfers*, 97.

9. For a more detailed comparison and breakdown of the structure of the arms trade see, S. Neuman, "The Arms Trade and American National Interests," in *Power and Policy in Transition*, ed. Vojtech Mastny (Westport, Conn.: Greenwood Press, 1984). In 1963, the superpowers together delivered 81 percent of the military equipment exported to the Third World. By 1983, their share had declined to 60 percent. See also S. Neuman, "Trends in the Conventional Arms Trade," *National Forum*, Special Issue on "The Militarization of the Globe," Fall 1986.

10. The Leiss et al. study presents a typology of five government-to-government supply relationships. (See Leiss et al., *Arms Transfers*, 54, 97). However, because the number of combatants in this study is so small, I merged Leiss's five categories into two basic transfer patterns: *monopoly/principal*, where one supplier provides 50 percent or more of an LDC's military assistance; and *diversified/multiple*, where two suppliers each contribute 45 percent or more of a state's military assistance, or where three or more donors are so involved, none of which provide over 49 percent of a combatant's military assistance.

11. For the purposes of this chapter, *prewar period* refers to the two to three years prior to the outbreak of hostilities. The dollar values for those years are summed and averaged in the following tables.

12. Afghanistan, Somalia, Vietnam, Iraq, Syria, Iran, and Israel.

13. For the purposes of this study, a long war is one in which armed hostilities continue for two years or more. The dollar values for those years are summed and averaged in table 7–5 and the appendix to this chapter, from which tables 7–3 and 7–4 are derived.

14. Even Nicaragua is not an exception. Although tables 7–3 and 7–4 suggest that Nicaragua changed its procurement patterns during hostilities, in fact the Nicaraguan government altered its bloc orientation only after the Sandinista victory in 1979 and before the present confrontation with its neighbors. Despite the initial willingness of the United States to continue providing military assistance, the Sandinista government drew closer to Eastern bloc suppliers for political and ideological reasons. Unlike the other cases, the change in its procurement patterns was not due to war-connected supplier restrictions or demands and occurred before the cross-border conflict reached its current intensity.

15. Exceptions are Argentina and Iran, which were embargoed by their former principal suppliers, and Honduras. The war period for Argentina, however, lasted only one and a half months, and its military purchases in the months following more than compensated for any interruption in deliveries. The apparent "decline" in wartime military assistance to Honduras is due to an unusually large procurement during the prewar period. Israel completed delivery of "an air force" (Mystere fighters and Arava transports) in 1978 that constituted two-thirds of Honduras's total military expenditures for that period.

16. Central Intelligence Agency (CIA), *Arms Flows to LDCs: U.S.-Soviet Comparisons, 1974–1977*, ER 78-10494U (Washington, D.C., November 1978), p. 5.

Soviet military industries produce large numbers of weapons with the export market in mind, permitting fast delivery particularly in wartime emergencies. Twelve to eighteen months have generally elapsed between sales agreements and deliveries of Soviet weapons; U.S. lead times have averaged about three years. For a comparison of U.S. and Soviet transport capabilities, see the discussion in Neuman, *Military Assistance in Recent Wars.*

17. During the mid-1960s, John L. Sutton and Geoffrey Kemp made a similar observation when they compared the amount of military aid going to the Middle East and to sub-Saharan Africa in "Arms to Developing Countries, 1945–1965," *Adelphi Papers*, no. 28, (October 1966): 33.

18. In 1981–82 Argentina's inventory included 169 combat aircraft, 150+ helicopters, 200 tanks, and 375 armored fighting vehicles. Their average vintage was eighteen years. In Africa, Ethiopia's force structure was by 1979–80 the largest. It included combat aircraft (100), helicopters (49), tanks (680), and armored personnel carriers (APCs) (582). Their average age was twenty years old. Morocco's inventory although considerably smaller was somewhat more modern, averaging sixteen to seventeen years in age, primarily because of recent helicopter deliveries. The force structures of Asian states contain the oldest equipment (ranging from the PRC's average of twenty-five years, to an average of twenty-one years for Vietnam [including captured U.S. equipment], to twenty-four years for Afghanistan). In size they vary also, from the huge PRC inventory, to the medium-sized Vietnamese arsenal (485 combat aircraft, 165 helicopters, 2,500 tanks, and 2,300 APCs), to the smaller and fluctuating Afghanistan force structure.

19. For further discussion of training and its impact on the outcome of recent wars see Neuman, *Military Assistance in Recent Wars,* chap. 5.

20. The category support equipment is composed of "nonlethal" or dual-use items such as trucks, communications equipment, cargo aircraft, and so forth. (Defense Security Assistance Agency [DSAA], *Weapons Analysis Report*; interview with DSAA official, June 1985).

21. Statistical breakdown provided by Dr. Andrew Semmel, Department of Defense, March 1984.

22. Roger E. Kanet, "Soviet Military Assistance to Eastern Europe," in *Communist Nations' Military Assistance,* ed. John F. Copper and Daniel S. Papp (Boulder, Colo.: Westview Press, 1983), 39–71.

23. Data are not available for the dollar value of Soviet–Warsaw Pact training programs, but one can assume, given the disparity in *numbers* of personnel trained, that the dollar value is considerably less than that of the United States.

24. On the eve of the Iranian revolution, for example, some analysts reported that of the 450 combat aircraft in inventory, considerably fewer than 50 were operational (Robert Selle, "Iran Said to Be Training Pilots for Suicide Strikes against U.S.," *FPI News Service*, Jan. 9, 1984; *MILAVNEWS*, Aug. 1983). Other intelligence analysts have speculated that both the number of planes in inventory and the number that were operational was somewhat higher (interview with author, Dec. 1983). However, although there are differences in opinion regarding exact numbers, there is general agreement that Iran's air force had been drastically and negatively affected by the revolution.

25. The Lebanon war is an anomaly in which Israel retained both the quantitative and qualitative edge.

26. For a lengthier discussion on the effectiveness of military assistance in recent wars, see Neuman, *Military Assistance in Recent Wars*, chap. 5.

27. Although most analysts attribute a rapid and generous response on the part of the Soviet Union to the Ethiopian request for aid, in fact even before the war when approached by the *Dergue* in 1975, the Soviet Union reacted cautiously, "far from convinced . . . that a convergence of interest yet existed between Moscow and the *Dergue*." It was not until October 1977, eight months after fighting began in the Ogaden and after the Carter administration had denounced the Mengistu regime on human rights grounds and announced the end of military aid to Ethiopia, that the Soviet Union began to assist the new government. In the United States, the long debate and indecision of the Carter administration regarding aid to Somalia continued throughout the war. U.S. military assistance to Somalia did not actually start until after the armed conflict had ended, when small amounts of U.S. training and equipment deliveries began in 1981. (For further discussion, see William Lewis, "Ethiopia-Somalia (1977–1978)," in *The Lessons of Recent Wars in the Third World*, vol. 1, eds. Robert E. Harkavy and Stephanie G. Neuman (Lexington, Mass.: Lexington Books, 1985), 102–106.

28. A Senate Foreign Relations Committee report observed that the Soviet Union decided in the spring of 1982 to abandon its earlier policy of "neutrality" and to support Iraq, calculating that the neutral stance "risked permanently alienating Iraq without compensating gains in Iran." In fact, according to Dennis Ross, the Soviet Union had imposed transfer restrictions on the Iraqis, refusing to provide direct and new arms supplies to them, fulfilling only prior contracts for small arms and munitions. At the same time, the Soviets offered military and other forms of assistance to Iran (Dennis Ross, "Soviet Views toward the Gulf War," *Orbis* 28, no. 3 (Fall 1984), 438). But despite Soviet efforts, Iran during the early 1980s took a consistently anti-Soviet position, rejecting direct military aid and suppressing the pro-Moscow Tudeh party. In the summer of 1982 the Soviets began supplying arms again to Iraq (Ross, "Soviet Views," 439). However, according to the Senate Foreign Relations Committee report, the Soviet move may have been too late. Although the Soviets subsequently delivered several billion dollars worth of military equipment to Iraq, "the Iraqis will not forget that the Soviet Union embargoed weapons and sided with Iran in the early stages of the war." A great deal of distrust between Iraq and the Soviet Union remains. (See *War in the Gulf*, a Staff Report prepared for the Committee on Foreign Relations, United States Senate, Aug. 1984, p. 10.

29. For a discussion of Soviet moderation in the transfer of offensive weapons such as surface-to-surface and air-to-surface missiles, see "Iraq: Those Reports of New Weapons," *Defense and Foreign Affairs Daily*, June 25, 1984, 1–2. In 1983, the Soviet Union heavily reequipped the Iraqis with T-72 tanks and new MiG-23s, and SAMs were also reported to have been placed around Baghdad and other cities. However, the Soviets have not provided long-range missiles that would enable the Iraqis to seriously disrupt oil tanker traffic at Kharg Island or to "change the strategic balance in the region—meaning that Iraq has received no long range missiles that could reach Israel" (John Kifner, "Unlikely Allies Emerge over Persian Gulf War," *New York Times*, July 17, 1984; "USA and Soviets Balancing Arms Sales to Iran-Iraq," *Jane's Defence Weekly*, July 21, 1984, p. 60; see also, Vladimir N. Sakharov, "Soviets Pursue a Wary Iran-Iraq War Policy Line," *San Diego Union*, July 22, 1984, p. C7).

30. "Soviets Reportedly Replace Syria's Summer Weapons Losses," *Washington Post*, Dec. 3, 1982. Interview with State Department analyst, Jan. 1984.

31. Ibid; "One Hard Lesson," *Wall Street Journal*, Nov. 9, 1983; Anthony H. Cordesman, "Soviet-Syrian Challenge," *Near East Report*, Oct. 14, 1983, p. 33; Alexander J. Bennett, "Arms Transfers as an Instrument of Soviet Policy in the Middle East," *Middle East Journal* 39, no. 4 (Autumn 1985), pp. 745–74.

32. Michael Richardson, "The F-16 for Southeast Asia: Arms Race or Strategic Balance?" *Pacific Defence Reporter* 11, no. 11 May 1985, pp. 17–19; "New Arms, Troops Expand Soviet Military Role in Southeast Asia," *Washington Post*, Dec. 21, 1983, p. 1, and interview with State Department official, Jan. 1984. The SU-22 is a downgraded Fitter-F (1977) aircraft with a less capable engine and avionics.

33. In early 1984, the Soviet Union deployed fourteen MiG-23s, four Bear-D long-range naval reconnaissance aircraft, four Bear-F antisubmarine warfare planes, and sixteen Soviet Tu-16 ("Badger") medium-range bombers, and submarines, as well as surface and support ships at Cam Ranh Bay (Michael Richardson, "The F-16 for Southeast Asia," pp. 17–19; Drew Middleton, "Soviet Buildup in Far East Causing U.S. Concern," *New York Times*, Jan. 30, 1984, p. A2; "New Arms, Troops Expand Soviet Military Role in Southeast Asia," *Washington Post*, Dec. 21, 1983, p. A1, A34).

34. See table 7–5 for Soviet military assistance figures. Estimates of total annual Soviet expenditures on the war in Afghanistan vary widely. There is general agreement that by 1984 the Soviets had increased their financial involvement by adding new air bases and support facilities in Afghanistan. Analysts differ vigorously, however, over the percent rise and real cost of the war to the Soviets. Their estimates range from "several hundreds of millions of dollars" (interview with State Department official, Jan. 1986) to several billion dollars. One source calculated the cost at $1.5 billion (*Economist*, July 14, 1984, pp. 37–39, 41), while a Chinese report estimated that expenses had risen to $2.2 billion in 1984 (*Intelligence Digest*, March 1, 1984, p. 7). But before the buildup in 1984 and since then, even larger expenditure estimates have appeared in the literature. In 1983 and 1985, for example, different sources claimed that the Soviets were spending between $3 billion and $5 billion annually. (See "Afghanistan," *Bulletin of Atomic Scientists* 39, issue 6 [June–July 1983]: 23; Joseph J. Collins, "The Soviet Experience in Afghanistan," *Military Review* [May 1985]: 21; James B. Curren and Phillip A. Karber, "Afghanistan's Ordeal Puts Region at Risk," *Armed Forces Journal International* [March 1985]: 98.) But regardless of variation, based on the Organization of Joint Chiefs of Staff's calculations of Soviet defense expenditures in 1984 ($245 billion), none of the above estimates amounts to more than 1 or 2 percent of the total Soviet military budget—a sum considerably less than that spent by the United States during the Vietnam War. As one source notes, in 1969 the U.S. war effort amounted to 23 percent of the U.S. defense budget (James B. Curren and Phillip A. Karber, "Afghanistan's Ordeal," 98).

35. By 1986 there were some indications that this might be changing. Stung by criticisms leveled at the performance of their systems during the Lebanon war, the Soviet Union may be offering favored clients more modern equipment, such as MiG-29s to India.

36. H. Joachim Maitre, "The Pentagon Unloads Junk on Hapless El Salvador," *Wall Street Journal*, June 8, 1984, p. 29.

37. For a balanced analysis of the strategic benefits accruing to the Soviet Union, see Lief Rosenberger, "The Soviet-Vietnamese Alliance and Kampuchea," *Survey* 27, no. 118–19 (Autumn–Winter 1983): 212–13; also, "Cam Ranh Bay—Forward Base of the Soviet Pacific Fleet," *Jane's Defence Weekly*, July 21, 1984, p. 66; Middleton, "Soviet Buildup in Far East," p. A2; "New Arms, Troops, Expand Soviet Military Role in Southeast Asia," *Washington Post*, p. 1.

38. Judith Miller, "Syrian Fear: Soviet Shift," *New York Times*, Feb. 14, 1984, p. A5. Anthony Cordesman believes the 7,000 figure used by some analysts is too high and that the number of Soviet advisers in Syria is closer to 5,000. (Cordesman, "Soviet-Syrian Challenge," p. 33.)

39. For the pros and cons of the debate, see James E. Dougherty, "The Polisario Insurgency: War and Minuet in North-West Africa," *Conflict* 2, no. 2 (1980): 93–120; John Maclean, "State Department Divided from within over Tank Sale to Morocco," *Defense Week*, Nov. 3, 1980, p. 7. See also William Lewis, "War in the Western Sahara," in *The Lessons of Recent Wars in the Third World*, vol. 1, ed. Robert E. Harkavy and Stephanie G. Neuman (Lexington, Mass.: Lexington Books, 1985), 132.

40. The Shah of Iran had been deposed, President Anastasio Somoza of Nicaragua had fallen, and the Sandinistas had come to power; the Soviet Union had invaded Afghanistan; U.S. allies and conservative Arab countries were expressing public consternation over U.S. resolve to defend its allies and friends; some of the most vigorous congressional opponents to Moroccan aid had been electorally defeated.

41. The Soviets, on the other hand, were not more forthcoming to the opposition. Although Soviet allies reportedly provided some indirect assistance to the *Polisario*, the Soviet Union did not recognize the *Polisario*, nor did it break off its trade relations with Morocco. See staff report, "Polisario's Ongoing War Against Morocco Has Ramifications in Tactical Warfare," *Defense and Foreign Affairs* (April 1980): 1–2.

42. U.S. Department of Defense, "Security Assistance Programs," *Congressional Presentation, FY 1983*, p. 106. To the Reagan administration concerned about access to the southern Mediterranean and to the Persian Gulf after the fall of the Shah, Morocco's strategic location at the mouth of the Strait of Gibraltar and its deep-water harbors offered the United States a convenient staging or refueling post for U.S. forces and could provide alternate transit rights for U.S. aircraft if Spain and Portugal denied them. (Martha Wenger, "Reagan Stakes Morocco in Sahara Struggle," *MERIP Reports*, May 1982, pp. 22–26.)

43. Stockholm International Peace Research Institute, *SIPRI Yearbook* (London and Philadelphia: Taylor & Francis, 1984), pp. 198–99.

44. For a more detailed description of this form of procurement see Neuman, *Military Assistance in Recent Wars*, chap. 3.

45. Indirect transfers no longer provision only guerrilla forces. East and West now use them to resupply all sides in conventional and unconventional wars. In a historic reversal of roles, there are as many insurgencies being fought by anti-Communists against Marxist regimes (for example, the Contras in Nicaragua and the Afghan rebels) as are being fought by leftist insurgents (for example, the *Polisario* and the Sandinistas).

46. See Copper and Papp, eds., *Communist Nations' Military Assistance*, particularly Trond Gilberg, "East European Military Assistance to the Third World," 72–95. Gilberg notes: "The Soviets provide most of the arms, the transportation facilities, and strategic clout; the Cubans provide the necessary manpower; and the East

Germans supply the highly sophisticated technical and administrative expertise so desperately needed in the emerging states" (p. 83). See also Richard Shultz, "The Role of External Forces in Third World Conflicts," *Comparative Strategy* 4, no. 2 (1983): 1–17; Robert M. Cutler, Laure Despres, and Aaron Karp, "Aspects of Arms Transfers and of Military Technology Transfers in East-South Relations," paper prepared for presentation to session 1, "Changes in Development Strategies and North-South Economic Relations," of the Research Committee on Emerging International Economic Order, at the Twelfth World Congress of the International Political Science Association, Paris, July 15–20, 1985; Aaron Karp, "Eastern European Arms Production and Arms Transfers, 1945–1985," paper presented to the Twenty-sixth International Studies Association Convention, Washington, D.C., Mar. 5–9, 1985; Gavriel D. Ra'anan, "Surrogate Forces and Power Projection," paper prepared for the conference, "Projection of Power: Perspectives, Perceptions and Logistics," ninth annual conference of the International Security Studies Program, the Fletcher School of Law and Diplomacy, Tufts University, Apr. 23–25, 1980; James J. Townsend, "Countering Soviet Proxy Operations," paper prepared for the Twenty-fifth Annual Convention of the International Studies Association, Mar. 27–31, 1984, in Atlanta, Georgia.

47. Although the Soviet Union had officially embargoed arms sales to Iraq, the German Democratic Republic (GDR), Poland, and Romania continued to deliver T-54/55 tanks and other materiel to help Iraq compensate for its vast losses.

48. For further discussion of the Soviet use of "surrogate" or "proxy" suppliers, see Neuman, *Military Assistance in Recent Wars*, chap. 6.

49. Richard Halloran, "Peking Reported to Offer More Guns to Afghan Rebels," *New York Times*, Jan. 17, 1980, p. 3; "Egypt Says It Is Training Afghans to Fight Soviet-Supported Regime," *New York Times*, Feb. 14, 1980; "U.S. Supplying Afghan Insurgents with Arms in a Covert Operation," *New York Times,* Feb. 16, 1980; "U.S. Weapons for Afghanistan," *Chicago Tribune*, July 22, 1981; "Caravans on Moonless Nights," *Time*, June 11, 1984, pp. 30–40.

50. Bernard Weinraub, "U.S. Is Considering Having Asians Aid Nicaragua Rebels," *New York Times*, March 6, 1985, pp. A1, A10; " 'South Korean Aid' to Contras," *Jane's Defence Weekly* 4, no. 8 (Aug. 24, 1985); 344.

51. Philip Taubman, "Nicaragua Rebels Reported to Have New Flow of Arms," *New York Times*, Jan. 13, 1985, pp. L1, L11.

52. Edy Kaufman, "The View from Jerusalem," *Washington Quarterly* 7, no. 4 (Fall 1984): 40–51; "Argentina Sends More Weapons to Central America," *Washington Post*, June 10, 1984, p. A1; "Ortega Charges Israel," *Boston Globe*, Aug. 9, 1985, p. 11; Philip Taubman, "Nicaragua Rebels," pp. L1, L11.

53. "U.K. Offers Military Training to El Salvador," *Financial Times*, Feb. 13, 1985, p. 4; "El Salvador Seeks Aid," *Jane's Defence Weekly* 3, no. 8 (Feb. 23, 1985): 291; "W. Germany to Resume Aid to El Salvador," *Washington Post*, July 18, 1984, pp. A1, A20.

54. The sale included two Alouette III helicopters, two coastal patrol boats, forty-five trucks, one hundred helicopter-mounted rocket launchers, and seven thousand rocket rounds (*Newsweek*, March 29, 1982, p. 17; Jonathan C. Randal, "France Stalls on Helicopters for Nicaragua," *Washington Post*, March 31, 1982, p. A20).

55. In 1984, Mexico was reported to be backing away from its strong support of the Sandinista government. It halted all shipments of oil to Nicaragua, pending

payment of overdue bills, began pressuring guerrillas living in Mexico to stop their public activities, and stopped endorsing the Salvadoran guerrillas. The reason for Mexico's change, according to Prof. George Dominguez, is that the "Mexican leaders also felt they were getting too close to a break with Washington over Central America and wanted to head off pressures, particularly given the precarious state of the Mexican economy." This at a time when President Reagan had signed a directive authorizing diplomatic efforts with the Mexican government "to reduce its material and diplomatic support for the Communist guerrillas" in El Salvador and "its economic and diplomatic support for the Nicaraguan Government" (Leslie H. Gelb, "Mexico Is Cooling on Latin Rebels U.S. Officials Say," *New York Times*, July 19, 1984, pp. A1, A2).

56. *Washington Post*, Jan. 24, 1978, p. A9.

57. David Ignatius, "Egypt's Russian Policy Grows More Hawkish in Mideast and Africa," *Wall Street Journal*, Feb. 9, 1981, p. 1.

58. Both superpowers closely monitor this war, the U.S. with the American-manned AWACS aircraft on loan to Saudi Arabia, the Soviets by satellite (Edgar O'Ballance, "The Battle for the Hawizah Marshes: March 1985," *Asian Defence* (June 1985): 8, 9).

59. Author interview, June 26, 1985.

60. Roy Gutman, "U.S. Willing to Use Air Power to Keep Iran from Beating Iraq," *Long Island Newsday*, May 20, 1984, p. 3; and Charles J. Hanley, "In the Gulf War, a High Price Paid for a Stalemate," *Philadelphia Inquirer*, Aug. 1, 1984, p. 2.

61. British ships, a tanker and two logistics ships, Swiss Pilatus PC-7 trainers, and the Italian-Swiss Skyguard antiaircraft system were said by their producers to fall into this category and were delivered. The export of Italian-produced helicopters, Ch-47s, which had been ordered by the Shah, was halted by the Reagan administration when it bought the 11 helicopters still outstanding from the manufacturer. (Interview with State Department official, March 1985; Anthony H. Cordesman, "Arms Sales to Iran: A Working Note," unpublished paper, Jan. 29, 1985, p. 11; "Iranian Navy Warns Against Cargoes to Iraq," *Jane's Defence Weekly* 4, no. 6 (Aug. 10, 1985): 254).

62. "Israel Halts Arms Supplies to Iran in New Gulf Policy," *Jane's Defence Weekly* 3, no. 13 (Mar. 30, 1985), p. 554; James R. Schiffman, "Both Koreas Supplied Weapons to Iran," *Wall Street Journal*, May 2, 1984, p. 5.

63. Cordesman, "Arms Sales to Iran," 6. According to some skeptics, the Chinese restraint may have been only temporary. Interview with State Department official, Jan. 1986.

64. "Defense News Digest," *Army Quarterly and Defense Journal* 114, no. 2 (1984): 215. Brazil's sales were mainly to the Middle East in 1984.

65. Albert L. Weeks, "Host of Soviet Advisers Reported in Iran," *New York City Tribune*, May 1, 1985, p. 1. Shahram Chubin, "Israel and the Iran-Iraq War," *International Defense Review* (March 1985): 304. Interview with State Department official, Nov. 1985.

66. For example, 30 percent of each Tornado plane produced jointly by the United Kingdom, West Germany, and Italy reflects imported U.S. equipment ("Special Report," *Defense Electronics*, May 1979, p. 58).

67. It is estimated that the United States spends three to four times more than Europe on conventional military research and development, which has meant that individual European countries have had to depend on U.S. R&D efforts for many

systems. One U.S. official, attempting to explain why the United States is reluctant to buy European weapons, observed: "We spend four times as much on conventional research and development as they do. You can't have a two-way street in weapons production when one party has the production that we have. It's like 13 dwarfs trying to cooperate with one giant" (quoted in Bernard Weinraub, "Allies Say U.S. Shuns Their Arms," *New York Times*, Nov. 12, 1978, p. 22. See also Paul Lewis, "Europe's Fighter Jet Program," *New York Times*, Nov. 13, 1979, D1, D14; "Special Report," p. 58). See also Neuman, "The Arms Trade and American National Interests," 147–82, for a discussion of the comparative production capabilities in the international system.

Appendix

Military Assistance to Third World Combatants (through 1983)
Averaged $ Value (millions) and % of Total Value (deliveries)

| | Prevar[a] | | | | | | | | | | | | | |
| | Eastern Europe | | USSR | | Western Europe[b] | | United States | | Third World | | Other Significant Supplier | | Total SP[f] | |
	$	%	$	%	$	%	$	%	$	%	$	%	$	ID/M
Ethiopia	1.8	3.9	0.06	0.1	5.5	11.9	22.9	49.4	16.1	34.7	—	—	46.4	DM[g,l]
Somalia	0.1	0.1	79.5	98.6	1.0	1.2	—	—	—	—	—	—	80.6	M[h,m]
Afghanistan[c]	—	—	27.9	98.6	0.03	0.1	0.2	0.7	0.2	0.7	—	—	28.3	M[m]
Morocco	—	—	2.0	1.0	159.3	76.9	38.5	18.6	7.4	3.6	(FR	42.5)	207.2	DM[l]
Nicaragua	—	—	—	—	2.1	24.7	2.6	30.6	3.8	44.7	(IS	36.0)	8.5	DM[l]
Honduras	0.8	5.2	—	—	0.5	3.2	3.2	20.6	11.0	71.0	(IS	66.5)	15.5	P[i,l]
El Salvador	—	—	—	—	0.1	2.9	1.8	51.4	1.6	45.7	(IS	45.7)	3.5	DM[l]
Vietnam[d]	4.1	10.1	36.3	89.6	0.1	0.2	—	—	—	—	—	—	40.5	M[m]
PRC[d]	—	—	31.4	27.9	77.1	68.5	0.3	0.3	3.7	3.3	(UK	58.0)	112.5	I/P[i,l]
Iran	0.2	—	258.0	12.7	187.1	9.2	1530.1	75.4	54.5	2.7	—	—	2029.9	P[k]
Iraq	254.1	13.7	1209.2	65.4	357.9	19.4	0.03	—	28.4	1.5	—	—	1849.6	P[m]
Argentina	—	—	—	—	281.0	75.2	23.3	6.2	69.3	18.5	—	—	373.6	I/DM[l]
Syria[e]	127.2	5.8	1893.6	85.9	153.6	7.0	0.07	—	28.7	1.3	—	—	2203.2	P[m]
Israel	—	—	—	—	1.5	0.2	883.5	99.8	—	—	—	—	885.0	I/M[k]
$ Total	388.3		3538.0		1226.8		2506.5		224.7		—		7884.3	
% Total		4.9		44.8		15.6		31.8		2.8				

War[a]

	Eastern Europe		USSR		Western Europe[b]		United States		Third World		Other Significant Supplier		Total SP[f]	
	$	%	$	%	$	%	$	%	$	%	$	%	$	
Ethiopia	41.0	5.4	650.0	84.9	15.3	2.0	35.3	4.6	24.1	3.1	(EG	29.0)	765.7	P[m]
Somalia	2.0	1.3	26.0	17.0	61.6	40.3	—	—	63.2	41.4	(IT	24.0)	152.8	DM
Afghanistan[c]	1.5	1.1	130.8	98.7	—	—	0.2	0.2	—	—	—	—	132.5	M[m]
Morocco	2.8	0.8	0.3	0.1	247.9	69.1	91.4	25.5	16.4	4.6	(FR	52.8)	358.8	P[l]
Nicaragua	1.4	24.6	25.8	55.6	1.9	4.1	0.02	—	7.3	15.7	(GDR	17.0)	46.4	P[m]
Honduras	—	—	—	—	1.6	20.8	5.1	66.2	1.0	13.0	—	—	7.7	P[k]
El Salvador	—	—	—	—	5.5	18.3	24.1	80.1	0.5	1.7	—	—	30.1	P[k]
Vietnam[d]	—	—	—	—	—	—	—	—	—	—	—	—	—	—
PRC[d]	—	—	—	—	—	—	—	—	—	—	—	—	—	—
Iran	22.0	2.8	74.8	9.5	191.4	24.4	—	—	496.0	63.2	(NK	29.0)	784.2	DM
Iraq	652.8	19.8	1091.6	33.2	961.2	29.2	—	—	586.2	17.8	—	—	3291.8	DM
Argentina	11.1	11.1	—	—	27.7	27.6	—	—	61.4	61.2	(PR	60.4)	100.2	I/P[l]
Syria[e]	—	—	—	—	—	—	—	—	—	—	—	—	—	—
Israel	—	—	—	—	—	—	—	—	—	—	—	—	—	—
$ Total	734.6		1999.3		1514.1		156.1		1256.1				5660.2	
% Total		12.9		35.3		26.7		2.8		22.2				

Appendix (Continued)

	Postwar[p]													
	Eastern Europe		USSR		Western Europe[b]		United States		Third World		Other Significant Supplier		Total SP[f]	
	$	%	$	%	$	%	$	%	$	%	$	%	$	
Ethiopia	7.8	2.7	266.0	93.0	6.2	2.2	—	—	6.0	2.1	—	—	286.0	M[m]
Somalia	2.4	2.3	—	—	78.0	73.8	7.7	7.3	17.6	16.7	(IT	70.0)	105.7	P[l]
Afghanistan[c]	—	—	—	—	—	—	—	—	—	—	—	—	—	—
Morocco	—	—	—	—	—	—	—	—	—	—	—	—	—	—
Nicaragua	—	—	—	—	—	—	—	—	—	—	—	—	—	—
Honduras	—	—	—	—	—	—	—	—	—	—	—	—	—	—
El Salvador	—	—	—	—	—	—	—	—	—	—	—	—	—	—
Vietnam[d]	0.8	0.1	690.4	99.9	0.2	—	—	—	—	—	—	—	691.4	M[m]
PRC[d]	—	—	32.8	26.9	88.3	72.7	0.4	0.3	—	—	(UK	43.0)	121.5	I/DM
Iran	—	—	—	—	—	—	—	—	—	—	—	—	—	—
Iraq	—	—	—	—	—	—	—	—	—	—	—	—	—	—
Argentina	—	—	—	—	652.6	78.4	16.3	2.0	162.7	19.6	(FRG	65.0)	831.6	P[l]
Syria[e]	110.0	7.2	1200.0	78.9	166.7	11.0	—	—	44.5	2.9	—	—	1521.2	P[m]
Israel	—	—	—	—	—	—	790.4	100.0	—	—	—	—	790.4	I/M[k]
$ Total	121.0		2189.2		992.0		814.8		230.8				4347.8	
% Total		2.8		50.4		22.8		18.7		5.3				

Source: Derived from U.S. government sources.

CU = Cuba, EG = Egypt, FR = France, FRG = Federal Republic of Germany, GDR = German Democratic Republic (East Germany), IS = Israel, IT = Italy, NK = North Korea, PR = Peru, UK = United Kingdom.

a*Prewar Period:* 2–3 years prior to onset of war; dollar value averaged.

bCanada, Japan, and Australia included (represent small amount of total).

cWar years for Afghanistan calculated from 1978–82; dollar value averaged; prewar years 1954–77 dollar value averaged.

dPostwar years up to and including 1982.

eTotal dollar value of Soviet resupply for Syria in 1983 not included.

fSP—Supply pattern.

gDM—Diversified or Multiple suppliers: two suppliers each with 45 percent + of the market, or 3 + suppliers none of which provides more than 49 percent of a recipient's military assistance.

hM—Monopoly: one supplier provides 90 percent + of all military assistance.

iP—Principal supplier: one supplier provides 50–89 percent.

jI—Indigenous production capability for major weapons.

kUS.

lWestern Bloc.

mUSSR.

nEastern Bloc.

o*War Period:* Up to and including 1983 (estimate for 1983 only); dollar value averaged.

p*Postwar Period:* Years after the cessation of hostilities, up to and including 1983 (estimate for 1983 only); dollar value averaged.

8
Third World Military Industries: Capabilities and Constraints in Recent Wars

Stephanie G. Neuman

As wars have become endemic in the Third World, much has been written about their incidence and probable cause. Only recently has the role of LDC (less developed country) military industries been called into question by some analysts who believe that their increasing number and capabilities tend both to raise the level of conflict in the international system and to lower the ability of the superpowers to contain its intensity. As one study observes: "The introduction of new, more potent [LDC produced] weapons heightens the possibility of conflict while reducing the ability of the major powers to limit the intensity of potential warfare."[1] Another claims that "the threat of runaway escalation is further accentuated by the intensive creation of other armament production plants in some forty of the developing countries."[2] And a third concludes that "the greatest threat to U.S. security probably arises from the fact of technology diffusion itself. By contributing to the arms-making capabilities of foreign powers, the United States automatically contributes to the *war*-making potential of those countries—as well as to any third countries they supply with U.S.-designed weaponry—and thus inevitably increases the world's total capacity for military violence."[3]

In spite of the increased attention Third World industries have attracted, there is little research to support or refute the above speculations. This chapter considers some of the evidence at hand. It examines recent wars in an effort to learn more about the part LDC defense industries have played. Three general questions are addressed: (1) What are the production capabilities of Third World countries? (2) How do they affect the conduct of wars in the Third World and the capabilities of the LDCs to fight them? (3) What are the implications for the future of conflict and stability in the international system?

The eight wars described and analyzed in volume 1 of *The Lessons of Recent Wars in the Third World* are used here for illustrative purposes: the Horn (Ethiopia/Somalia); The People's Republic of China (PRC)/Vietnam; the Western Sahara (Morocco/*Polisario*); Afghanistan; Iran/Iraq; Central America

(Honduras/Nicaragua/El Salvador/Contras); Lebanon (Israel/Syria/Palestine Liberation Organization [PLO]; the Falklands (Britain/Argentina). In each, the role of Third World suppliers is examined during the prewar, war, and postwar periods.[4]

The Effect of War on LDC Arms Transfers

There is little question that recent wars have dramatically increased the role of Third World suppliers in the arms trade. The sharp rise in the developing countries' share of the global arms trade from less than 3 percent in 1977 (when the Ethiopian-Somalian war began) to over 9 percent in 1982 at the height of the Iran-Iraq conflict, reflects their wartime involvement (see table 8–1).

Table 8–1
The World Export Market by Value of Deliveries:
A Comparison of 1963 and 1983
(constant 1981 $ millions)

Suppliers by Country/Region	1963 Dollar Value	1963 Percent of World Total	1977 Dollar Value	1977 Percent of World Total	1982 Dollar Value	1982 Percent of World Total
NATO Europe[a]	1,445.2	9.9	5,057.0	16.3	7,197.0	19.2
United States	9,173.0	62.8	12,934.0	41.8	12,348.4	32.9
Canada	153.8	1.1	97.0	0.3	226.0	0.6
Other Europe[b]	124.7	0.9	957.0	3.1	1,141.0	3.0
Japan	23.9	0.2	41.0	0.13	56.0	0.15
Soviet Union	3,232.3	22.1	9,157.0	29.6	10,281.0	27.4
Other WTO[c]	387.2	2.7	1,790.0	5.8	2,822.0	7.5
Oceania[d]	10.7	0.07	41.0	0.13	9.0	0.02
Developing[e]	47.8	0.3	908.0	2.9	3,491.0	9.3
Total	14,598.6		30,982.0		37,571.4	

Source: U.S. Arms Control and Disarmament Agency (ACDA), *World Military Expenditures and Arms Transfers, 1963–1973 and 1985* for all countries except the United States. The dollar value of U.S. exports was derived from the Department of Defense Security Assistance Agency (DSAA), Fiscal Year Series (as of September 30, 1983 and 1984), which includes deliveries of construction, training, and other services. The ACDA data includes these services in the dollar value of exports for all countries other than the United States. The DSAA figures for the United States were used rather than ACDA's so the U.S. and non-U.S. export figures would be comparable.

[a]NATO Europe = Belgium, Denmark, France, Federal Republic of Germany (FRG), Greece, Iceland, Italy, Luxembourg, Netherlands, Norway, Portugal, Turkey, United Kingdom.

[b]Other Europe = Albania, Austria, Finland, Ireland, Malta, Spain, Sweden, Switzerland, Yugoslavia.

[c]Other WTO = Bulgaria, Czechoslovakia, German Democratic Republic (GDR), Hungary, Poland, Romania.

[d]Oceania = Australia, New Zealand.

[e]Developing Countries = Africa, Asia (without Japan), Latin America, Middle East.

Third World states have been responsible for roughly 22 percent ($3.6 billion) of all military aid to LDC combatants during hostilities, in contrast to less than a 3 percent share during prewar periods and about a 5 percent share during postwar periods (see figure 8–1). It is interesting to note that thus far the Iran-Iraq war has consumed over 70 percent of all military assistance given to combatants during recent wars and about 90 percent (!) of all LDC transfers. From an economic standpoint, the Iran-Iraq war has provided a lucrative market for LDC suppliers (see table 8–2).

Who Supplies What to Whom

Five Third World arms producers—China, North Korea, Brazil, Egypt, South Korea—have contributed over 75 percent of the LDC military assistance that has gone to nine of the warring LDCs.[5] Libya, although it does not produce arms indigenously, is the sixth largest LDC supplier. The breakdown is as follows: China has delivered 24 percent of all LDC aid to combatants; North Korea, 19 percent; Brazil, 16 percent; Egypt, 10 percent; South Korea, 10 percent; and Libya, 9 percent. However, the proportion of LDC aid delivered has varied considerably from combatant to combatant, determined largely by the extent to which each has been cut off from a principal industrialized supplier.[6] For example, during the Horn war, the Soviet Union sent large amounts of aid to Ethiopia, so that only 3 percent of Ethiopia's materiel came from other LDCs, in contrast to 41 percent of Somalia's. Thus far in the Iran-Iraq war, Iran has purchased 63 percent of its military supplies from other LDCs, whereas Iraq's LDC deliveries account for just 18 percent of its total procurement, with France and the Soviet Union providing a large number of its major systems. Argentina relied on Peru for most (60 percent) of its arms imports during the Falklands war, while the proportion of Third World assistance to Morocco, Honduras, Nicaragua, and El Salvador ranged between only 2 percent and 16 percent of their total deliveries (see table 8–2).

The Composition of LDC Transfers to Combatants

Because Third World countries have different production and export capabilities, the kinds of equipment and services they deliver and how much of them, varies widely. First, although the dollar value of Third World military assistance has climbed in response to wartime demand, the proportion of indigenously produced major weapon systems supplied has not been large. (See the appendix to this chapter for a listing of selected military items currently produced and planned by Third World countries.) In fact, only three countries, Brazil, China, and South Africa have transferred domestically produced major systems

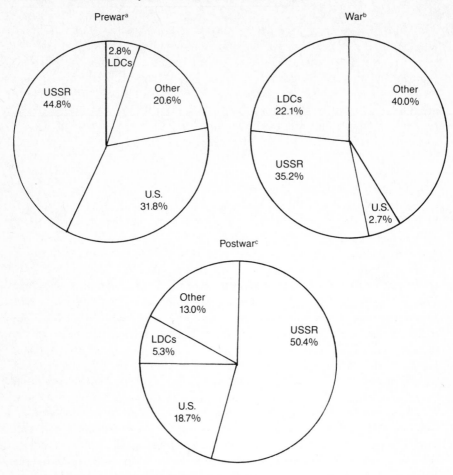

Prewar[a]

2.8% LDCs

USSR 44.8%

Other 20.6%

U.S. 31.8%

War[b]

LDCs 22.1%

Other 40.0%

USSR 35.2%

U.S. 2.7%

Postwar[c]

Other 13.0%

LDCs 5.3%

USSR 50.4%

U.S. 18.7%

Source: Derived from appendix to chapter 7.

[a]Prewar period: two to three years period to start of war, $ value of total deliveries averaged per year.

[b]War period: $ value of total deliveries to combatants during periods of armed conflict, up to and including 1983 (estimate only), averaged.

[c]Postwar period: $ value of total deliveries to combatants during years after cessation of hostilities up to and including 1983 (estimate) averaged.

Figure 8–1. Military Assistance to LDC Combatants during Prewar, War, and Postwar Periods

to other LDCs during wartime. In 1977 and 1979 South Africa sold Morocco its Eland and Ratel armored cars. China sold Iraq F-7 (MiG-21) aircraft, artillery, and tanks, and Brazil supplied Iraq with Cascavel and Urutu armored vehicles. (Argentina, after the Falklands war, ordered Embraer's [Brazil] Xavante trainer and maritime reconnaissance aircraft, which in early 1985

Table 8-2
Third World Military Assistance to Combatants during Conflict[a]
(dollar value millions)[b]

Suppliers	The Horn		Western Sahara	Central America			Iran/Iraq		Falklands	Total	
	Ethiopia	Somalia	Morocco	Honduras	Nicaragua	El Salvador	Iran	Iraq	Argentina	$	% LDC Total
Algeria	—	—	—	—	NA	—	4.0	—	—	NA	—
Argentina	—	—	4.5	—	0.7	—	—	—	—	9.2	—
Brazil	—	—	—	—	7.3	—	—	572.2	—	579.5	16.0
Chile	—	—	—	negl.[d]	—	2.4	—	—	—	2.4	—
China (PRC)	3.0	—	1.0	—	—	—	144.0	735.5	—	883.5	24.4
Cuba	NA	—	—	—	23.7	—	—	—	—	23.7	—
Ecuador	—	—	—	—	—	—	—	—	0.7	0.7	—
Egypt	0.4	88.0	22.0	—	—	—	3.0	250.5	—	360.5	9.9
India	—	0.2	—	—	—	—	—	1.0	—	4.6	—
Iran	—	3.0	—	—	—	—	—	—	—	3.0	—
Israel	5.4	—	—	5.0	2.0	—	24.5	—	0.2	36.9	1.0
Jordan	—	0.2	—	—	—	—	—	—	—	0.2	—
Morocco	—	—	—	0.1	—	—	—	—	—	0.1	—
North Korea	1.0	—	—	—	—	0.2	671.9	153.7	—	672.9	18.6
South Korea	16.0	—	2.4	—	—	—	170.7	3.0	—	343.0	9.5
Kuwait	—	—	—	—	—	—	—	—	—	6.0	—
Libya	20.0	20.8	—	—	3.0	—	314.8	15.0	—	334.8	9.2
Pakistan	—	—	—	—	—	—	18.8	—	—	54.6	1.5
Peru	—	—	—	—	—	—	—	—	60.5	60.5	1.7
Saudi Arabia	—	—	—	—	—	—	—	NA	—	14.1	—
Singapore	—	14.1	—	—	—	—	14.1	NA	—	14.1	—
South Africa	—	—	68.7	—	—	—	—	—	—	68.7	1.9
Sudan	—	NA	—	—	—	—	—	5.0	—	5.0	—
Syria	—	NA	—	—	—	—	120.2	—	—	120.2	3.3
Taiwan	—	—	—	—	—	—	2.0	—	—	2.0	—
Turkey	—	—	—	—	—	—	—	2.8	—	2.8	—
Yemen (Aden)	2.4[c]	—	—	—	—	—	—	—	—	2.4	—
Yemen (Sana)	—	—	—	—	—	—	—	20.0[c]	—	20.0	—
Venezuela	—	—	—	—	—	NA	—	—	—	NA	—
LDC Total	48.2	126.3	98.6	5.1	36.7	2.6	1,487.8	1,758.7	61.4	3,625.	
Grand Total[b]	1,532.2	305.5	2,153.4	38.4	232.7	150.5	2,352.4	9,875.5	100.2	16,741	
% LDC/Grand Total	3.1	41.3	4.6	13.0	15.8	1.7	63.2	17.8	61.3	22.0	

Source: Derived from U.S. government data for war years, up to and including 1983 (estimate for 1983 only).

[a] There were no Third World military deliveries to the governments of Afghanistan, the PRC, Vietnam, Syria, or Israel during conflict.

[b] Total dollar value of military assistance from all suppliers.

[c] grant-aid

[d] negl. = negligible amount of military equipment transferred.

had yet to arrive.)[7] In all, the dollar value of LDC indigenous major systems (approximately $700 million)[8] transferred to combatants during wartime constituted roughly 19 percent of LDC military aid (and only about 4 percent of the military assistance received from all suppliers).

Second, some developing countries have retransferred to warring LDCs older major systems, most of them dating from the 1950s and 1960s, and originally acquired from another supplier. This type of equipment is particularly attractive to Third World buyers because of the short delivery time and its compatibility with existing inventory. Nevertheless, these so-called third country transfers have been relatively small in terms of numbers and dollar value. For example, Libya retransferred Soviet helicopters (two Mi-2s [vintage early 1950s][9]), five Czech L-39 trainer aircraft (1972), and two patrol boats (?) to Nicaragua in 1982; Yemen gave three Mi-8 helicopters (1960) to Ethiopia in 1977, and Egypt contributed twenty Soviet medium tanks (probably T-54s [1954]) to Somalia in 1977. In the case of Iraq, the number of third country transfers has been somewhat larger. Egypt, for example, delivered twenty-five MiG-21-Fishbed (mid-1950s) and ten SU-7 Fitter fighters (early 1960s) to Iraq. For the most part, however, the major suppliers' retransfer prohibitions, the political costs and logistical difficulties involved in attempting to evade them (particularly for large military items),[10] and the severe financial constraints restricting most LDC buyers have all combined to limit the number of major systems retransferred. Thus the level of third country deliveries has amounted to approximately 6 percent (about $200 million) of total (LDC) military-related deliveries to Third World combatants during hostilities (through 1983).

Third, ground forces equipment, ammunition, small arms, quartermaster supplies, spare parts, and wheeled vehicles have made up most of LDC transfers, composing about 70 percent of all Third World military assistance during conflicts.[11] It is not easy, however, to distinguish between indigenous and third country transfers in this category of weapons. Worldwide production of infantry items and combat consumables has greatly increased in recent years, often obliterating the distinction between indigenous and licensed or pirated systems. Note in the appendix to this chapter the large number of LDC manufacturers of ground forces equipment and ammunition compared with those producing aircraft, large naval vessels, and missiles. Inevitably, as their number has grown and their production capabilities have increased, the design origin of older infantry weapons has become less clear and the original producer's third party transfer restrictions less enforceable—developments which explain in large part why embargoes have proved ineffective for ground forces consumables in recent wars.

Over the years most of the industrialized states have granted licenses containing provisions that restrict sales to third parties. (Licenses for the more complex aerospace, naval, communications, and ground systems have been fewer and more recent.) In some cases these restrictions have been lifted with the assent of the supplier. In other cases they have been violated by the recipient through covert sales or by slightly modifying the licensed product and selling it as an indigenous model.[12] Many of these items are easily concealed and transportable, making it relatively easy to evade supplier export prohibitions. As a result most types of light ground forces equipment and ammunition are readily available without restriction on the international market for cash customers. For example, U.S.-made spares, ammunition, and small arms continue to flow into Iran each year despite a U.S. Department of State ban on all weapons sales to that country. Illegal retransfers from U.S. allies blend imperceptibly with "indigenous" models of U.S. arms, spares, and parts into a large subterranean trading system that supplies embargoed countries like Iran.[13]

A fourth type of LDC military transfer, one often overlooked in the arms transfer literature, is financial assistance for arms purchases. Saudi Arabia, for example, although it does not have an arms industry, has given generous cash grants for arms purchases by poorer Moslem combatants, such as Somalia and Morocco. It is estimated that in 1980 alone, Arab OPEC states financed two-thirds of all arms purchased by other Third World states.[14]

Finally, Third World states are providing more training and technical assistance to other LDCs. This form of aid is particularly difficult to document, but it has been playing a significant role in recent conflicts. Those countries with successful combat records in either conventional or insurgency wars offer specialized training in their area of expertise—for example, Israel's experience with the PLO created a demand for its services in several Central American and African countries. And the Sri Lankan minister of defense announced that Israelis would help train Sri Lanka's security forces to deal with the Tamil insurgency in the northern part of the state. South Korea is also reported to have sent military experts to advise the Nicaraguan counterrevolutionaries (Contras) in military tactics.[15]

Given the various forms of LDC military assistance and the complexities involved in accounting for them, it is evident that estimates of their number and dollar value can be only approximate. First, information about defense-related transfers generally is considered at least confidential and often is more highly classified by the recipient or supplier (and sometimes by both). It therefore is publicized infrequently. Second, even when an itemized list of LDC weapon deliveries is available, estimating its dollar value is not easy, especially when the origin of manufacture is in question. And even when the product is recognized as an indigenously fabricated product, there is little agreement in the field as to real LDC production costs. Assessing the value of technical services, training, and personnel is still more problematic. Finally, excluded from the dollar estimates presented here are indirect LDC transfers to insurgent groups for which there is little documentation. In sum, because of the softness of the data, the quantitative values presented here should be considered as only supplementary comparative measures to be used in conjunction with more qualitative estimates of LDC military assistance capabilities.

LDC Exports to Third World Combatants during Recent Wars

In general, Third World military exports are less advanced items. As figure 8–2 shows, half the total dollar value of all LDC military sales between 1976 and 1982 were ground forces equipment and consumables, with more advanced systems, such as aircraft and naval vessels, composing only about one-quarter of total transfers. Of the latter, propulsion, electronic, and weapon systems make up most of their dollar value—items, with few exceptions, that have been procured from Western suppliers and then incorporated into the indigenously produced product.[16] Contracts for construction projects make up another 20 percent of LDC sales.

Exports to combatants from LDC suppliers have reflected this general pattern. As a rule, because weapons must be compatible with the inventory of forces committed, at least during the first phase of engagement, Third World countries that produce equipment of Soviet or U.S. origin have become important alternate sources of supply for Third World countries. And countries

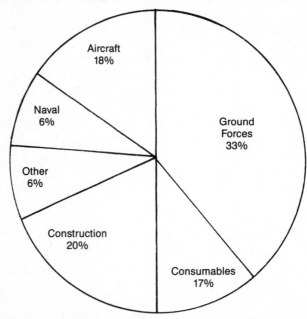

Source: Based on U.S. government data. Interviews with U.S. State Department officials and extrapolations from U.S. Department of State, *Conventional Arms Transfers in the Third World*, Special Report No. 102, August 1982, pp. 12–13; U.S. Arms Control and Disarmament Agency, *World Military Expenditures and Arms Transfers, 1985*, 135.

Figure 8–2. Third World Arms Sales by Type of Equipment, 1976–82 (Percent U.S. $ Billions)

such as Libya, which retransfers Soviet equipment, also play an important role in providing materiel to combatants.

However, what holds for the general pattern of LDC arms transfers is even more characteristic of LDC resupply during combat. As described earlier, Third World suppliers have provided primarily unsophisticated military systems, largely ground forces items, to their warring neighbors and allies, and although the dollar value of Third World arms exports has been inflated by the demand, they have not risen above 9 percent of the total world arms trade (see table 8–1). The following section investigates why the Third World has established this supply pattern and why its exports have remained limited. It describes the military production and export capabilities of the major LDC suppliers and examines the economic, political, and technological constraints on their ability to resupply combatants.

China (PRC). China's national defense industry was born after the Chinese revolution in 1949. During the 1950s, the Soviet Union assisted China and a number of Soviet turnkey factories were established to produce Soviet-designed weapons. But the internal upheavals of the 1960s and 1970s, combined with China's political isolation and the end of Soviet assistance in 1960—all served to retard seriously the growth of China's military industrial sector. As a result, although China today produces, in large quantities, all categories of major weapon systems, as well as less sophisticated military items (see appendix to this chapter), most still reflect design concepts that are twenty to thirty years old.

In the past, China played a relatively small role as an arms exporter, in part because demand from China's own armed forces for military equipment was so great. Arms when they were transferred were used for political purposes and were generally given away. However, the demand for older Soviet systems generated by recent wars has represented irresistible trade opportunities to the foreign exchange–hungry Chinese, particularly sales to solvent customers such as Iraq and, to a lesser extent, Iran that pay cash and can offer oil in exchange.[17] This combination of outside demand and economic need has served to expand China's military sales. Exports quadrupled in 1982, catapulting China into the exclusive one-billion-dollars-and-over club of world arms exporters.[18] In all, China, the largest LDC supplier, contributed 24 percent of all military aid to the combatants during wartime.

Most of China's exports have gone to Iraq. Out of the total dollar value of China's arms deliveries to combatants ($884 million) Iraq received 83 percent (see table 8–2), only about 12 percent of which were aircraft (F-7s [MiG-21s]).[19] Most of China's military transfers to Iraq have been ground forces equipment, some Type-69 tanks[20] and field artillery, but primarily light vehicles, spares, quartermaster supplies, small arms, and ammunition.[21] In addition, China has augmented its foreign exchange earnings by exporting human capital to the Persian Gulf. Twenty-thousand Chinese contract laborers have built Iraqi factories and repaired oil pipelines, reportedly earning most of the $2 billion China nets from this type of export to the area.[22]

Furthermore, China has given more arms and supplies to insurgency groups than any other state, most of which goes unreported.[23] For the purposes of this chapter, much of that aid is irrelevant since it has gone to groups fighting in Southeast Asia[24] (conflicts that are important to China's national interests but are not considered in this chapter). China has sent some equipment to the Afghan rebels, but again it is difficult to determine the size and content of that contribution.[25] What the Afghan rebels receive, for the most part Soviet-design small arms, bombs, mortars, and ammunition, could originate from many other places (such as from Soviet stores within Afghanistan that the guerrillas periodically raid or from deserting Afghan government soldiers), and locating the exact source is more often than not impossible. Whatever the proportion, however, China has been providing aging Soviet materiel, mostly small arms and consumables, to the Afghan rebels and to other guerrilla groups.

North Korea. North Korea is the second largest supplier of military assistance to combatants, providing 19 percent of the total (see table 8–2). Like China, North Korea established its military industries with Soviet help (after the Korean War). As a result, North Korea's products are primarily either direct copies of older Soviet designs or modified versions. Until recently it was believed that North Korean industries produced only naval vessels, small arms, ammunition, and artillery pieces. However, by the early 1980s some sources were claiming that T-54, T-55, and T-62 tanks had been in production for some time[26] and that the manufacture of antitank missiles had begun.[27]

Again, as in the case of China, the Iran-Iraq war has been a lucrative market for North Korea. Iran has been the primary recipient, procuring almost 100 percent of North Korea's wartime deliveries ($672 million; see table 8–2). Only Ethiopia received a small amount of assistance from North Korea during its war with Somalia. Over three quarters of all North Korea's transfers to Iran have been light infantry equipment, some artillery, spares, and ammunition. Tanks (T-62s)[28] and tank-related items have made up about 20 percent of their sales.[29]

Some question has been raised about the ability of North Korea's factories to manufacture enough tanks and heavy guns to accommodate Iraq's needs, and so there has been speculation that some of the heavier items delivered to Iran actually are retransfers from North Korea's own inventory.[30] However, in the category of small arms and ammunition and consumables, North Korea's industrial capacity has proved to be more than adequate. Not only have these items constituted most of North Korea's arms exports, furnishing Iran with Soviet calibers for captured Iraqi-, Syrian-, and North Korean-supplied equipment, but the North Koreans also have been able to retool production lines quickly to provide Iran with compatible ammunition for its U.S.-origin systems.[31] In addition to hardware, like China, North Korea has exported human capital, providing large numbers of military instructors to Iran.[32]

From the Iranian perspective, North Korean aid has been vital, supplying almost 30 percent of its total military assistance deliveries (see table 8–2). Iranian Boeing 747s have reportedly been making weekly visits to North Korea to collect arms purchases, including artillery shells, mortars, light weapons, and Soviet-designed infantry personnel equipment.[33] Cut off from direct supplies from either NATO or the Soviet Union, Iran has been forced to rely heavily upon North Korean supplies to sustain its military response to Iraq.[34] From the North Korean perspective, sales to Iran not only earn valuable foreign exchange but ensure vital oil deliveries. According to some reports, the North Koreans and Iranians signed an oil-for-arms agreement at the beginning of the war which includes "a quarter of a million tons of crude oil over a four year period, presumably at below market rates."[35]

North Korea has also furnished military assistance to other developing countries. Several African and Latin American states have sent military personnel to North Korea for training or have invited North Korean instructors to demonstrate antiguerrilla tactics. Nicaragua, Ethiopia, Somalia, and Libya are only some of their reported clients.[36] Beyond these government-to-government arrangements, the full extent of North Korean military aid is difficult to ascertain since much of it goes to insurgent groups and much of it consists of financial grants, training, small arms, and ammunition—all very difficult to trace.

In general, however, knowledgable observers believe that other than the sizeable arms shipments to Iran, North Korean military transfers have consisted largely of training and small arms in modest quantities.[37] As one State Department official commented, "The list of countries that at one time or another received military advice and assistance from the North Koreans would extend to at least a dozen. Pyongyang seems to be motivated by a desire to bolster its nonaligned status and to earn much needed hard currency."[38]

Brazil. Brazil is the third largest LDC supplier to Third World combatants (16 percent). Brazil's arms industries have had a long, erratic history that, unlike China's and North Korea's histories, reflects European and U.S. influence, exerted primarily through licensing agreements and subsidiaries. Prior to the 1960s, various tasks on imported U.S. and European aircraft and naval craft were performed domestically, but small arms and ammunition were Brazil's primary military-industrial product then and still are an important segment of its industry. The manufacture of military trucks began in the mid-1960s, and in the late-1960s indigenously designed armored (wheeled) military vehicles were added to the line; both remain the mainstay of Brazil's export business.[39]

By the mid-1970s, Brazil was also producing its own Bandeirante light transport, the licensed Italian Xavante jet fighter-trainer, along with other licensed and domestic-design prop trainers, light naval craft, and a licensed destroyer. In the late 1970s to early 1980s two missile systems were being produced under license, a main battle tank and other missiles were in development, two licensed submarines were planned, and a 90 millimeter gun and turret was available for export to retrofit obsolete armored vehicles in other countries[40] (see the appendix to this chapter). Over time, production capabilities have grown, permitting Brazil to offer a rather wide range of weapon systems to prospective customers. Many of the designs, components, raw materials, and tooling devices are still acquired from abroad,[41] but some items reflect real indigenous technological development.

Despite its long history of arms production, Brazil became a significant exporter of arms only recently. Arms exporting did not begin until 1975, and total sales did not rise above $150 million until 1982 when the dollar value rose to $300 million (current dollars).[42] Like their competitors, Brazil's rising exports have been stimulated by wartime demand. About 99 percent of Brazil's resupply to combatants went to Iraq, much of it in exchange for oil.[43] Other than Iraq, only Nicaragua received a small amount of military assistance (about 1 percent of Brazil's total exports; see table 8–2). Reports have circulated that Brazil indirectly supplied Iran with equipment as well; however, if true, the dollar value of these exports is not available.[44]

Given the structure of Brazil's industry, most of that nation's arms deliveries have been ground forces equipment, consisting primarily of military vehicles and some small arms, ammunition, bombs, air-to-surface and antitank missiles, and a variety of spare parts.[45] For example, Cascavel armored vehicles, Urutu armored personnel carriers (APCs), and trucks delivered to Iraq in 1981 amounted to almost 20 percent of the sale. And trucks made up the total value of Brazil's transfers to Nicaragua.[46]

Egypt. Egypt, the fourth largest supplier of military assistance to combatants in recent wars, is responsible for 10 percent of the total. However, the scale of its military assistance program is much smaller than that of the previously discussed donor states, amounting to only about one-half that of China's or North Korea's or Brazil's. In other respects, though, Egypt's military-industrial history, production capabilities, and the character of its exports bear comparison.

Egypt's defense industries, like those of other LDC producers, have followed an uneven development course, and they remain dependent upon outside sources for economic and technological assistance. During the 1960s various plants produced small arms, rockets, ammunition, and spare parts of Soviet origin with Soviet technical assistance. Since the government's decision in 1975 to reduce dependence on outside sources of supply, particularly the Soviet Union, the Egyptians have concentrated on purchasing Western arms and diversifying the capabilities of their indigenous defense industries. The main vehicle for this was to be the Arab Organization for Industrialization (AOI), which would also provide neighboring Arab countries with arms produced by Egyptian factories and skilled manpower—all to be financed with Saudi Arabian and Kuwaiti capital.

The project foundered after the Camp David accords in 1979 when Saudi Arabia and Kuwait refused to fund the project. Egypt then reorganized the AOI as an Egyptian enterprise[47] and negotiated with Western Europeans and the United States for the assembly and licensed production of various military systems. Currently, the older factories still manufacture Soviet-designed small arms, rockets, and ammunition, and a partly indigenous armored personnel carrier, the Walid, developed in 1967 (which is still used by the armed forces of Algeria, Egypt, Israel, and North Yemen).[48] Newer plants are assembling Alpha jet trainers (Dassault) and Swingfire antitank guided missiles (British Aerospace Public Limited Company [BAe]) of Western origin, and a production line has been started for Egypt's version of the Soviet SA-7 Grail infantry SAM (known locally as the Hawkeye), possibly in collaboration with France.[49] (See the appendix to this chapter.)

Egypt, like Brazil, is a newcomer to the arms export business. From 1963 to 1981, Egypt's yearly exports did not rise above $90 million (current dollars). Only in 1982 did arms transfers soar to over $300 million[50] in response to the Iran-Iraq war. Seventy percent (approximately $250 million) of Egypt's total military aid to combatants went to Iraq (see table 8–2).

Along with China and North Korea, Egypt has served as an alternate supplier of Soviet-compatible equipment in recent wars. Exports include systems produced in Egypt's defense industries, as well as third party transfers from Egypt's inventory or reserves of Soviet weapons. For example, ammunition, mines, and spares for Soviet aircraft, many of which are produced in Egypt's factories for its own armed forces, and Soviet-built T-54 and T-55 tanks and spares from the Egyptian army's reserves compose most of Iraq's arms purchases from Egypt.[51] Unfortunately, the exact proportion of indigenous manufactured items to retransfers, either in dollar value or number, is unknown.

Egypt has also sent a number of Soviet-origin aircraft to Iraq—Soviet MiG-21s (probably from Egypt's own inventory) and the Chinese version (F-7s). The latter have been reassembled after shipment from China by the Egyptian Air Force with the assistance of technicians from the PRC and then sent to Iraq. It has also been reported that Egyptian instructor pilots have been operating with the Iraqi Air Force providing training and flying "occasional air patrol sorties."[52]

Smaller amounts of aid have been sent to Somalia and Morocco as well.[53] Constrained by Western and Warsaw Pact countries' resupply restrictions, both recipients received sorely needed small arms, ammunition, T-54 tanks, and training from Egypt during their respective wars with Ethiopia and the *Polisario*. Despite the end of overt hostilities in the Horn, aid to Somalia has continued since 1978.[54] Egypt also extends assistance to various rebel groups in the

Third World. For example, Egyptian military advisers in Pakistan are helping to train Afghan guerrillas, and Egyptian factories are supplying "most of the ammunition the Afghans need for their captured Soviet weapons".[55]

The recent rise in Egypt's exports, however, has not reduced its reliance upon outside sources of support. Even the arms sales themselves are often directly dependent upon the largesse of Egypt's wealthier neighbors and friends. Thus, Iraq's purchases from Egypt reportedly have been paid for by the Gulf States—out of the $30 billion interest-free loans they have granted to Iraq.[56] Saudi Arabia has also granted financial aid to Morocco and Somalia, making their Egyptian acquisitions possible. And rumors have circulated that it has been U.S. monies funding the sale of Soviet-built SA-7 man-portable surface-to-air missiles from Egypt to the Afghan rebels.[57]

In addition to economic dependency, Egypt's defense industries suffer from technological constraints. Industrialized suppliers continue to infuse major technical assistance into them, furnishing not only hands-on training, but also much of the necessary manufacturing equipment, raw materials, and advanced components. In sum, despite expanding production capabilities, Egypt's industries remain reliant upon others for much of their economic and technological viability. In combination, these factors undoubtedly have made Egypt sensitive, as an arms supplier, to the political needs of its major donors.

South Korea. South Korea is the fifth largest Third World purveyor of military assistance to LDCs at war, accounting for almost 10 percent of the total. Prior to the 1970s, the Republic of Korea (ROK) felt little need to devote much of its industrial capacity to defense because of the large military aid program from the United States. However, various developments during the 1970s encouraged a drive toward military-industrial self-sufficiency, not the least of which was the U.S. threat to reduce its aid and force commitment to South Korea. By the mid-1970s, the country had begun producing (based largely on imported U.S. materials and technology) an assortment of small arms, munitions, small naval craft, and a basic trainer. In 1981, South Korea began assembling under license the F-5E/F fighter (Northrop)[58] and had established production lines for all major weapon systems other than tanks and missiles. By 1983, an indigenous tank (the ROKIT) was in development.[59] Currently South Korean industries are producing infantry equipment,[60] small naval vessels (an exception is a 1,600-ton frigate, which has been indigenously produced and is now in service), and aircraft.[61]

Most of South Korea's products, particularly ground forces equipment, are thought to be of excellent quality which can be marketed for less than their U.S. equivalents. However, because they are produced by benefit of licensing, coproduction, or coassembly agreements, and with U.S.-furnished tooling equipment in some cases, these items are also subject to retransfer prohibitions, which constrain South Korea's export potential considerably.

Little wonder then that South Korea's exports to the nine LDC combatants have been relatively modest: $343 million (or about half the dollar value of its northern, less industrially capable neighbor's), of which Iran and Iraq have consumed 95 percent.[62]

Because of the political constraints on South Korea's export trade and its compelling need to earn foreign exchange to pay for its own military purchases, there have been some attempts to circumvent U.S. political restrictions. For example, there have been some charges of reverse engineering (small arms and ammunition), and a few occasions when the South Koreans have been accused by U.S. companies of modifying licensed items and offering them for sale as indigenous products.

South Korea is reported also to have secretly supplied both sides in the Iran-Iraq war during the early 1980s. Iran is said to have received quartermaster supplies, as well as small arms and ammunition, and wheeled vehicles—some directly from South Korea and some through indirect channels. Pakistan, for instance, is believed to have made purchases of U.S. equipment on the international market, including in South Korea on Iran's behalf, despite a State Department embargo.[63]

But since mid-1984, U.S. pressure and South Korea's political dependency have combined to stop South Korean exports to Iran.[64] In the end South Korea's reliance on the United States for technological assistance and political/military support encouraged general observance of retransfer prohibition agreements.

These factors then have worked to contain the level and composition of South Korea's exports to combatants. Most have been technologically less sophisticated items: some small arms and ammunition that are not license produced, or those systems approved for retransfer by the U.S. government or U.S. manufacturers. To supplement these sales, the South Koreans have developed a large trade in quartermaster supplies, for example, uniforms, helmets, tents, boots, canteens, and so forth. Iraq's buy from the ROK, for example, was composed entirely of ground forces equipment (jeeps, howitzers, ammunition, explosives, radios) and quartermaster supplies; only quartermaster supplies were sold to Somalia and Morocco.

Libya. Although Libya has transferred about the same amount of military aid as South Korea (about 9 percent of the LDC total)—of which 94 percent went to Iran—because it does not produce its own weapons domestically, Libya is not included in this discussion. Unlike the other major LDC arms suppliers, Libya exports weapons exclusively from its own arsenal. It also provides financial aid to LDC clients and friends for arms purchases from other suppliers.

Israel. Israel's military-industrial capabilities far exceed those of the preceding producers. Yet it has been a relatively small exporter of military equipment and services to the combatants. In all, Israel's resupplies have amounted to only about $37 million, or about 1 percent of total LDC military deliveries during recent wars (see table 8–2). It is included here not because Israel ranks as a major supplier, but because it presents an interesting picture of the political and economic factors that restrain the exports of Third World industries irrespective of their technological sophistication.

Four types of enterprise compose Israel's defense industry: state-owned; joint ventures between Israeli companies (private and public) and foreign partners; privately owned firms with little or no government participation; and the wholly owned subsidiaries of foreign corporations.[65] However, most of Israel's indigenous production is conducted by state firms that together employ some 20 percent of the state's industrial work force.[66]

These industries field a wide array of products, which include not only the small arms, ammunition, mortars, explosives, light vehicles, and quartermaster supplies typical of most other Third World industries, but also air, naval, and infantry major systems and sophisticated communications and other electronic equipment. Furthermore, unlike other Third World industries, there is a close interface between the Israeli armed forces and the defense industries. Former military personnel are employed in large numbers, bringing with them Israel's war experiences, which are then incorporated into the design of the next generation of weapons. The added fact that the civilian scientists, engineers, technicians, and mechanics who produce Israel's weapon systems also use them during war has produced a high-quality line of military products designed to meet the specific needs of the Israeli armed forces.

But despite the relative size and innovativeness of Israel's defense industry, it is still very dependent upon the United States for technology transfers, some materials, certain subassemblies, and financial assistance, and therefore, indirectly, for export markets. To date all modern Israeli indigenous major weapon systems contain at least one major U.S. component bringing them under U.S. third country transfer regulations.[67] For example, both the Kfir aircraft and Merkava tank, two Israeli-manufactured major systems, are powered by U.S. engines.[68]

These constraints have determined, to a great extent, the character of Israel's arms trade. First, a high proportion of Israel's weapon sales is accounted for not by large, major systems such as aircraft, ships, and tanks, but rather by small arms, crew-served weapons, ammunition, electronic accessories, computers, technical information, the sale of licenses, and so on—products that have no U.S. components and do not, therefore, fall under U.S. arms control jurisdiction. Also, some Israeli sales (including those from huge caches of Soviet weapons acquired in the 1967, 1973, and 1982 wars) are apparently not made directly through government-to-government sales, but rather via indirect conduits such as private traders, intelligence services, disguised brokers and middlemen, and such, where they are less easily traced. In addition, there are the more visible refinished, upgraded, older technologies—often of European origin—that constitute the bulk of Israel's major weapons transfers. Because of their age and their high indigenous content they escape supplier restrictions in effect for newer systems.[69]

Second, Israel's status as a pariah state, particularly among Moslem states, further limits its export market. Some of the world's wealthiest customers in the Middle East are essentially denied to Israel's industries. This has meant that Israel's sales have of necessity been concentrated in other, less affluent areas of the Third World. Latin America, for example, accounts for most Israeli arms exports (which include a large number of refurbished French Mirage aircraft),[70] with individual countries in Asia and Africa making up the balance. South Africa has been a particularly interested customer, buying not just equipment but production know-how as well.[71]

These patterns characterize Israel's supplier relationships with Third World states and explain to some degree the modest role Israel has played in the wartime resupply market and the limited number of its customers. Argentina, Central American states, and Ethiopia have been the main recipients of Israel's wartime resupply aid.

Argentina, a regular peacetime customer, received Israeli resupplies, most of which arrived after the Falklands war (April 2–June 15, 1982) had ended. By March 1983 it was reported that Argentina had replaced a large proportion of the about 120 aircraft and helicopters it had lost in the war—twenty-two of the replacements were refurbished Mirage IIIs from Israel.[72]. In Central America, although the relative dollar value of its exports is small, Israel has been a major supplier to incumbent regimes, assisting Somoza's Nicaragua, Honduras, and El Salvador. Recently, Israel has been supplying weapons captured from the PLO to Honduras for use by the Nicaraguan rebels, and also is selling some Western-origin equipment apparently with the acquiescence of the United States. Training for Salvadoran and Honduran troops is also underway.[73]

Recent wars have created strange resupply situations for Israel. During the Horn war, for example, Israel continued its peacetime military support of Ethiopia[74] and found itself in concert with Ethiopia's new allies, the Soviet Union, Cuba, and East Germany.[75] And, during the Iran-Iraq war, despite its virulent anti-Israel stance, Khomeini's Iran continued to buy military equipment from Israel. Limited to consumables, such as tires for Iran's F-4s, small arms, mortars, and ammunition,[76] by 1984 even these transactions had all but stopped.

Thus, in spite of Israel's considerable technological and production capacity, the volume and dollar value of its military transfers have been significantly reduced by political/economic factors—a situation in which other, less capable Third World producers also find themselves.

In general, although the exports of Third World producers to combatants have been confined to essentially older, unsophisticated military equipment, primarily infantry items, the impact of these transfers on recent wars has not been insignificant. From the recipients' point of view they have often represented the difference between an armed response or defeat. As the Iran-Iraq and Western Sahara wars have demonstrated, LDC military assistance to one combatant can help prolong conflicts indefinitely, depriving both sides of a clear-cut victory or defeat.

This capability perhaps has perpetuated an exaggerated impression of the role Third World military producers have played in determining the outcome of recent wars. As we have seen, even the most sophisticated LDC manufacturers remain dependent upon outside sources for either weapons designs, production technology, raw materials, or advanced components, and often for the financial and technical wherewithal to make it all happen. They are, therefore, particularly vulnerable to supplier-imposed restrictions on transfers of major systems, particularly to belligerents. Other Third World producers with less advanced capabilities tend to manufacture basic technologies and therefore do not have more sophisticated domestic products to sell. Thus LDC exports to combatants have been less than state-of-the-art items which, in some instances, may have prolonged wars but could not and did not raise the level of sophistication at which they were fought.

The Role of the Combatants' Own Domestic Arms Industries

The preceding section discussed the role LDC exports have played in recent wars. This section[77] examines the part played by the combatants' own indigenous defense industries. If, as some suspect, the "war-making potential" of Third World countries is enhanced by their military-industrial capabilities, then one might logically expect that a large number of LDC producers would have been actively involved in Third World conflicts. However, only three of the twenty- seven LDC major weapons producers were combatants in recent wars.[78] One might also assume that the indigenous military-industrial skills of the combatants would have lent important support to their own war-fighting capabilities. But recent wars do not support this conclusion either.

The sample of countries for our analysis is of course rather small. Among the combatants, only China, Argentina, and Israel produce major weapon systems domestically, and only two of them have demonstrated significant production capabilities—China in quantity and Israel in quality. Argentina's military industries remain largely assembly operations. But given the spread and variety of their industrial skill levels, these countries represent potentially interesting test cases of the differential impact various manufacturing capabilities have on the process and outcome of war. Contrary to expectation, in all three cases, regardless of technological proficiency, indigenously produced military equipment did not appear to have tipped the balance in favor of the producer.

Argentina. Argentina's defense industries turn out a wide assortment of primarily licensed items, most of them largely assembled in Argentina. Included are the IA-58 Pucara (a twin turbo prop, ground-attack aircraft), armored vehicles (VCI-ICV and the TAM tank), a corvette, 155 millimeter artillery, and a variety of small arms, mortars, ammunition, and missiles (see appendix to this chapter).

Despite these capabilities, Argentina's indigenously produced systems took little part in the war over the Falklands. According to Argentine accounts, six sorties were flown from mainland bases by Pucaras in antihelicopter patrols.[79] Other Pucaras, based at Goose Green and Stanley airfields, proved no match for the British Harriers and remained inactive after the first days of the ground war, and no British casualties were attributed to them.[80] Five had been shot down in combat, nine or more were destroyed on the ground, and the rest were captured intact on the airfields after the Argentine surrender.[81] Of the sixty Pucaras in service with the Argentine Air Force, twenty-five—the entire complement based on the Falklands—were lost.[82]

The role of Argentina's major systems in the ground defense of the Falklands was also minimal. Although some armored vehicles were fielded by the Argentines, because of their weight they bogged down in the muddy Falklands terrain and took no part in the fighting.[83] In all, Argentina lost about 120 planes and helicopters,[84] a cruiser, a submarine, and the entire weapons and equipment of three army brigades, costing a minimum of $800 million.[85]

In spite of its indigenous capabilities, Argentina found that fighting an offshore war, even against an overextended enemy, required more sophisticated equipment and better support and training[86] than its factories or military could provide.

China (PRC). The lessons learned by China from its engagement with Vietnam were no less sobering. In fact an argument can be made that China's reliance on its own defense industries served to constrain rather than enhance its war-fighting capabilities.

By any standard, the PRC-Vietnam confrontation in 1979 was a limited war. China committed no aircraft for combat or troop support, and only light infantry formations, with some supplementary armor, marched across the PRC-Vietnam border to "teach the Vietnamese a lesson." It was a war that the world's largest armed forces, supported by the Third World's largest defense industry should have easily won. Vietnam was not only smaller, but it also had no significant defense industry and was completely dependent upon the Soviet Union for its military supplies.[87]

As it turned out, the war was not a clear victory for China. First, China did not achieve its primary political purpose—to relieve pressure on Kampuchea by drawing away elite Vietnamese troops to the Chinese border. Second, although China succeeded in destroying Vietnamese border installations and captured five provincial capitals, it did so with great difficulty and high casualties.[88]

Third, the war demonstrated the backwardness of China's aging equipment, for the most part derived from Soviet models of the late 1940s and early 1950s. There is some evidence to suggest that China's limited military commitment was in part due to the military's assessment that its equipment would prove to be inadequate against the more modern inventories of the battle-hardened Vietnamese. One study concludes that the PLAAF's (People's Liberation Army Air Force) Mig-17s/19s/21s would have been "at critical risk in any engagements with the air units of the SRV (Socialist Republic of Vietnam)." It judges that the air defense environment created by the SAMs and the interceptor capabilities of the SRV would have placed the PLAAF's bombing and attack planes, the IL-28s and F-6bis, at similar risk. "Any significant losses in major air combat and ground support craft which might have resulted would have revealed major weaknesses within the PLAAF, so the Chinese Communist military command apparently opted not to disclose these deficiencies."[89]

For the Chinese leadership, the war highlighted, among other things, the drawbacks of outmoded equipment, antiquated doctrine, and indigenous production without foreign technical assistance or procurement. As Yang Dezhi, the deputy commander of the Chinese forces observed: "This battle has brought up a number of new questions for our military, political, and logistical work, and also provided us with new experiences. All of these will have a profound influence on the revolutionization and modernization of the army."[90]

Today, China's leadership is faced with the dilemma of balancing the need for military modernization with the fear of economic and political dependency. Thus far the government has moved slowly, procuring "dual-use technologies" such as computer and civilian aircraft designs, which will help modernize both civilian and military industries.[91] They are also upgrading existing platforms with new weapons and components, reportedly with some Israeli technical assistance.[92] There is some skepticism among analysts, however, about whether China can effect military modernization during a time of financial stringency and political uncertainty. One predicted that it might be the late 1980s or beyond before mid-1970s technology could be absorbed: "The qualitative gaps between indigenous output and the state-of-the-art will remain at least ten years."[93]

Israel.[94] The lessons learned from Israel's experience with its own equipment are more difficult to assess. Unlike Argentina and China, Israel fought three kinds of war in Lebanon: a tank war, the attacks on the Syrian SAMs, and the air-to-air battles. Because of the number of different systems involved and the reticence of the Israelis regarding their strategy and tactics, reliable information about which systems were used for what purpose and how they performed is not readily available, and there has been much controversy among analysts on this question.

Various sources believe Israel's homemade weapons were a major factor in Israel's fast victory over Syria.[95] One commentator has claimed that some of Israel's equipment is superior to anything yet deployed by either NATO or the Warsaw Pact.[96] Others believe it was U.S. technology that won the war. They point out that U.S. equipment heavily outweighed Israeli products in inventory then and that Israel continues to be dependent upon the United States for many systems,[97] not to mention the financing of its own military and industrial programs.[98] But whether the "winning" weapons were of truly indigenous design and domestic manufacture or not, there is a consensus among defense analysts that weapons were not crucial to the outcome of the Lebanon war. This conclusion is not meant to denigrate the role played by U.S. and Israeli equipment. Without it the attacks surely would have been less successful and more costly.[99] But most observers believe that whether of indigenous design and manufacture or not, the technologies themselves were less responsible for the Israeli military victory than the qualitative human factors of innovation, planning, training, and command.[100] As one U.S. observer put it: "The Israelis developed an integrated, advanced command and control network involving air-to-ground data links which worked. They were the first to make it work as a system. They fought the war of the future. Equipment didn't matter. If you switched the weapons the results would have been much the same!"[101]

In our discussion thus far there has been no mention of the role played by small arms, ammunition, and spare parts factories in expanding the war-fighting capabilities of producer countries. Many specialists believe that indigenous production of these items mitigates the need for resupply during conflict. However, because so many countries manufacture this type of equipment—and because indirect, discreet means of delivery are readily available—the advantages associated with its indigenous production may be overestimated, particularly for short conflicts. Furthermore, the fact that Israel stockpiles these items (a "lesson learned" from the 1973 Middle East war) suggests that "surge" production capabilities, even in Third World countries with relatively sophisticated industries, may be more of a problem than is generally acknowledged.[102]

Because the producers examined here all fought short wars, it is difficult to evaluate the role indigenous defense industries might play in longer, low-intensity conflicts. Under those circumstances, domestic production might contribute at least some of the necessary materiel—and make a difference. But for Argentina, China, and Israel indigenous industrial and (in the case of China and Argentina) logistical facilities have proved insufficient to resupply their own troops involved in high-intensity, high-attrition combat. The evidence from recent wars indicates that the military production efforts of warring states have had limited impact on the outcome of recent wars. For Third World combatant-producers, the ability to produce consumables during peacetime has not translated into an ability to deliver sufficient resupplies to the battlefront.

Conclusion

The evidence presented above suggests that Third World military production efforts have had limited impact on the outcome of recent wars. Ironically, because the developing states remain dependent upon foreign suppliers for transfers of technology, money, sophisticated components, and often raw materials to expand their production capabilities, they are also vulnerable to political pressure that restricts their export potential, particularly to combatants.

Furthermore, the performance of arms producers in recent wars has raised serious questions about the contribution military industries have made to their own national security. In China's case the defense-industrial capabilities of its factories have determined the age and quality of its army's inventory, generating considerable pessimism among U.S. analysts over China's ability to defend itself.[103] Argentina's industries were unable to prevent or moderate the country's humiliating defeat. And not even Israeli equipment has been credited with victory.

Recent developments indicate that constraints on Third World military resupply capabilities will continue, at least for the foreseeable future. Virtually all the arms producers discussed in this chapter are experiencing serious economic difficulties and/or foreign debt problems. Israel, for example, has been forced for the first time in its history to cut its defense budget in an effort to assist the country's tottering economy and to begin paying back its enormous debt. Argentina's postwar government, working with the International Monetary Fund, has reduced military expenditures in order to help stabilize the economy and deal with its foreign debt crisis. Economic difficulties have kept China's military modernization at a low priority level. These financial problems, exacerbated by the world economic recession, are endemic to Third World countries. Most have reduced their defense spending, in effect shrinking the market for LDC defense products, even their own.

Furthermore, Third World producers cannot offer the financing arrangements and grant-aid programs extended by major suppliers, particularly the United States. Hungry for foreign exchange earnings to finance their own military expenditures, Third World suppliers are forced to demand cash payments from countries increasingly unable to afford them. Given the declining price of oil, even those Middle East states formerly able to finance their own and other LDC's military purchases will find doing so more difficult in the future.[104] As a result the volume of LDC military sales is bound to remain limited, at least until the world economy picks up again.

From an arms control perspective, the situation is complicated but not completely discouraging. Intricate networks of arms transfers from Third World industries can and do evade arms embargoes sought by major producers. Any effort to control the flow of small arms, light infantry weapons, and consumables now produced in many countries all over the world is difficult and perhaps futile. But for modern major weapon systems, third party restrictions and supplier leverage have proved very effective in recent wars. A tacit arms control system for new sophisticated military technology appears to be firmly in place. Given the probability of continuing Third World dependence on industrialized suppliers for these items, this situation gives little indication of change.

The implications for the prevalence of violence in the world, however, may be less comforting. Although Third World industries will not produce weapons that are directly competitive with the most advanced state-of-the-art systems manufactured in the industrialized world, over time they will undoubtedly raise the number and technological sophistication of their exports. These indigenous LDC products, unsophisticated relative to the industrialized world's new emerging technologies (which will continue to be controlled by the major producers), nevertheless will have the potential of sustaining longer, ever more destructive conflicts. Clearly, the increasing capabilities of LDC industries do not improve the chances for a world with less combat. Armed conflict as a means of resolving intractable political differences has characterized relations between sovereign states or factions within states since ancient times and gives little sign of abating. As Herman Melville lamented in the 19th century:

> At the height of their madness
> The night winds pause,
> Recollecting themselves;
> But no lull in these wars.[105]

Notes

1. U.S. Arms Control and Disarmament Agency, *World Military Expenditures and Arms Transfers, 1969–1978* (Washington, D.C.: ACDA, 1980), p. 21 (hereafter *WMEAT*).

2. Ulrich Albrecht et al., "Arming the Developing Countries," *International Social Science Journal* 28, no. 2 (1976): 326–40.

3. Michael T. Klare, "The Unnoticed Arms Trade: Exports of Conventional Arms-making Technology," *International Security* 8, no. 2 (Fall 1983): 86.

4. These conflicts include conventional and guerrilla forms of war (and in the case of the Lebanon war a mixture of the two). Statistical data on arms transfers are collected regularly by government agencies but include only government-to-government sales and deliveries. Indirect forms of assistance, particularly those to guerrilla forces, in this case the *Polisario*, the Afghan rebels, the PLO, the Contras, and Nicaraguan-aided guerrillas in Central America are more difficult to collect, less available, and less reliable. Therefore, only government-to-government deliveries are statistically analyzed in this chapter.

5. Only five wars lasted long enough for supplies to reach the recipients during combat: the Horn (Feb. 1977–Mar. 1979); the Western Sahara (late-1978–); Central

America (1979–); the Horn (late 1978–); Iran-Iraq (Sept. 1980–). During the two-and-a-half-month Falklands war (Apr. 2, 1982–June 15, 1982) some supplies did arrive and continued into 1983 despite a British-U.S. embargo. The short PRC-Vietnamese and Syrian-Israeli-PLO engagements precluded resupply, and the government of Afghanistan, since 1980, has received supplies only from the Soviet Union and Eastern Europe.

6. See discussion on patterns of procurement in chapter 7 of this book.

7. Information drawn from the author's files on Third World industries, which are culled from U.S. and foreign newspaper and journal articles. (Hereafter referred to as Neuman data.)

8. Author interview with U.S. State Department official, April 1984.

9. Dates within parentheses and brackets indicate year of first production.

10. Neuman data; Stockholm International Peace Research Institute (SIPRI), *World Armaments and Disarmament Yearbook* (New York: Taylor and Francis, various years); author interviews with U.S. State Department officials, April 1984. Large military items can be identified by satellite surveillance and are difficult to conceal from observers on the ground as they are unloaded from ships, trains, aircraft, or other transport vehicles. Furthermore, few LDCs have transports capable of delivering heavy items expeditiously.

11. Author interview with U.S. State Department official.

12. For example, South Korea and the United States have disputed the status of a series of small arms and ammunition manufactured in South Korea.

13. "Arms for the Ayatullah," *Time*, July 25, 1983, 26.

14. Saudi Arabia has been especially forthcoming to its moderate neighbors. In 1977, Egypt received $2.5 billion in economic and military aid; Syria was granted $1 billion to help pay for its military forces in Lebanon; Jordan was given $500 million, and North Yemen $150 million (Andrew J. Pierre, *The Global Politics of Arms Sales* [Princeton: Princeton University Press, 1982], 178). This form of assistance has not been limited to Middle Eastern donors. Argentina, for example, is reported to have given Peru a credit line of $20 million to permit the Peruvian armed forces to set up their own manufacturing industry ("Argentina Funds Defence Production in Peru," *Jane's Defence Weekly*, Jan. 19, 1985, 97).

15. " 'South Korean Aid' to Contras," *Jane's Defence Weekly*, Aug. 24, 1985, 344.

16. Interview with U.S. State Department official, April 1984.

17. Falling oil revenues and foreign reserves combined with rising military expenditures of some $1.5 billion per month has created a large war debt and has created doubt in the international community about Iraq's creditworthiness. In response to this problem, Kuwait and Saudi Arabia have joined to provide an oil loan to Iraq under which they will supply Iraq's customers with crude oil and allow revenues to be paid directly to Iraq. In addition, some arms suppliers are paid directly for their deliveries. Saudi Arabia, for instance, is reported to have given China about $1 billion for 260 T-69 tanks for Iraq (*MILAVNEWS*, March 1983 and April 1983).

18. The dollar value of China's exports between 1973 and 1981 averaged about $200 million per year. In 1982 it rose to $1 billion and in 1983 to $1.4 billion in constant 1982 dollars. Between 1973 and 1981 membership in the over-$1-billion-in-military-exports-club was limited to France, Italy, West Germany, the Soviet Union, the United Kingdom, and the United States. During that period Italy entered the club only in 1981, West Germany in 1979, the United Kingdom in 1978, and France in 1976. (See *WMEAT*, 1985.)

19. Interview with U.S. State Department official, April 1984.

20. According to *Jane's Armour and Artillery, 1984–85,* the Type-69 main battle tank (MBT), which entered production in China in 1969, is obsolete by Western standards (p. 3).

21. "Birth of an Arms Salesman," *The Economist,* Nov. 17, 1984, 40; "China Plays Both Sides in Persian War," *Washington Post,* Jan. 13, 1983, p. A21.

22. Ibid., "China Plays Both Sides."

23. John F. Copper, "China's Military Assistance," in *Communist Nations' Military Assistance,* eds. John F. Copper and Daniel S. Papp (Boulder, Colo.: Westview Press, 1983), 97.

24. Rebel groups in Southeast Asia that have received Chinese assistance at one time or another since the 1950s include: the Khmer Rouge and Son Sann, a leader of anti-Vietnamese guerrillas in Kampuchea; Meo and Lao tribes in Laos; groups in Burma, Thailand, Malaysia, Indonesia, and the Philippines. China has also assisted insurgency groups in other parts of the world, for example, India, Algeria (where revolutionaries from Angola, Mozambique, Portuguese Guinea, and South Africa were trained and equipped indirectly by China after Algeria's independence), Congo, Morocco, North and South Yemen, Syria, the PLO, Somalia, Central African Republic, Angola, Zimbabwe-Rhodesia, among others in sub-Saharan Africa (Ibid., 115–22).

25. One State Department official estimated that one-fifth of the Afghan rebels' supplies originate in China (author interview, September 1984).

26. Donald R. Cotter and N.F. Wikner, "Korea: Force Imbalances and Remedies," *Strategic Review* 10, no. 2 (Spring 1982): 64; speech by Gen. Robert Sennewald in Seoul, Korea, as reported in the *Korea Herald,* June 17, 1983, 1; *Jane's Armour and Artillery, 1984–85,* 49, comments only on the probability: "The T-62s probably now are made in North Korea."

27. Author interview with South Korean industry officials in Seoul, Korea, August 1983.

28. The T-62 MBT is a light tank that was developed from the earlier T-54/T-55 series and entered production in the Soviet Union in 1961. It is obsolete by Western standards and is no longer produced in the Soviet Union. Production ended in 1971–72. (*Jane's Armour and Artillery, 1984–85,* 67.)

29. Author interview with U.S. State Department official, February 1984.

30. "Iran/Iraq: Arms Deliveries Increasing," *Defense and Foreign Affairs Daily,* Jan. 30, 1983, 1–2.

31. Most ammunition factories can convert a production line to manufacture other caliber small arms or artillery ammunition within a few weeks. It entails a relatively simple readjustment of tooling machinery since the same materials and skills are used to produce most types of ammunition. Basically, the market determines the feasibility of conversion. If there are enough buyers to make it economically worthwhile, any number of countries can do so. Recent conflicts have apparently created such a demand. North Korea reportedly supplies Iran with ammunition that is compatible with its U.S.-origin systems. (Interview with State Department official, May 1984.) Bulgaria, too, operates a factory that produces NATO-standard ammunition. This particular round has been found in only three places in the West: in a small southern town in El Salvador; in the Sandinista Army in Nicaragua; and in 1973–74 in the Dominican Republic, held by a group of Cuban-supported insurgents ("El Salvador Arms Trade," *Jane's Defence Weekly,* Oct. 6, 1984, 564). In the West, Israel began producing copies

of the Soviet 240 mm BM-24 artillery rocket after the 1967 Middle East war. This rocket is now well integrated into the Israeli Defense Forces (IDF) service and is used from captured launchers mounted on Israeli trucks (*Jane's Defence Weekly*, July 7, 1984, 1109).

32. "Iran/Iraq; Arms Deliveries Increasing," "North Korea Reported to Step Up Arms Sales and Training Abroad," *New York Times*, Nov. 29, 1983, pp. A1, A9.

33. "Hormuz Straits Defence 'Global Responsibility'," *Jane's Defence Weekly* 1, no. 8 (March 3, 1984): 310.

34. "North Korea Said to Be Arming Iran," *New York Times,* Dec. 19, 1983, p. A1.

35. "Iran/Iraq: Arms Deliveries Increasing," 1–2.

36. Nack An and Rose An, "North Korean Military Assistance," in *Communist Nations' Military Assistance*, eds. John F. Copper and Daniel S. Papp (Boulder, Colo: Westview Press, 1983), 171–75.

37. "North Korean Advisers Arrive to Train Force in Zimbabwe," *Washington Post*, Aug. 11, 1981, 1; interview with U.S. industry representative and State Department official, May 1984.

38. Author interview, May 1984.

39. It is estimated that Brazil sells about one thousand armored cars and armored fighting vehicles annually to the Middle East and Africa. Its three largest sellers are the amphibious Urutu, an armored car (the Cascavel), and the Jararaca, a light reconnaissance vehicle. (Drew Middleton, "Smaller Nations Crack Arms Market," *New York Times*, Aug. 28, 1983.

40. Neuman data.

41. Even Brazil's "indigenous" systems are often derivative in design, and the more complex components, such as engines, communications and electronic devices, and armaments are procured from abroad. For example, the chassis of the EE-T1 Osorio main battle tank being developed by the Engesa company in Brazil is scheduled to start trials in June 1984. However, when complete it will be powered by a West German water-cooled diesel engine and transmission. The suspension system is designed by a British aerospace firm (Dunlop), and the tank will be offered with a choice of main armament from either Britain or France. ("Engesa MBT to Start Trials in June," *Jane's Defence Weekly* 1, no. 16, Apr. 28, 1984): 640–41.

42. *WMEAT, 1973–1983.*

43. "Brazil-Iraq: Arms Bartered for Oil," *Defense and Foreign Affairs*, July 26, 1979. Middleton, "Smaller Nations Crack Arms Market."

44. *SIPRI Yearbook, 1984*, 198–99.

45. "Iraq Claims 'Devastating' Weapon Built in Brazil," *Foreign Broadcasting Information Service* (PY141407, São Paulo. *O Estado de São Paulo* in Portuguese, Feb. 12, 1983, p. 5).

46. Interview with State Department official, May 1984.

47. Today, the AOI is organized into five divisions which employ among them about fifteen thousand workers. Approximately three thousand more are employed by the AOI's four subsidiaries. (*Jane's All the World's Aircraft, 1984–85*, 48.)

48. *Jane's Armour and Artillery, 1979–80*, 191.

49. *MILAVNEWS*, November 1983, 8.

50. *WMEAT, 1973–1983.*

51. *MILAVNEWS,* May 1983.

52. *MILAVNEWS,* November 1983, 8, and July 1982, 8. Egypt is also reported to have sold Iraq Swingfire missiles.

53. North Yemen, the Sudan, and other sub-Saharan states are also recipients of Egyptian equipment. (*MILAVNEWS,* November 1983, 8.)

54. Egyptian military advisers have trained Somali troops for their ongoing skirmishes with Ethiopia, and armored vehicles, antitank rockets, other infantry weapons and ammunition have continued to arrive from Egyptian stores and factories. ("Egypt's Russian Policy Grows More Hawkish in Mideast and Africa," *Wall Street Journal,* Feb. 9, 1981.)

55. Ibid.

56. *MILAVNEWS,* June 1982, 23. See note 17 above, for further discussion of the Gulf States' financial aid to Iraq.

57. "U.S. Funded Sale of SA-7s to Afghan Rebels," *Defense Electronics,* October 1982, 14.

58. Deliveries to the ROK Air Force began in Autumn 1982. (*Jane's All the World's Aircraft, 1984–85,* 164.)

59. South Korea's tank production program, initiated in 1978, began with the modernization of U.S. M-48 tanks and today includes the development of the ROKIT. The latter is to be domestically produced with design assistance from the Chrysler Corporation. (See appendix to this chapter and *Jane's Armour and Artillery, 1984–85,* 49.)

60. South Korean production of ground forces equipment now includes machine guns, submachine guns, rifles, mortars, light antiaircraft guns (M55 Quad 127 mm SP), towed howitzers (105 mm M101A1 and 155 mm M114A1), ammunition for all these weapons, hand grenades, mines, and wheeled vehicles (e.g., trucks, cars, jeeps, and an armored personnel carrier; see appendix to this chapter).

61. The country has extensive repair, overhaul, and assembly capabilities for many U.S. aircraft in the South Korean Air Force, such as the F-5s, F-4s, and various helicopters.

62. Other wartime recipients have been Ethiopia (5 percent) and Morocco (less than 1 percent); El Salvador has received a small amount of ammunition.

63. *MILAVNEWS,* August 1983.

64. See discussion in chapter 7 of this book. For a lengthier discussion on the relationship between the superpowers and LDC suppliers see S. Neuman, *Military Assistance in Recent Wars,* chapter 6.

65. For a more detailed discussion on the structure of Israel's defense industry see Robert E. Harkavy and Stephanie G. Neuman, "Israel's Arms Industry," in *Arms Production in Developing Countries: An Analysis of Decision-Making,* ed. James E. Katz (Lexington, Mass.: Lexington Books, 1984). See also Gerald Steinberg, "Israel," in *The Structure of the Defense Industry,* eds. Nicole Ball and Milton Leitenberg (London: Croom Helm, 1983), 284–85; Aaron S. Kleiman, *Israel's Global Reach* (New York: Pergamon, 1985), chapter 5.

66. Ibid.

67. See Stephanie Neuman, "Third World Military Industries and the Arms Trade," in *Arms Production in Developing Countries,* ed. James E. Katz (Lexington,

Mass.: Lexington Books, 1984), and "International Stratification and Third World Military Industries," *International Organization* 38, no. 1 (Winter 1984): 167–97.

68. Ibid., and Harkavy and Neuman, "Israel's Arms Industry."

69. Harkavy and Neuman, "Israel's Arms Industry." Israeli industries have been particularly innovative in this regard. Several major programs for modernizing combat aircraft have been initiated which include the F-4 Phantom and the A-4 Skyhawk. These aircraft have been upgraded for the IDF, and the Israelis are offering them for export as well. The Mirage III and Fouga-Magister also have been upgraded for sale to foreign airforces. These programs involve aerodynamic equipment and systems modifications designed to improve performance, maintainability, and survivability. According to one report, changes to the Mirages and Skyhawks derive from the IDF's "extensive combat experience" and include such items as radar warning indication, flare and chaff dispensers, additional weapon hardpoints, advanced avionics and head-up displays. (*MILAVNEWS*, January 1982, 18.).

70. Only in 1981 did the United States lift its veto on the sale of the Kfir to Ecuador ("U.S. Lifts Veto on Israeli Jet Sales to Ecuador," *Washington Post*, Mar. 21, 1981, p. 8). There have been rumors that other Latin American states will be the next purchasers of these aircraft, but thus far they have not been confirmed (*SIPRI Yearbook, 1982*; Harkavy and Neuman, "Israel's Arms Industry").

71. The sale of Israeli small arms to Belgium and a license to West Germany for the production of Israel's M-111 tank shell, as well as certain buy-back agreements with the United States for F-16 components, account for some of Israel's non–Third World sales. It has also been reported that the U.S. Navy has purchased Tadiran's Mastiff remotely piloted vehicle (RPV). (*MILAVNEWS*, April 1984, 7.) More recently, Israel has leased to the U.S. Navy Kfir fighter aircraft to serve in an aggressor squadron. Israel has also negotiated a contract to maintain and repair the leased aircraft.

72. *MILAVNEWS*, March 1983, 2.

73. "Israel Said to Aid Latin Aims of the U.S.," *New York Times*, July 21, 1983, pp. A1, A4; "Israel Said to Step Up Latin Role Offering Arms Seized in Lebanon," *New York Times*, Dec. 17, 1982.

74. Mainly small arms, ammunition, quartermaster equipment, training, and technical assistance were supplied.

75. Steven David, "Realignment in the Horn: The Soviet Advantage," *International Security* 4, no. 2 (Fall 1979): 86.

76. "Arms Are a Crucial Export for Israel," *New York Times*, Aug. 24, 1981, p. 3; *MILAVNEWS*, February 1983.

77. This section is drawn from a longer work, *Military Assistance in Recent Wars: The Dominance of the Superpowers*, The Washington Papers, no. 122 (Washington, D.C.: Center for Strategic and International Studies, Georgetown University, with Praeger Publishers, 1986).

78. See S. Neuman, "International Stratification and Third World Military Industries," *International Organization* 38, no. 1 (Winter 1984): 167–97; Herbert Wulf, "Arms Production in the Third World," *World Armaments and Disarmament, SIPRI Yearbook 1985*, (London and Philadelphia: Taylor and Francis, 1985), 329–43, for a description of Third World military-industrial capabilities.

79. Reported in *MILAVNEWS*, April 1983.

80. Harry G. Summers, Jr., "Ground Warfare Lessons," in *Military Lessons of the Falkland Islands War: Views from the United States,* eds. Bruce W. Watson and

Peter M. Dunn (Boulder, Colo.: Westview Press, 1984), 70; Jeffrey Ethell and Alfred Price, *Air War South Atlantic* (London: Sidgwick & Jackson, 1983), 223.

81. *MILAVNEWS*, December 1982.

82. *MILAVNEWS*, December 1982 and June 1983. Argentina had two counter-insurgency (COIN)/training squadrons of Pucaras in inventory; apparently one was based on the Falklands and one on the mainland. (See International Institute for Strategic Studies [IISS], *Military Balance, 1981–1982,* [London: IISS, 1981], 92.)

83. David C. Isby, "Falklands War Weapons: The Best Men and Arms Won," *Soldier of Fortune* (August 1983): 36, 69. According to Isby the British Scorpion and Scimitar exert "only half the ground pressure of a penguin. They could traverse the boggy Falklands terrain where other vehicles immediately got stuck and troops sank to their knees." (p. 69).

84. *MILAVNEWS*, March 1983.

85. *MILAVNEWS,* February 1983.

86. Recent assessments of the Falklands war agree that the lack of antisubmarine warfare systems, all-weather fighting capabilities, airborne reconnaissance and early warning facilities, air-refueling devices, and secure communications were all important contributing factors to Argentina's poor military performance. However, inadequate training in tactics, maintenance, and operations is cited as the most compelling reason for its defeat. (See Watson and Dunn, eds., *Military Lessons of the Falkland Islands War*; Isby, "Falklands War Weapons"; Julian S. Lake, "The South Atlantic War: A Review of the Lessons Learned," *Defense Electronics* (November 1983): 86ff. See also S. Neuman, *Military Assistance in Recent Wars*, chapter 5, for a discussion on the role of the human factor in recent wars.

87. Vietnam produces a light machine gun and some grenades.

88. June Teufel Dreyer, "China's Military Power in the 1980s," a paper distributed by the China Council of the Asia Society, August 1982.

89. James B. Linder and A. James Gregor, "The Chinese Communist Air Force in the 'Punitive' War Against Vietnam," *Air University Review* (September/October 1981): 67-77.

90. Quoted in Dreyer, "Chinese Military Power," 11.

91. China received U.S. authorization to buy military hardware in June 1984. The first U.S. sale, reported in August 1985, was for gas turbine engines to be used in two Chinese-designed and -built destroyers. A second agreement followed in September 1985 which involved about $100 million in sales of equipment and technical help to modernize a large caliber artillery plant. Included in the sale was about $6 million worth of fuses, primers, and detonators for 155-mm artillery. China has also purchased 24 Sikorsky dual-use transport helicopters for $140 million (Kerry B. Dumbaugh and Richard F. Grimmett, *U.S. Arms Sales to China* [Washington, D.C.: Library of Congress, Congressional Research Service, July 8, 1985], 16; Paul Mann, "Study Forecasts No Change in Weapons Sales to China," *Aviation Week and Space Technology* [Sept. 30, 1985]: 82; "U.S. Reported Close to Arms Sale to China to Modernize Air Force," *New York Times*, January 25, 1986, p. A3.)

92. Chinese tanks have been reported to have new Israeli-made cannons mounted on them. ("Secret Military Deals Between Israel and China," *Jane's Defence Weekly* [November 24, 1984]: 915.)

93. Quoted in Dreyer, "China's Military Power," 22.

94. Some of the issues presented here are discussed at greater length in Robert E. Harkavy and Stephanie G. Neuman, "Israel," in *Arms Production in Developing*

Countries, James Everett Katz, ed. (Lexington, Mass.: Lexington Books, 1984), 193–224.

95. See among others *Military Electronics/Countermeasures*, special ed., January 1983, 106–45, and "Lessons of Lebanon," *Defence Attache*, no. 4 (1982): 23–35.

96. See for instance Edward Luttwak, "Gauging Soviet Arms," *New York Times*, Dec. 31, 1982, p. A19.

97. Author interview with U.S. Department of Defense official, April 1983; Anthony Cordesman, "The Sixth Arab-Israeli Conflict: Military Lessons for American Defense Planning," *Armed Forces Journal International* (August 1982): 29–32.

98. The extent to which Israel's defense industries are dependent upon the United States is suggested by the financial and technical assistance Israel has sought for its two major programs. U.S. FMS (Foreign Military Sales) funds were used to help finance the development and production of the Merkava tank (author interview with General Tal in Tel Aviv, August 1982); and more recently the United States has again agreed to allow Israel to use $250 million of FMS funds for R&D expenditures on the Lavi aircraft in Israel and another $300 million in the United States. The engine of the former, and major parts of the latter (including the engine) will be procured in the United States. ("Major Boost for Israel's Lavi Plans," *Jane's Defence Weekly* 1, no. 8 (Mar. 3, 1984): 311; "U.S. Offers Israel More Military Aid," *Washington Times*, Dec. 12, 1983.

99. From the Israeli viewpoint, a short war with minimal casualties is an important military goal. Innovations and technologies, especially in electronic warfare, that provide the Israelis with the ability to react quickly and save lives have a high payoff and are considered a decided military advantage. For them the process and outcome of war are inseparable.

100. Cordesman, "The Sixth Arab-Israeli Conflict," 31. Author interviews with Department of State and Department of Defense officials, March 1983, December 1983, and January 1984.

101. Author interview with Department of State official, March 24, 1983. The point made here by the informant is that because of the superior Israeli training, education, and organization, even if the weapons were exchanged, the Israeli military would be able to extract 100 percent efficiency from the Syrians' Soviet equipment, whereas the Syrian army, already experiencing operational difficulties with what it had, would have been further handicapped by the more sophisticated U.S.-Israeli technologies.

102. Israel produces much of its army's needs in small arms and ammunition. The Galil assault rifle and Uzi submachine gun are both of indigenous design and manufacture and are standard issue for the IDF. The Israeli army, however, also uses the U.S. M-16 rifle in large numbers. (*Jane's Infantry Weapons, 1983–84* [London: Jane's Publishing Inc.], 167.)

103. See Dreyer, "China's Military Power"; and Linder and Gregor, "The Chinese Communist Air Force in the 'Punitive' War Against Vietnam."

104. In January 1986, the price of crude oil had fallen to less than $20 for a forty-two-gallon barrel, approximately one-half what it was at its peak in 1981. In 1981, oil sold for $36 a barrel under long-term contracts and for $42 a barrel in the spot market (Nicholas D. Kristof "Economic and Political Shifts Seen If Oil Price Fall Persists," *New York Times*, Jan. 27, 1986, p. A1).

105. Herman Melville, "The Armies of the Wilderness," *The Battle-Pieces of Herman Melville*, ed. Hennig Cohen (New York: Thomas Yoseloff, 1963), 100.

Appendix

Selected Weapon Systems Produced in the Third World, 1982–83

Type of Weapon	In Production	Planned	Producing Country	Notes
Aerospace:				
Fighters		AMX[a]	Brazil	
	Ajeet		India	
	MiG-19 (F-6)		China	Fighter-bomber, radically modified MiG-19
	MiG-21 (F-7)		India, China	
	Q-5 (A-5)		China	
		MiG-27[b]	India	
	Kfir		Israel	
		Lavi	Israel	
		MiG-21[b]	N. Korea	
	F-5E[b]		S. Korea, Taiwan	
Heavy bombers	H-5 (Il-28)[e]		China	
	H-6 (Tu-16)[e]		China	
Attack/trainer	IA-58 Pucara		Argentina	
		IA-63	Argentina	
	EMB-326[b]		Brazil, S. Africa	
	CJ-6		China	
	MiG-17 (JJ-5)[e]		China	
	Alpha-Jet[b]		Egypt	
	Jaguar[b]		India	
	HJT-16 Mk-1 Kiran		India	
		MB-339[b]	Peru	
		XAT-3	Taiwan	

Utility	EMB-111		Brazil
	Brazilia ASW		Brazil
	Y-5 (AN-2)[e]		China
	Y-8 (AN-12)[e]	AN-32[b]	China
			India
	Arava IAI 201		Israel
	Westwind		Israel
Helicopters	Gaviao (Lama)[b]		Brazil, India
	Esquito (Ecureuil)[b]		Brazil
		Z-6[c]	China
	Alouette III[b]		India
	Hughes MD-500[b]		S. Korea
Remotely piloted vehicles/decoys	Scout		Israel
	Mastiff		Israel
		X[c]	S. Korea

Ground Forces:

Pistols	9 mm FN HP[b]	Argentina
	9 mm FN HP Pindad	Indonesia
	9 mm Taurus PT-92	Brazil
	9 mm Beretta[b]	Brazil, Israel
	9 mm Type-59[e]	China
	7.62 mm Type-51/54[e]	China
	7.62 mm Type-68	N. Korea
	7.65 mm Type-64/67[e]	China
	7.65 mm Type-64[e]	N. Korea — Copy of Browning Model 1900

Appendix (Continued)

Type of Weapon	In Production	Planned	Producing Country	Notes
Submachine guns	9 mm PA3-DM		Argentina	
	0.45 INA MB 50[f] & Model 953		Brazil	
	9 mm BSM 9 M3 SMG[b]		Brazil	
	9 mm Uru Mekanika SMG			
	9 mm MD-1 & ND-1A1 IMBEL		Brazil	
		9 mm SM Model 02 LAPA	Brazil	
	9 mm BA-52		Burma	
	7.62 mm Types-43/50[e]		China	
	9 mm UZI SMG		Israel	
	5.56 mm SMG		S. Korea	
	9 mm SANNA 77[e]		S. Africa	
Rifles	7.62 mm FN[b]		Argentina, India	
	7.62 mm caliber M1 Garand modified		Brazil	
	7.62 mm modified Mauser		Brazil	
	7.62 mm Mosque-FAL	5.56 mm OVM assault carbine	Brazil	
	7.62 mm Type-56/56-1		Brazil	
	7.62 mm Type 68		China	Assault rifle
	5.56 mm & 7.62 Galil AK-47/AKM[b]		China	Assault rifle
	5.56 mm R4[b]		Israel	
			N. Korea	
	5.56 mm M16[b]		S. Africa	Modified Galil
			Singapore, S. Korea	
			Philippines	
	5.56 mm M60[b]		S. Korea	
	5.56 mm Type-65	5.56 mm Type-68	Taiwan	
			Taiwan	

Machine guns	7.62 mm Uirapuru Mekanika GPMG	Brazil	
	12.7 mm Type-54 DPM[e]	China	Soviet copy
	7.62 mm Types-53/56/58[e]	China	Soviet copies
	7.62 mm Type-67 LMG	China	
	5.56 mm & 7.62 mm ARM Galil	Israel	
	5.56 mm Ultimax 100 LMG	Singapore	
	5.56 mm M60[b]	S. Korea, Taiwan	
Ammunition	9 mm	Argentina, Brazil, Burma, Cambodia, Cameroon, Chile, Colombia, Dominican Republic, Egypt, Ethiopia, India, Indonesia, Iran, Israel, Malaysia, Morocco, Nigeria, Pakistan, Peru, Saudi Arabia, Singapore, S. Africa, Sudan, Syria (?), Taiwan (?), Thailand, Upper Volta	
	5.56 mm	Brazil, Cambodia, Chile, Dominican Republic, Israel, S. Korea, Malaysia, Mexico, Philippines, Saudi Arabia, Singapore, Thailand, Upper Volta	
	7 mm	Brazil, Chile	

Appendix (Continued)

Type of Weapon	In Production	Planned	Producing Country	Notes
Ammunition (continued)	7.5 mm		Cambodia, Cameroon, Morocco, Upper Volta	
	7.62 mm		Argentina, Brazil, Burma, Cameroon, Chile, China, Colombia, Dominican Republic, Egypt, Ethiopia, India, Indonesia, Iran, Iraq, N. Korea, S. Korea, Malaysia, Morocco, Nigeria, Pakistan, Peru, Philippines, Saudi Arabia, Singapore, S. Africa, Sudan, Syria (?), Taiwan, Thailand, Upper Volta	
	7.65 mm		Argentina	
	7.92 mm		Egypt, Israel	
	.45 ACP		Argentina, Brazil, Dominican Republic, Iran, S. Korea, Mexico, Philippines	
	.30 carbine		Dominican Republic, S. Korea, Mexico, Morocco, Philippines	
	.303		Egypt, Pakistan, Singapore, S. Africa	

			Countries
	30-06		Argentina, Cambodia, Dominican Republic, Ethiopia, Iran, Israel, S. Korea, Mexico, Pakistan, Philippines
	12.7 mm		Brazil, Chile, China, Colombia, Dominican Republic, Egypt, India, Indonesia, Iran, Iraq, Israel, N. Korea, S. Korea, Mexico, Morocco, Pakistan, Philippines, Saudi Arabia, S. Africa, Syria (?), Thailand
	14.5 mm		China, Egypt, Iraq, N. Korea
Mortars	81/120 mm[b]		Argentina
	81/120 mm		India
	60/81/82/160[e] mm		China
	52/60/81/120/160 mm		Israel
	60/81 mm		Philippines, S. Korea, Taiwan
	60/81 mm[e]		S. Africa
	4.2 inch		S. Korea
	107/120 mm		Taiwan
Tanks	TAM		Argentina
		XMB-3	Brazil
		X-30[c]	Brazil
	X1A2 MT		Brazil
	T-59 MBT[e]		China
	T-63 LT		China
	T-62 LT		China

Appendix (Continued)

Type of Weapon	In Production	Planned	Producing Country	Notes
Tanks (continued)	Vijayanta^b		India	
		T-72^b	India	
	Merkava 1/2 MBT		Israel	
	Sherman (various)		Israel	
	T-55 (?) or T 62 (?)		N. Korea	
		ROKIT	S. Korea	
Other armored vehicles	VCI ICV		Argentina	
	EE-17 Sucuri TD		Brazil	
	EE-9 Cascavel AC		Brazil	
	EE-3 Jararaca ARV		Brazil	
	EE-11 Urutu APC		Brazil	
	K-63 APC		China	
	T55/56 AC^e		China	
	Walid APC		Egypt	
	RBY MK 1 ARV		Israel	
		RAM V-1 ARV	Israel	
	Eland AC		S. Africa	
	Ratel 20 ICV		S. Africa	
	Buffel APC		S. Africa	
	Fiat-OTO Melara 6614 APC^b		S. Korea	
Artillery	155 mm		Argentina	
	122 mm SP		China	
	T-63 SPAA		China	
	Variety of Soviet copies		China	
	105 mm, 155 mm SP		Israel	
	TCM-20 20 mm AA		Israel	
	75/105 mm		India	
	105 mm, 155 mm^b		S. Korea	
	Cactus SAM		S. Africa	

Category	System	Designation	Country	Notes
Artillery rockets	108R		Brazil	
		X-20, X40[c]	Brazil	
	107 mm T-63		China	
	132 mm (& possibly others)		Egypt	
	Zeev (Wolf)		Israel	
	BM-24 240 mm		Israel	
	SS-17(?)		N. Korea	
	120–150 mm (?)		S. Korea	
		Nike-Hercules	S. Korea	
Missiles:				
Air-to-air		MAA-1 Piranha	Brazil	
	CAA-1/2	CAA-3	China	
		Matra-550[b]	India	Similar to Matra-550
	Shafrir 2/3		Israel	
	Kukri		S. Africa	
	AIM 9-J (Sidewinder)[b]		Taiwan	
Antitank	Mathago		Argentina	
	Cobra-2000[b]		Brazil	
	AT-3		China	
	Swingfire[b]		Egypt	
	AT-1/3		Egypt, N. Korea	
	SS 11-1B[b]		India	
		Milan[b]	India	
	Picket		Israel	
	Kun-wu		Taiwan	

Appendix (Continued)

Type of Weapon	In Production	Planned	Producing Country	Notes
Antiship	CSS N-2	X[c]	Brazil	
	Gabriel 1/2	Gabriel 3	China	
	Gabriel 2[b]		Israel	
			S. Africa, Taiwan	
Antiaircraft	SA-7[b]		India, N. Korea	
	SA-2		N. Korea, China	
		SAKR-Eye	Egypt	
		Nike-Hercules	S. Korea	
	R440 Crotale[a]		S. Africa	Cactus
Air-to-surface	Martin Pescador	MAS-1	Argentina	
			Brazil	
	CAS N-1		China	
		VAP-1	Egypt	
	Luz-1		Israel	
Naval warships *(over 500 tons):*				
Frigates	Niteroi (3,800)		Brazil	
	Kiang-Hu (1,800)		China	
	Kiang Nan (1,350)		China	
	Jiannghu (?)		China	
	Godvari (3,000)		India	
	Ulsan		S. Korea	

Corvettes	Meko-140 ("Espora"-class)[b] (1,200)	Argentina
	X(1,600)[c]	Brazil
Submarines	Romeo (1,400)[e]	China
	Sauro[b](?)	Brazil
	Type-1400[b]	Brazil
	Type-1500[b]	India

Sources: Jane's *All the World's Aircraft; Weapon Systems; Armour and Artillery; Weapon Systems; Fighting Ships;* (various years); and Neuman data.

[a]Codeveloped with foreign partners.

[b]Produced under license. May involve the manufacture of small components and the assembly of imported major subsystems. Third country sales restrictions probably in effect.

[c]An X denotes a weapon under development that lacks nomenclature.

[d]Production ended.

[e]Copy without benefit of license. (Most Chinese systems are derivative of earlier Soviet designs.)

[f]Copy, with manufacturing rights.

9

The Use of Proxy Forces by Major Powers in the Third World

Steven R. David

Introduction

Throughout history great powers have used proxies to advance their interests. It was not until the 1970s, however, that the use of proxies assumed such a central role in international politics. During this decade, the United States and (to a much greater extent) the Soviet Union employed proxies to achieve foreign policy objectives that otherwise would have been lost. While the actual and enduring value of these gains can be questioned, the significance of the manner in which they were won is beyond doubt. It is now impossible for either superpower to maintain its range of interests in the Third World without being prepared to use proxies or respond to their use by others.

Any understanding of the importance of proxies must begin with a clear idea of just what is meant by the term *proxy*. In its most basic form, a proxy is an individual or group empowered to act for another. In the context of great power–third world relations (and for the purposes of this study), a proxy situation exists only when five criteria are met. First, there must be the presence of foreign military and security forces in the country that is the target of the proxy involvement. Economic advisors, teachers, technicians, and such, do not constitute a proxy presence. Second, the involvement of these forces must serve the interests of some stronger power. If Libya's invasion of an African country (for example, Chad) meets the interests of Libya but no greater power, such an action cannot be considered an invasion by proxy. Third, the stronger power must provide critical, ongoing, and direct assistance to the country supplying the troops, enabling the latter to intervene on a larger scale than otherwise would have been possible. While the 1982 Israeli invasion of Lebanon could not have taken place without prior U.S. assistance, it was not a proxy intervention since the U.S. aid was neither directly connected to the Israeli action nor administered in such a way so as to ensure the success of the intervention. Fourth, for a proxy intervention to take place, interests must not be at stake that are vital to either the dominant power or the state that supplies the fighting troops. During the early days of World War II, the U.S. policy of lend-lease did not make proxies of British and Soviet armies since both were fighting for the defense of their countries. Similarly, South Vietnamese troops in the Vietnam War were not U.S. proxies since they were fighting to preserve their state. Finally, a proxy relationship is characterized by a division of labor in which the proxy forces carry out tasks the stronger power is capable of doing but has chosen not to do so. Proxies are not employed because the greater power lacks the *ability* to reach an objective, but because it feels (usually for political reasons) that it is best that some other state do the job for it.

To clarify further what is meant by a proxy, it is useful to consider what a proxy is not. Proxies need not be the "puppets" of the power that is backing them. Proxy forces may disagree with their patron over aspects of their own involvement and/or may be serving some interests of their own by intervening. Simply because it is possible to demonstrate that a foreign intervention might not have followed the dictates of a great power to the letter, or may have met some of the interests of the intervening force's country is not sufficient to declare that the intervening forces were not proxies. Proxy forces should also not be confused with mercenaries. Proxy forces are organized units loyal to the country of their nationality—not individual soldiers for hire. Moreover, while the proxy relationship involves cooperation between two countries to advance their common interests (three, if one counts the country to which the troops are sent), it is not an alliance of equal powers. In a proxy relationship, a hierarchy exists, with the country supplying the troops subservient to another country whose interests are realized by the proxy forces' actions.

As defined by these criteria, the use of proxies by the United States and the Soviet Union escalated sharply in the mid-1970s. Throughout the Third World, with special attention on Africa (especially Angola and Ethiopia) and the Middle East (especially South Yemen), Cubans, East Germans, Moroccans, and others served the interests of their superpower patron with stunning effectiveness. Virtually every Third World conflict of concern to the superpowers either involved proxies or threatened to involve them.

Why Proxies Are Important

Why have proxies taken on such an important role in superpower relations with the Third World? Part of the answer lies in the attitudes toward superpower intervention that have developed in the wake of decolonization. A new egalitarian ethic has taken hold in international politics, making armed intervention a more visible and (at times) less justifiable alternative. No longer is it accepted that "the strong do what they can and the weak do what they must," as the international hierarchy (at least in rhetorical terms) has eroded. This change in international ethics will not prevent the United States or the Soviet Union from intervening in the Third World. It does, however, make such interventions more difficult and, consequently, less frequent.

Developments in the superpower nations themselves also explain the rise in the use of proxies. It has become much more difficult for the superpowers (particularly the United States) to use direct force to achieve their objectives. Because of the U.S. experience in Vietnam, the high costs of direct intervention (in human and economic terms), and the fear of a confrontation with the Soviet Union, it is highly unlikely that the United States would use large numbers of U.S. troops in a protracted Third World conflict for any but the most vital of interests. Moreover, a policy of direct protracted intervention for other than vital purposes (and perhaps for vital purposes as well) will not be supported by the American people. As the Korean and Vietnam wars so painfully demonstrated, the American people and Congress will not back a protracted U.S. involvement in a Third World conflict. So long as the United States cannot ensure that its intervention will be rapid and decisive (a goal its Third World adversary would work to frustrate), such an intervention would not be a viable policy choice for any but the most pressing of interests.[1]

While the Soviet Union faces fewer domestic constraints in the use of force (a major advantage for it in the competition for the Third World), it too must set limits on the expenditure of scarce resources for Third World adventures and be wary of provoking dangerous confrontations with the United States. That the Soviet invasion of Afghanistan in 1979 was the first major use of Soviet troops in a Third World conflict indicates that the Kremlin is quite prudent when committing its own forces to battle. The inability of Soviet troops to achieve a decisive victory in Afghanistan will most assuredly reinforce this sense of caution.

Since the superpowers are reluctant to intervene directly to meet any but vital interests in the Third World, there will be few opportunities for direct intervention. This is so because if a vital interest is defined as one that is so important that its maintenance is necessary to the continued existence of the state in question, then the interests of the United States and Soviet Union in the Third World, while significant, are overwhelmingly not vital. Given the limited salience of most Third World interests to the superpowers, the means used to protect and advance those interests will also usually be limited. Proxies represent an effective "middle ground" between direct intervention and doing nothing, allowing the superpowers to meet their interests with actions commensurate with the importance of those interests. While it is beyond the scope of this study to examine each of the Third World interests of the superpowers in terms of their respective significance to the United States and the Soviet Union, a few general points about the nonvital role played by most of these interests is helpful in understanding why proxies—and not the superpowers themselves—are so active in the Third World today.

Militarily, it is difficult to see how any Third World state or group of states can be considered truly vital to the United States or the Soviet Union. The fundamental security of the superpowers depends on the credibility of their respective nuclear deterrents. Undermining this deterrent relationship can come about through a technological breakthrough (for example, in strategic defense) and/or through a large imbalance in their nuclear forces. The Third World has no effect on the realization of either of these developments. This is not to suggest that the Third World is irrelevant to the military balance of power. Alignments and realignments to and from the superpowers are significant as are the use of bases in strategic areas of the world and cooperation with Third World military forces. Nevertheless, these and similar developments will not affect the basic security of the United States or the Soviet Union, nor will they provide the margin of military superiority to one side or the other.

Economically, the Third World is more of a convenience than a necessity to the superpowers. This is especially true of the Soviet Union, whose volume of trade with the Third World has consistently been only a fraction of that of the United States. For the Soviets, autarky is not attractive, but neither is it impossible. As a major economic power, the United States is more dependent on trade than is the Soviet Union. Still, with U.S. trade to the Third World only amounting to about 0.3% of GNP and U.S. investment accounting for only 3.7% of gross business earnings, the Third World is also less than economically vital to the United States.[2] Moreover, Third World raw materials (with the possible exception of oil) are not vital to either of the superpowers. The Soviet Union possesses virtually every mineral it needs, and those few it does not have it can easily obtain elsewhere. The situation is more difficult for the United States but nowhere nearly as critical as some assert. While the United States does depend on the Third World for such minerals as platinum, chromium, and cobalt, its dependence does not preclude adaptation to sudden shortages. Stockpiling, recycling of existing supplies, conservation efforts, and research to find substitutes are all policies that prevent the loss of any Third World country from vitally affecting the U.S. economy.[3]

None of this means that the Third World is not important to the superpowers or that specific interests cannot at times be vital to their very existence. Clearly, if the United States is faced with the loss of Persian Gulf oil or either superpower is confronted with a Third World nuclear threat, direct intervention would be undertaken for self-protection. Nevertheless, for perhaps the first time in history, the dominant powers in the world do not need and cannot be militarily conquered by the lesser powers of the world. Such an eventuality cannot help but lessen the competition for the Third World while promoting caution lest the superpowers directly confront one another. In this situation the use of proxies to achieve limited ends and to avoid direct conflict between the superpowers can readily be understood.

Proxies are also increasingly important because neither of the superpowers has enough military resources to meet all of the commitments it maintains in the Third World. The largest share of the U.S. military effort is devoted to the defense of western Europe. Much of the remaining conventional preparations deal with contingencies involving the Persian Gulf and, to a lesser extent, Central America. As the Korean and Vietnam Wars so forcefully demonstrated, even a "limited" conflict in a nonvital area can seriously drain U.S. resources to the point that the nation's ability to meet more central concerns is called into question. It is little wonder that one of the strongest opponents to direct military intervention of U.S. troops to less than vital areas is the U.S. military itself.[4] Similarly, the Soviet Union must balance its most important commitments (preserving its position in Eastern Europe, defending the border with the People's Republic of China) with less significant interests throughout the Third World. Afghanistan has proved to be a costly effort for the Soviet Union that may have already constrained the Kremlin's policy choices in other, more important areas. The Soviets cannot afford many other commitments with similar costs.

If the superpowers cannot meet their existing commitments in the Third World it would appear that they have three choices open to them. First, they could reduce their commitments to a level commensurate with their available resources. The problem with this approach is that it would mean the sacrifice of a great number of important interests by the superpower choosing this policy. So long as the United States and the Soviet Union consider themselves to be great powers, such a voluntary curtailment of their interests is not likely. Second, the United States and the Soviet Union could raise the levels of their military expenditures to meet the commitments they maintain. Given the high cost of conventional weaponry, domestic opposition in the United States, and the meager (and unsure) returns from Third World adventures, neither the Soviet Union nor the United States can be expected to choose this policy. Finally, both superpowers can employ proxies to narrow the gap between commitments and capability. While there are many problems inherent in this approach (especially for the United States), it is easy to see why getting others to meet one's own commitments is an option that would appeal to both the Soviet Union and the United States.

The increasing use of proxies by the United States and the Soviet Union can also be explained by the nature of much of the Third World. With a few notable exceptions, Third World armies tend to be relatively small and weak. Their experience is often limited to internal, policing functions. As such, many Third World armies are especially poor in the use of armor and air power. Should a conflict arise between two armies, the introduction of a few thousand well-trained and disciplined troops on one side can often provide the margin of victory and do so in a relatively short time.

Furthermore, many Third World states are characterized by very low levels of meaningful political participation and penetration of government power. Their regimes often lack legitimacy or established procedures of succession. With the government in effect limited to a few individuals in the capital city, the prospect of assassination or coup d'état becomes the greatest threat to the continued survival of the regime (and of the interests of the superpower supporting that regime). Because these threats (like the regime they challenge) are so narrowly based, the introduction of a few hundred well-trained proxies can be a critical element in determining the survival of the government. Depending on the behavior of the leadership, the proxies could defend the regime against internal threats or act to replace the regime with one more amenable to its patron's interests. In any event, the knowledge that their continued existence in power depends on the support of the proxy forces should, in most cases, be sufficient to make certain that the Third World's leaders' policies are in line with their protectors' wishes.

The significance of proxies has also been enhanced due to the nature of the U.S.-Soviet competition in the Third World. Both superpowers recognize that a critical means of gaining influence in the Third World lies in meeting the security concerns of friendly Third World leadership elites. Both the United States and the Soviet Union realize that proxies can play a central role in meeting and raising those security concerns. The difference between the superpowers lies in the role that threatening and defending Third World regimes with proxies must play. For the Soviet Union, manipulating the security concern of Third World leaders (often with proxies) represents the best way it can extend its influence throughout the Third World. By making short-term security considerations paramount (something well within Soviet capabilities), the Kremlin is able to prevent the competition for influence in the Third World from moving into other areas where the United States could capitalize on its strengths. For the United States, meeting the short-term challenge presented by Soviet proxies is necessary so that it can exploit its superiority in other aspects of its competition with the Soviet Union, most notably its economic strength. Although the United States realizes that it has long-term advantages over the Soviet Union, it also recognizes that those strengths are meaningless if it cannot protect friendly Third World regimes in the short term. The result is that security considerations, and the role of proxies in affecting them, is likely to remain a crucial element in the superpower competition for the Third World.

Finally, proxies are becoming increasingly important because they are often in a better position to meet superpowers' objectives than are the superpowers themselves. The advantages of proxies depend of course on the specific proxy employed, but it is nevertheless possible to delineate some general strengths they provide. Since they are by definition not superpowers, proxies can intervene in Third World conflicts with less visibility and worldwide opposition. Their lack of an imperialist past and their less threatening capability for challenging the sovereignty of Third World states make them more welcome than forces from the Soviet Union or the United States. The acceptance of proxies is further enhanced when they come from a Third World state, speak the language of the country they are supporting, and/or are of a race similar to that of the belligerents. Finally, proxies might be better suited for fighting in the type of Third World conflict they are sent to than either the Soviet Union or the United

States. The unorthodox tactics of guerrilla warfare and counterinsurgency might be accomplished more effectively by proxy forces trained in this area than by the more conventionally trained armies of the superpowers.

The Cases

Cases that illustrate the use of proxies in military conflict that will be considered more fully include Angola in 1975, Ethiopia in 1977–78, and Zaire in 1977–78. In the Angolan episode, 15,000 Cuban troops, equipped and transported by the Soviets, provided the margin of victory for the Soviet-backed faction in an ongoing civil war. In Ethiopia, 15,000–20,000 Cuban troops, equipped, transported, and *led* by the Soviet Union defended a beleaguered pro-Soviet regime from a very nearly successful invasion by Somalia. The Zairian case examined how France, in 1977, encouraged and assisted the intervention of 1,500 Moroccan troops to Zaire's Shaba province, where they defeated an armed force bent on toppling the Mobutu regime. When the invaders reappeared in a more potent form a year later, the United States backed and provided critical support to French and Belgian troops, enabling them to intervene and protect Zaire's pro-Western regime.

These cases were selected because they collectively demonstrate the value of proxies in furthering the interests of other powers. In each case, important interests of major powers required prompt military action. For political reasons the major powers were unwilling to intervene directly. Only by employing proxies were the major powers able to secure their interests at a justifiable cost. Moreover, these cases illustrate the respective strengths and weaknesses of the United States and the Soviet Union in employing proxies. As will be seen, while both superpowers retain the capability to use proxies in the Third World, their capabilities are far from equal.

The Two Invasions of Shaba

The two invasions of Zaire's Shaba province in 1977 and 1978 demonstrate the importance of proxies in defending a strategic state that is too weak to protect itself.[5] Both invasions were launched by Katangese exiles based in Angola. The exiles were descendants of those who unsuccessfully fought for secession from Zaire in the early 1960s when Zaire was called the Congo and the Shaba province was known as Katanga. Organized in a group named the FNLC (Front de Liberation Nationale Congolaise), the rebels sought to replace Zaire's President Mobutu with someone more sympathetic to their demands for autonomy in Shaba.

The first invasion of Zaire began on March 8, 1977, when small groups of Katangese crossed into Shaba province by foot and bicycle. Since the rebels belonged to the same ethnic group as Shaba's inhabitants, their presence was not immediately noticed. After entering Shaba, the approximately 1,500-man force quickly overran several key towns. Encountering virtually no resistance from the 70,000-man Zairian army, the Katangese reached a point only twenty-five miles from the provincial capital (and mining center) of Kolwezi.

While the invasion itself hardly came as a shock, many observers were surprised that Zaire's 70,000-man, North Korean–trained army could not halt the advance of 1,500 lightly armed insurgents. Although the army subsequently pointed to poor roads to excuse their slow response, there was no denying the abysmal performance of the Zairian forces. Beset by purges and poor pay, the Zairian army responded to orders to defend Shaba with defiance and mutiny. Elite units that might have acted more effectively remained in Zaire's capital because of President Mobutu's ever-present fear of a coup d'état.[6] In the meantime, the rebels expanded and tightened their hold on Shaba.

By the end of March the situation in Zaire was becoming increasingly desperate. One third of Shaba was already occupied by the FNLC. Even more alarming was the continuing rebel advance on Kolwezi. Should that strategic city fall, Zaire's mining operations and thousands of European inhabitants would be threatened. Such a shock might be enough to cause the downfall of the Mobutu regime. In this context, with the Zairian Army showing no signs of coming to life, President Mobutu appealed for outside assistance to save his government.

Mobutu's plea for help was directed primarily at the states with the greatest economic and political stakes in Zaire: Belgium, the United States, and France. At first glance, Belgium would appear to be a likely source of assistance. With over $1 billion invested in Zaire and over two thousand citizens in the Kolwezi area (Zaire had been a colony of Belgium), Belgium had the most to lose as a result of the Shaba invasion.[7] In spite of all this, Belgium quickly rejected the prospect of providing direct assistance to Zaire. The Belgians felt a profound distaste for the Mobutu regime and did not want to be placed in the uncomfortable position of ensuring its survival. Moreover, with elections upcoming, the Belgian government was especially wary of becoming involved in an unpopular intervention. As long as Belgian citizens were not yet attacked, Belgium chose to remain aloof from the fighting in Zaire.

The United States watched the unfolding events in Zaire with concern. Zaire's strategic location in central Africa and its vast mineral wealth (Zaire is the world's largest exporter of cobalt and industrial diamonds) made it a country of considerable importance to the West. The United States was also disturbed by allegations made by President Mobutu that the Cubans were behind the invasion. Coming so soon after their victory in Angola, another Cuban success would be a serious blow to U.S. interests in Africa.

And yet the United States also decided against directly helping President Mobutu. Influenced by Vietnam and considerations of human rights, the newly elected Carter administration was not willing to intervene directly in another war to preserve a corrupt regime. The Carter administration dismissed the assertion that the Cubans were behind the invasion, preferring to believe that the crisis in Zaire was an African problem requiring an African solution. With the East-West dimension of the conflict minimized, and the threat posed by the ragtag insurgents seen as relatively mild, the United States limited itself to an offer of $15 million in "nonlethal" equipment (for example, rations and trucks).[8]

The Belgian and U.S. decisions effectively to ignore President Mobutu's request for assistance focused attention on the French. With few French citizens living in Zaire and with a relatively modest financial investment in the country (about $20 million) it would not ordinarily be expected that France would play a major role in the crisis. Nevertheless, the French were intensely concerned about the unfolding events in Zaire. In part, their concern stemmed from traditional French interests in African stability. By defending President Mobutu, the French would reassert their commitment (backed by garrisons of French troops based in several African states) to protect existing regimes. Moreover, Zaire was of particular interest to France because of its enormous economic potential. Equally important, the French were convinced that the insurgent threat could be defeated with minimal effort.

French interest in Zaire, however, was not synonymous with French intervention. While the French might gain influence as a result of a successful effort to defend President Mobutu, such a gain was considered simply not worth the risks and costs of sending troops to fight in Zaire. Thus France, like the United States and Belgium, was apparently prepared not to become involved in the rapidly escalating crisis.

At this point the role of Morocco became critical. Unlike the other states observing Zaire's plight, Morocco was willing to send troops to save President Mobutu. Its willingness to become directly involved in the conflict is not difficult to understand. The leader of Morocco, King Hassan, was genuinely concerned about the extent of Communist intervention in Africa. The prospect of a Cuban-backed movement's overthrowing a pro-Western state so soon after Angola frightened the Moroccan king. Furthermore, King Hassan sought support for the West in Morocco's own struggle with rebels seeking to establish an independent state in the Moroccan-claimed Western Sahara. A demonstration that its troops could successfully serve Western interests in Africa would do much to ensure friendly treatment for Moroccan requests.

Morocco's willingness to intervene directly in Zaire depended upon two conditions' being met. First, Morocco required logistical support for its troops. The Moroccan armed forces did not have anywhere near the airlift capability to fly large numbers of soldiers to Zaire in time to meet the rebel threat. Second, Morocco required political support. As a small African state with no direct interests in Zaire, Morocco needed the backing of a major Western power to justify its actions. Despite King Hassan's enthusiasm for intervening, if these conditions were not met there would be no Moroccan troops sent to Zaire.

While it is not clear who took the initiative, the French agreed to meet the Moroccan conditions, thus laying the basis for the subsequent intervention. In early April, approximately one month after the initial Katangese incursion, 1,500 Moroccan troops were flown to Zaire in French aircraft. The French also sent twenty secret service men to organize Kolwezi's defense (should it be necessary) and additional arms for the Zairian army.

The arrival of the Moroccan troops had an immediate impact. The listless Zairian Army began fighting with vigor and, together with the Moroccans, was able to stiffen its resistance to the FNLC. Having failed to achieve a lightning *fait accompli* victory and realizing that the momentum had now shifted, the badly outnumbered FNLC melted back into the countryside or returned to Angola. The threat to Mobutu that appeared so frightening just a short time ago disappeared without a single major battle's being fought.

Nevertheless, the successful defense of Shaba had a number of serious qualifications. First, although the rebels retreated they were not defeated. Their military infrastructure remained intact, and they could still count on the support of many of Shaba's people. Second, the insurgents retained the support of Angola because of Zaire's continuing assistance to the Front for the National Liberation of Angola [FNLA]) and Cuba. Finally, and most important, the conditions that led to the initial Shaba invasion were not corrected. Instead of instituting reform to deal with the economic crisis and the rampant corruption, President Mobutu contented himself with a purge of those he felt were responsible for the near success of the 1977 invasion. The result was an even further weakening of the Zairian armed forces at a time when the conditions for a repeat invasion were ripe.

The second invasion of Shaba began on May 11, 1978, when some 4,500 FNLC troops entered Zaire from bases in Angola. Once in Shaba they joined with hundreds of FNLC irregulars who had been infiltrating the province for months preceding the invasion. Although the attack appeared at first to be a repeat of the March 1977 affair, it quickly became apparent that there were differences. The invasion force was larger, better organized, and equipped with more modern weapons than its predecessor. Most important was the speed with which it acted. Having been cheated out of victory once before because (in part) of its slow progress in Shaba, this time the FNLC headed straight for Kolwezi. The change in strategy proved effective as, despite the presence of 8,000 Zairian troops (who true to form offered little resistance), the insurgents were able to capture Kolwezi just a few days after the invasion began.

Once in Kolwezi, the FNLC committed a fatal error. Instead of consolidating their gains and using their strategic position for further attacks on the Mobutu regime, the discipline of the FNLC broke down. FNLC insurgents (along with some Zairian troops) rampaged through the city. Scores of Europeans and

Africans were brutally murdered in actions that were publicized throughout the world. This massacre radically changed the importance of the Shaba invasion for the West. Those arguing that the situation in Zaire was essentially a local matter with no wider implications were undercut by the horror of the ongoing murders. While the West might have accepted the fall of the increasingly corrupt Mobutu regime, it could not ignore the reign of terror following the fall of Kolwezi.

The Kolwezi massacre galvanized Belgium, France, and the United States into action. Of the three, the Belgians were the most reluctant to intervene, fearing that such a move would be seen as approval of the Mobutu regime. Nevertheless, with over two thousand Belgians living in the Kolwezi area, they had little choice. The French were not bothered with similar inhibitions. They saw this second invasion as a further opportunity to demonstrate their role as protector of the Francophone countries and of Western interests in general in Africa. Moreover, the French may have felt that an effective response on their part would persuade President Mobutu to increase France's role in the mineral-rich Zairian economy at the expense of the cautious Belgians. As the Belgian foreign minister caustically remarked, French attention appeared to be directed "towards African countries that possess important resources." In any event, with the Moroccans not available, all that stopped the Belgians and French from quickly intervening was adequate air transport.

Like the Belgian response, the U.S. reaction to the second invasion of Shaba was in marked contrast to its policy of aloofness only a year before. Instead of divisive debate leading to inaction, the Carter administration was united in its belief that a forceful response to save President Mobutu was necessary. The reasons for this view varied. For those who favored a regional understanding of African affairs with an emphasis on humanitarian concerns (for example, Ambassador Andrew Young), Zaire presented the opportunity for the United States to save African and European lives without provoking an East-West confrontation. For those who favored a more geopolitical view (for example, National Security Advisor Zbigniew Brzezinski), Zaire could demonstrate that the United States had overcome its post-Vietnam malaise and could successfully defeat communist-inspired aggression against pro-Western governments. Finally, for President Carter, the invasion of Zaire presented the opportunity to answer his critics who claimed that he could not act decisively in a crisis.[9]

The actual intervention reflected the motives of each of the participants. The United States, with the least directly at stake in Zaire, played a supporting role by providing eighteen C-141 transport aircraft to the French and Belgian troops. The French made use of the planes first as 400 troops of the French Foreign Legion parachuted into Kolwezi on May 19. Once in Zaire they quickly engaged the FNLC in battle, forcing them to retreat for the first time since the invasion began. With the immediate threat to Kolwezi stalemated, the Belgians intervened on May 21. Approximately 1,200 Belgian troops flew to Shaba where they proceeded to evacuate the European residents from the combat area. Reflecting the ambivalence in which they held their mission, the Belgians left Zaire after just a few days without having once fought with the FNLC.

The intervention proved a resounding success. Despite some grumblings from the Belgians that the French interfered with their flights to Zaire, the two European powers managed to cooperate enough with each other and with the remnants of the Zairian army to defeat the rebel threat. Within days after the intervention, the FNLC was ejected from Kolwezi and forced to retreat to its bases in Zambia and Angola. Over two thousand Europeans were transported to safety by the Belgian forces. President Mobutu's regime was once again saved by outside assistance.

The cost of the intervention was relatively slight. The Belgians suffered no casualties, while the French Foreign Legion reported two dead. The rebels were harder hit with at least 300 killed. The necessity for the speed of the intervention was perhaps best underscored by the casualties of the hostages. Despite the rapidity of the rescue effort, 136 Europeans were massacred by the insurgents.[10]

The successful defense of Shaba did not solve the long-term security problems of President Mobutu's regime. After two invasions it was painfully clear that Zaire could not defend itself and that the Katangan threat was still very much alive. Since the French and Belgians were unwilling to establish a permanent presence in Zaire, an International African Force (IAF) was created to defend Shaba from further incursions. The IAF was composed of troops from former French colonies, with the earliest contingents coming from Morocco (1,500 troops) and Senegal (600 troops). Logistical support is provided by the United States, which (together with Saudi Arabia) finances the IAF. While far from a total solution to President Mobutu's plight, the IAF permitted the rapid disengagement of Belgian and French troops from Zaire and provides a modicum of security for Shaba's borders.[11]

Angola

Located in southwest Africa, Angola is a large (nearly 500,000 square miles) country sparsely populated with 6.5 million people. Rich in oil, diamonds, and coffee, Angola has potential that has always exceeded the reality of its poverty. Beginning in 1975, the relative obscurity of Angola ended as a local struggle for power transformed itself into a proxy war with international repercussions.

The origins of this conflict can be found in the nearly five hundred years of Portuguese rule. The Portuguese governed their vast colony through the "divide and rule" tactics used so successfully by the British. Unlike the British, however, the Portuguese did not prepare any individual or group to assume power once they had departed. Consequently, once the Portuguese government collapsed in April 1974 and efforts to bring about a peaceful transition to Angolan independence broke down in early 1975, there was no obvious or legitimate authority to replace the Portuguese. Instead, the three separate movements that had engaged in the anticolonial struggle now confronted each other to see who would rule Angola.

These three movements were the MPLA (Popular Movement for the Liberation of Angola), FNLA (Front for the National Liberation of Angola), and UNITA (National Union for the Total Independence of Angola). The MPLA (under the leadership of Dr. Agostinho Neto) drew its support from the Soviet bloc, Cuba (which first provided aid in the mid-1960s), the Portuguese left wing, and urban intellectuals. Its power base was located in the center of the country and included the capital city of Luanda. The FNLA received support from Zaire, the United States, and the People's Republic of China. Led by Holden Roberto, the FNLA's influence was concentrated in the north and was considered to be the principal rival to the MPLA. Jonas Savimbi's UNITA received its support not from foreign sources but from the Ovimbundu tribe located in southern Angola. Although the Ovimbundus made up 40 percent of Angola's population, UNITA suffered from lack of training and equipment, making it the weakest militarily of the three movements.

Despite their differences, the MPLA, FNLA, and UNITA had much in common. All followed the same basic economic and political policies. Each was essentially a nationalist party with a multiethnic leadership. Although they were regionally and tribally based, each of the movements denounced separatism and attempted to appeal to the Angolan people as a whole. Slight differences in ideological emphasis existed, but in the main their conflict was not one of ideas but of power.

The first phase of the war in Angola began with the failure of the Portuguese-sponsored ALVOR agreement in January 1975. The agreement was to have united the three movements politically and militarily but was undermined by the constant fighting that followed it. Much of this fighting centered around the FNLA's attempts to evict the MPLA from Luanda. The stronger FNLA might have succeeded (and thus taken control of Angola) except for Soviet support of the MPLA.

Beginning in March 1975, the Soviets greatly increased arms shipments to the beleaguered MPLA. Strengthened with these weapons, the MPLA successfully preserved its position in Luanda and was able to attack both the FNLA and UNITA in May. The MPLA counterattack brought UNITA into the fighting for the first time, precipitating the uneasy alliance between UNITA and the FNLA.

Although the MPLA held a dominant military position by the summer of 1975, its success was hardly assured. In July 1975, Zaire sent troops to assist the FNLA, and in August a small South African detachment entered Angola to protect a hydroelectric plant. Also in August the United States, which had thus far not provided any military aid to the Angolan movements, began delivering the first arms of a $32 million covert aid project to the FNLA and UNITA.[12] In light of this increasing threat and the fact that the MPLA could not operate much of the Soviet equipment (especially armor and artillery), the MPLA leadership requested that Soviet troops be sent to Angola.

Perhaps fearing the U.S. response, the Soviets refused the MPLA's request but suggested that they ask the Cubans for assistance. Castro agreed to help, and the first contingent of about fifty troops arrived in late July. By the end of September, as many as three thousand Cuban troops accompanied by several hundred Soviet advisers were actively assisting the MPLA.[13] Their involvement enabled the MPLA to overcome the renewed FNLA-UNITA threat and to extend its influence to the Angolan ports (thus precluding large-scale rearmament to its enemies). In October 1975 it appeared that the MPLA would achieve a de facto victory before the scheduled independence in November.

The tide of war took an abrupt turn, however, when South Africa directly intervened in the Angolan conflict on October 23. Approximately 1,500–2,000 regular South African troops led a column of UNITA, FNLA, and mercenary fighters up southern Angola. Although the South Africans did not commit their air force and armor, and played only a supportive role in the fighting, they succeeded in forcing the MPLA into a full retreat by November. In the meantime, a joint FNLA-Zairian force in the north had come to within a few miles of Luanda. The MPLA, whose fortunes had looked so bright just a short time ago, was now battling for its very existence.

The confusion on the battlefield was reflected in Angola's celebration of independence on November 11. Two governments were proclaimed that day. The MPLA (based in Luanda) established the People's Republic of Angola and the FNLA-UNITA coalition jointly set up the Democratic Republic of Angola (from their base in the city of Huambo). Since Portugal had ceded power only to the "Angolan people" and the Organization of African Unity (OAU) demanded a government comprised of all three movements, neither group could legally claim legitimacy. As a result, the MPLA was recognized by only the Soviet bloc states and by fewer than a third of the African countries; the FNLA-UNITA government was recognized by no one.

Even before formal independence, the Soviets and their allies realized that an internationally recognized government of Angola could only be achieved by a decisive military victory. With the MPLA facing a major military defeat and perhaps political oblivion, the Soviets and the Cubans acted quickly. Beginning in mid-October and accelerating dramatically after the South African intervention, Soviet and Cuban support flooded into Angola. The Soviets sent (mostly by sea) enormous quantities of rockets, tanks, small arms and even a dozen MiG-21 fighter aircraft. In early November, thousands of Cuban troops began to be flown from Cuba to Angola. When U.S. pressure prevented Cuban planes from refueling at Barbados, the Soviets supplied long-range IL-62 aircraft to Cuba (this episode may have heightened Cuban interest in securing a foothold in Grenada) and facilitated the transport of Cuban troops by sea. As a result, at the height of the fighting in January 1976, over eleven thousand Cuban troops (according to Western estimates) were in

Angola. The figure may even be higher, as Castro asserted that some thirty-six thousand Cuban troops were in Angola in 1976 (Western estimates put the peak at twenty thousand).[14]

The combination of Soviet arms and Cuban personnel dramatically changed the fortunes of the MPLA. Bolstered by its foreign support, the MPLA began an offensive in December that its opponents (despite some early victories) could not halt. Recognizing the tide of events (and influenced by Vietnam), the United States Senate voted to end additional assistance to the FNLA and UNITA. On January 23, the now isolated South Africans withdrew from the conflict. By February, the Soviet-Cuban-MPLA onslaught had essentially won the war.

The MPLA's victory on the battlefield (especially in the face of South African intervention) had an immediate political impact. The OAU voted to recognize the MPLA as the legal government of Angola on February 2. The European Economic Community (EEC) followed on February 17, and less than a week later Portugal recognized the MPLA. The United States continued to withhold recognition on the grounds that the MPLA survived only because of the continuing presence of Cuban troops. In spite of the U.S. decision, there was little denying that the Soviet-Cuban-backed MPLA had succeeded in becoming the internationally recognized government of Angola.

Ethiopia

The immediate origins of the Soviet-Cuban intervention in the Horn of Africa can be found in the 1974 coup d'état that deposed the Emperor Haile Selassie in Ethiopia. Prior to the coup, Ethiopia had been the closest ally of the United States in black Africa and had received the bulk of U.S. military aid directed toward that continent. The coup brought to power a military group (called the *Dergue*) that quickly adopted a Marxist, anti-Western stance. Although the United States continued to supply Ethiopia with arms (actually increasing from previous levels), it quickly became clear that the revolutionary, socialist regime in Ethiopia was uncomfortable with its U.S. ties. Not surprisingly, the *Dergue* turned increasingly to the Soviets for support.

At the time of the coup, the Soviets were the chief backer of Siad Barre's regime in Somalia. Somali irredentist claims on the Ethiopian province of the Ogaden (which was populated by ethnic Somalis but comprised about one-fifth of Ethiopian territory) had led to serious clashes between the two countries. The Soviets had no problem in supporting Somalia since, under Siad Barre, they were helping a "socialist" state against pro-Western, feudalistic Ethiopia. The coming to power of the *Dergue*, however, complicated Soviet policy and led to some delays in responding to Ethiopian overtures for assistance. The Soviets decided to proceed slowly, concluding a modest arms deal with the *Dergue* in December 1976 while holding up actual deliveries to see whether events would justify their risking strategic bases in Somalia for uncertain gains in Ethiopia.

In the end, the Soviets chose Ethiopia over Somalia for reasons not hard to understand. Ethiopia has approximately ten times the population and GNP of Somalia. Its location bordering several key states and its status as headquarters of the Organization of African Unity made it a better springboard for the spread of Soviet influence than was the case with Somalia. In supporting Ethiopia, the Soviets would be helping a state defend its borders (a policy supported by the OAU) rather than assisting in an illegal invasion. Because Ethiopia was more highly developed (some capitalism, and some industry) than the largely nomadic Somalia, in the eyes of the Soviets, it had a greater potential to produce a true Marxist revolution. Moreover, the Soviets were angry at the Somalis for refusing to join a federation of pro-Soviet states proposed by Fidel Castro (and including Ethiopia and South Yemen) in the Horn. Given this, when the pro-Soviet Haile Mariam Mengistu seized power in February 1977 (perhaps with Soviet encouragement), Moscow lost no time in providing military and political support.

The full realignment of Ethiopia from the United States to the Soviet Union became apparent in May 1977. During this month the United States suspended all military aid to Ethiopia in response to human rights violations and the expulsion of U.S. military advisors. The damage to the *Dergue* was far from serious, however, for the same month Mengistu concluded a major new arms agreement with the Soviets during a visit to Moscow. The arms agreement was valued at more than $500 million or nearly twice the arms assistance provided to Ethiopia by the United States since their military relationship began in 1952. Included in the agreement were MiG fighters, tanks, artillery, and armored personnel carriers.

Somalia reacted to the Soviet decision to arm Ethiopia with alarm. The Somali regime knew that a Soviet-backed Ethiopia was in a much better position to frustrate Somali aims of seizing the Ogaden than was the case with the U.S.-backed Selassie regime. This was due not only to the greater willingness of the Soviets to supply large amounts of sophisticated arms to the Ethiopians, but also to the Soviet ability to cripple the Somali military effort simply by withholding additional weapons and spare parts. At this point, the Somalis knew that if they had any hopes of military success in the Ogaden they had to act quickly before the strength of the Soviet Union could be brought to bear on the conflict. Any doubts the Somalis might have had about striking at Ethiopia were probably removed when on July 15 the United States (along with Britain and France) declared their willingness "in principle" to provide defensive weapons for Somalia.

The invasion of the Ogaden by Somali regular forces (a guerrilla conflict had been escalating in the region for months) came in midsummer 1977. The Somalis chose the timing of their attack well. Their armed forces were at the peak of readiness, while the Ethiopians, having been cut off by the United States and not yet receiving appreciable quantities of arms from the Soviets, were between suppliers. The result was a series of lightning Somali victories that put much of the Ogaden under Somalia's control by mid-August.

The Soviet reaction to the Somali invasion also came in August. In an article in *Tass* the Soviets revealed their decision to back Ethiopia over Somalia when they labeled the Somalis as aggressors in the conflict. The Soviets then quietly ended all arms shipments to Somalia and publicly revealed their decision to do so in October. The Somalis reacted to the Soviet policies by renouncing their treaty of friendship and cooperation with the Soviet Union in November. By that time, over Soviet objections and without Western assistance, the Somalis had apparently achieved a fait accompli victory in the Ogaden.

The Soviets, however, had a great deal at stake in their newly found client Ethiopia and were not about to lose their investment so easily. While the Ethiopian armies might have been routed, Moscow still commanded the loyalty of the Ethiopian leadership (who, after all, had nowhere else to turn) and were thus committed to that leadership's continued survival. Their most pressing problem concerned the city of Harar deep in Ethiopian territory. In November, Somali forces were mounting an armored and artillery attack on the city. Soviet arms were being rushed to Ethiopia by sea and air to stave off the assault, but there was not enough time for the U.S.-trained Ethiopian forces to learn their use and put them into action against the advancing Somalis. If Harar fell and the Somalis continued their onslaught, the survival of the Mengistu government—and the Soviet position in Ethiopia—could very well collapse. It was time for the Cubans.

Cubans began arriving in Ethiopia in late 1977. They came by air (from Cuba and Angola) and by sea (in Soviet ships). By November, their numbers reached approximately one thousand. They were already well versed in the use of Soviet weapons and were quickly put into battle against the Somalis in Harar. Their intervention proved decisive as the Somali offensive was halted before Harar fell.

With the immediate threat ended, the Soviets turned to the task of pushing back the Somalis. While the United States and other Western countries continued to refuse to supply Somalia with weapons (or to permit their allies to do so) as long as Somali troops were in Ethiopian territory, the Soviets acted. They began with a massive sea- and airlift of arms to Ethiopia beginning on November 24. In the airlift the Soviets flew over several countries and filed false flight plans to make their deliveries. Over twenty Soviet ships were deployed off the Ethiopian coast to protect the military supply operation.[15]

The Soviet effort was more than just for show. The weapons Moscow delivered (nearly $1 billion worth, or three times the amount supplied to Ethiopia by the United States in twenty-five years) were well used by the Cubans and the rapidly trained Ethiopians. In mid-January, an Ethiopian force, supplemented by an estimated ten thousand Cubans and led by Soviet Gen. Grigoriy Barisov (who previously headed the Soviet military mission to Somalia), began their counteroffensive. Spearheaded by Cuban mechanized units (under the overall command of Cuban Gen. Arnaldo Ochoa, who had been in Angola), the Somalis were forced to retreat. With their pleas for Western help still going unanswered, the Somalis announced their withdrawal from the Ogaden on March 9, 1978.

Having dealt with the Somali threat, the Soviets turned their attention to the ongoing conflict in the Ethiopian province of Eritrea. Ever since Ethiopia annexed the former colony of Eritrea in 1962, it has attempted to suppress Eritrean demands for greater autonomy or independence. By the time the *Dergue* took power, most of Eritrea was in rebel hands, with government troops restricted to only a few major cities. The Soviets knew that should the Eritrean revolt succeed not only would it cause Ethiopia to lose its only outlet to the sea, it would also encourage other secessionist movements throughout the state that could ultimately topple the *Dergue* (and the Soviet position).

That many of the Eritrean rebels were Cuban-trained, Marxist, and oppressed by the Ethiopian state did not provide them with protection from the Soviet-Cuban-Ethiopian forces. In June 1978, a Soviet-led and equipped Ethiopian army (the Cubans apparently balked at a direct involvement because of their past experiences as advisers to the Eritreans) once again confronted an enemy of the *Dergue*. Again they were successful, as the Eritrean rebels, who had been on the verge of victory, were soundly defeated and forced back into guerrilla warfare.

The Soviet-backed Ethiopian regime is still not out of danger. Guerrillas in the Ogaden and Eritrea continue to harass Ethiopian troops. Provincial secession movements remain a problem, as does the internal stability of the *Dergue*. Despite these difficulties, it is impossible to deny the critical gains the Soviets and the Cubans brought to the *Dergue* and especially to its leader, Colonel Mengistu. They transformed a country racked by invasion, rebellion, and secession into a country that has preserved the sanctity of its borders, maintained the survival of its ruling elite, and kept its empire intact. One may quarrel with Soviet methods, but, at least from the *Dergue*'s perspective, one cannot fail to appreciate their results.

Issues in the Case Studies

Two major issues relevant to the understanding of proxy war stem from the Zairian and Angolan case studies. In the Zairian case the issue raised was whether the Katangese were operating as Cuban (or Soviet) proxies when they invaded Zaire. Aside from its geopolitical implications, the issue is significant in that if the Katangese were proxies, their intervention in Zaire would mean that proxies were fighting proxies. On one side of the dispute was the Carter administration, which argued that the Cubans trained, equipped, and encouraged the Katangese invasion. Opposing this view are those who argue that the invasion was an independent act by disgruntled Katangese who had little or no outside support. This view is most strongly expressed by Fidel Castro, who vehemently denied any involvement in the invasion and declared that he did all he could to stop it.[16]

Despite the intensity of this controversy, some important points were not at issue. As part of its involvement in the Angolan civil war, Cuba supplied and trained Katangese exiles in Angola in 1975–76. Cuban troops also fought with the Katangese insurgents on the side of the MPLA in the last few months of the Angolan civil war. After the MPLA victory the Cubans maintained a large presence in the border regions (with Zaire) populated by the Katangese. Nevertheless, no Cubans (or other foreign troops) accompanied the Katangese into Zaire. The issue, therefore, concerned the nature of the Cuban relationship with the Katangese since 1976 and, more specifically, whether the Cubans assisted and/or encouraged the Katangese invasions of 1977 and 1978.

The argument denying Cuban involvement in the second invasion of Shaba is not without merit. While Castro's assertion that he broke off contact with the Katangese exiles following the end of the Angolan war is almost certainly untrue, the degree and direction of influence maintained by Cuba over the Katangese rebels are open to question. Supporting Castro's case is the lack of influence any outside power could be expected to maintain over the rebels because of divisions within the FNLC itself. Since the FNLC was filled with internal discord it is difficult to see how the Cubans (who occasionally were caught between fighting factions) could control the organization to the point of organizing an invasion.[17]

Moreover, it is argued in Castro's defense, the invasion of Zaire was not in Cuba's interests. Attacks back and forth across the Angolan border complicated Cuba's goal of pacifying the countryside and protecting Neto's regime in Angola. An invasion would certainly exacerbate the already tense Angolan security situation, making Cuba's task that much more difficult. Therefore, Castro asserts, what influence he did have over the FNLC was used to try to prevent the invasion. In support of this, Senate sources confirm that on May 17 (soon after the invasion began), Castro informed the United States that he only learned of the rebels' plans in early April and tried unsuccessfully to stop them.[18]

The Carter administration's case for Cuban involvement was based on a CIA report, the declassified version of which was released publicly in mid-June 1978. The report itself was not based on any "hard" evidence (for example, satellite surveillance) but rather on information collected from prisoners, diplomatic channels, and other African countries. Its conclusion included the following points:

> Since the summer of 1976 the Soviets and the Cubans pressed President Neto of Angola to support incursions into Zaire.

Cubans provided military training to the Katangese rebels before the 1977 and 1978 invasions.

The Cuban presence in Zaire was "pervasive"—very little could be done without its direct involvement.

The East Germans may have also been involved in the training of the Katangese for several years.

The Soviets have also been indirectly involved in the training of the Katangese (presumably through the East Germans and Cubans).

Both the 1977 and 1978 invasions took place with the cooperation of the Angolan government and Cubans.[19]

Whatever one's view as to the responsibility of the Cubans for the Shaba invasion, it is clear that the CIA information played a crucial role in the U.S. decision to assist the Franco-Belgian intervention. The CIA first asserted that the Cubans played a "vital" role in the Katangese invasion on May 19—the day the airlift was approved. Further information implicating the Cubans (as well as criticisms of the U.S. role in Shaba from the Congress) prompted President Carter to state publicly on May 25 that the Cubans trained the Katangese and "did nothing" to stop the attack.[20]

While critics continued to challenge the president's assertions, subsequent information gathered by U.S. intelligence appeared to placate all but the most fervent believers in Cuban innocence that there indeed was significant and substantial Cuban involvement in at least the second Shaba invasion and probably in the first as well.[21] The motive for Cuban (and indirect Soviet) support appears to have been to pressure Zaire's President Mobutu to stop supporting remaining FNLA troops in northern Angola. Following the second invasion, the Angolan goal was achieved as Mobutu agreed to halt further aid to the FNLA in exchange for Angola's (and presumably Cuba's and the Soviet Union's) preventing further Katangese incursions. Since the agreement, the Shaba border has been relatively quiet, giving additional credibility to the view that the Cubans maintain more influence over the Katangese rebels than they admit.

One of the major issues in the Angolan affair is the extent to which the Soviet-Cuban intervention was provoked by the United States and South Africa. Many have argued that large scale Soviet-Cuban involvement came about only in *response* to U.S. and then South African interference. According to this view, had the United States and South Africa remained aloof from the Angolan civil war, Soviet-Cuban intervention would have been minimal, the United States would not have suffered a political defeat, and a proxy war might have been avoided.

The record of external intervention indicates this view is mistaken. While the involvement of each of the outside powers influenced the others', the United States and South Africa were not fully or even primarily responsible for the

Soviet-Cuban intervention in Angola. Rather, that intervention can best be explained by the Soviet Union's desire to ensure an MPLA victory with the assistance of Cuban forces.

Those who blame the United States for the proxy war in Angola point first to the decision of the "40" Committee in January 1975 to give $300,000 to Roberto's FNLA. This decision, it is argued, accounted for the large Soviet escalation in arms deliveries in March. In mid-July 1975 Secretary of State Henry Kissinger requested $79 million in aid for Zaire, a good part of which was earmarked for arms for the FNLA. It is argued that this action and the approval of additional funds for covert aid to the FNLA precipitated an arms race with the Soviets that the United States subsequently lost. As for the Cubans, Fidel Castro (and others) have asserted that their presence was prompted by the South African invasion of October 23.

The flaws in these arguments are revealed by relating the extent and timing of the Soviet-Cuban involvement to Western actions. First, it is difficult to accept the notion that a mere $300,000 for political action (not arms) given to the FNLA prompted the multimillion-dollar flood of weaponry from the Soviets in March and April. This is especially true since the Soviets (as described previously) had already provided more than $50 million in aid to the MPLA before the U.S. decision was made. Furthermore, the magnitude of the March–April Soviet escalation indicates it was decided upon before the U.S. assistance to the FNLA became known.[22]

Similarly, increased Soviet arms deliveries and the arrival of several hundred Cuban troops during the summer of 1975 cannot be attributed to the U.S. decision to send additional weapons to the FNLA in mid-July. The mobilization, transport, and equipping of such large numbers of troops would take at least six weeks, placing the decision to send them to Angola in May.[23] Furthermore, while the U.S. decision to increase its involvement came in July, significant arms supplies to the FNLA did not arrive until September—well after the Soviet-Cuban escalation. It is also difficult to understand why the Soviets, if they were only responding to U.S. involvement, rejected Secretary of State Kissinger's plea (made before March 1975) that both the United States and the Soviet Union stay out of Angola.[24]

The role of South Africa in causing the massive Soviet-Cuban intervention that eventually won the war for the MPLA has also been grossly exaggerated. The magnitude of the Soviet-Cuban involvement increased dramatically in early October—three weeks *before* the South African invasion (and a month before Angola proclaimed its independence). At the time of the South African intervention there were already large numbers of well-armed Cubans fighting with the MPLA. While it is true that the South African invasion produced an even greater Soviet-Cuban response, the fact remains the Soviets and the Cubans were already deeply and directly involved in Angola *before* the South Africans became a major factor in the conflict.[25]

The most likely explanation for the series of Soviet-Cuban escalations beginning in the spring of 1975 was the Soviet-Cuban determination to ensure a victory for the MPLA. This required the Soviet-Cuban forces first to protect the MPLA base in Luanda from attacks by UNITA and FNLA so that the MPLA could control the capital when independence was proclaimed. Subsequent Soviet-Cuban assistance increased markedly when it was clear that the United States would not involve itself in a meaningful way and that South Africa would not confront the Soviets and Cubans alone. This Soviet-Cuban assistance (which in dollar terms was at least five times greater than the amount of aid provided by the United States) thereupon enabled the MPLA to achieve its final victory virtually unopposed by the West.[26] As such, outside powers (with the possible exception of China) were neither a major catalyst nor an ongoing rationale for Soviet-Cuban involvement. To the contrary, a more determined Western response (especially before Spring 1975) would more likely have lessened rather than increased the Soviet-Cuban involvement.

Lessons of the Case Studies

Although the U.S. and Soviet use of proxies took place in unique contexts, they provide useful lessons in understanding the overall nature of proxy wars. These lessons are best understood by focusing on the U.S. and Soviet use of proxies separately and then considering what generalizations about proxy wars emerge from their combined experience. Once this is accomplished, the role of proxy wars in the future can best be assessed.

There are a great many lessons to be learned from the Soviet use of Cuban proxies in Angola and Ethiopia.[27] First, the Soviet-Cuban intervention came about because of developments that the Soviets did not themselves create. The collapse of the Portuguese Empire and the overthrow of Haile Selassie opened up opportunities that the Soviets and Cubans exploited but could not have anticipated with any degree of certainty. The Soviet use of Cuban proxies in these countries was a responsive, opportunistic action to indigenous events rather than a part of some well-thought-out master plan.

Politically, the Soviet uses of Cuban proxies were low-risk operations. Not only were Soviet troops not directly involved in the fighting, but their assistance was provided to the side that enjoyed regional support. In Angola, the Soviet-Cuban-backed MPLA was supported by most of the African countries because it fought South African troops (who were assisting the other factions), and it controlled the capital city of Luanda (a crucial requirement for legitimacy in Africa). In Ethiopia, the Soviets responded to a call for assistance by the existing government that was threatened by an invasion from an irredentist state. Since the cardinal principle of the Organization of African Unity is the inviolability of colonial borders, the Soviet-Cuban defense of Ethiopia could not be expected to (and did not) produce much African opposition.

Soviet involvement in Ethiopia and Angola was also undertaken in the face of relative American indifference. In both countries, the Soviets escalated their involvement incrementally and cautiously. The United States, however, chose not to respond in a meaningful way. With the Vietnam experience still vivid (especially in Congress), and neither Angola nor Ethiopia perceived as being especially important or in Washington's sphere of influence, significant American resistance was quickly ruled out. It was at this point that Soviet involvement and the introduction of Cuban troops reached their height.

Militarily, the Angolan and Ethiopian cases revealed impressive Soviet capabilities. Especially with regard to Ethiopia, the Soviets demonstrated the capability and willingness to air- and sealift huge quantities of weapons and proxy troops in a very short time. Facilitating the Soviet operation were a variety of Soviet bases and staging areas throughout Africa (for example, Algeria, Guinea, Mali). Once in the combat area these weapons (which were all standard Soviet issue as opposed to the mixed origins of the arms used by the FNLA and UNITA) provided superior firepower to the MPLA. Especially effective were the "Stalin organ" rocket launchers, which had a devastating psychological impact on the pro-Western forces. Furthermore, the Soviets were able to use commanders and Cuban troops possessing detailed information about the country in which they were fighting and about their adversary. This information came from long experience in Africa and, in the Ethiopian case, from having trained and equipped the Somali army.

Most important, the Soviet involvement in Ethiopia and Angola revealed how proxies can make the difference between defeat and victory. Both the MPLA and the Ethiopian Army were facing defeat before the Soviet weapons arrived. The transfer of huge amounts of arms to those forces by the Soviets was impressive but ineffectual. This was so because the Angolans and Ethiopians did not know how to operate the Soviet weaponry and could not possibly have learned in time to stave off the attack by their enemies. The use of Cuban proxies allowed the Soviets to ensure that their clients, regardless of sophistication or prior training, would be able to utilize Soviet weaponry promptly and effectively without direct Soviet intervention. Such a crisis intervention capability proved decisive in Angola and Ethiopia and is all the more impressive because it is not matched by the United States.

The lessons of the Western response to the two invasions of Zaire are more mixed than the Soviet experience. On the positive side, the French use of Moroccan proxies and the U.S. use of French and Belgian proxies successfully preserved the pro-Western government of President Mobutu from foreign aggression. Consequently, the West demonstrated that it could defend its clients from military attacks when they are unable to protect themselves and when great power or superpower intervention is not expedient. Moreover, the Western proxy intervention in Zaire, like the Soviet proxy interventions in Angola and Ethiopia, was a low-risk operation. Since the intervention's purpose was to defend the borders of an African country it did not raise the ire of the OAU, and since Zaire was already in the Western sphere of influence the Soviets were not likely to become involved.

Nevertheless, the Western use of proxies in Zaire was not as impressive as it might have first appeared. In both Shaba I and Shaba II, the Western troops acted more like a quick reaction police force than an army. The Moroccans, French, and Belgians fought no real battles and (with the exception of the Moroccans) departed as soon as the threat had subsided. The positive impact of the proxy intervention was further diminished by the difficulties encountered by the French and the United States in persuading the Belgians to undertake even a limited intervention. While the Zairian affair may have reinforced the credibility of the Western use of proxies for some Third World leaders, for the vast majority (especially those facing a protracted conflict or who do not have a sizable American or European population) it could hardly be reassuring.

Several generalizations emerge from the proxy wars considered in this study. First, the use of proxies can be effective in meeting the interests of the super-powers in the Third World. Without the Cubans, the Soviet-backed MPLA faction might well have had to form a coalition government less friendly to the Kremlin. In Ethiopia, the absence of the Cubans could have brought down the Mengistu government and eliminated Soviet influence throughout the Horn. Similarly, without the Moroccans, French, and Belgians, the pro-Western government of President Mobutu might have been lost to forces hostile to the United States. In each of these conflicts the superpowers had good reasons not to intervene directly with their own troops, making the use of proxies vital to the protection of their interests.

In each of these conflicts, proxy troops demonstrated how a relatively small, well-trained, disciplined force can easily overwhelm motivated but unsophisticated indigenous fighters. In Zaire, the Moroccans and French encountered virtually no resistance in defeating the Katangese rebels. In Angola, the Cubans easily triumphed over the rival factions and their mercenary supporters. This is not to suggest that proxy forces will always be victorious. Cuban troops were defeated by South African troops in Angola, and Cuban forces reportedly did poorly against the Israelis in the Golan Heights in the October war. Nevertheless, where the opposition is on the relatively primitive level of most Third World armies, a few thousand skilled proxy troops can make a decisive difference in a conflict.

Finally, the Soviet use of proxies has to be judged more impressive than the use of proxies by the West. In Zaire, the success of the West was against minimal opposition, carried out over a very short time, and marked by political dispute. In Angola and Ethiopia, the Soviet-backed Cuban forces won two major wars, fought over a period of several months, remained in the countries to ensure internal security, and cooperated in relative harmony. The reasons for Soviet superiority in these proxy wars include the lack of domestic political constraints faced by the Soviets, the unique challenges posed by Angola and Ethiopia, and the fact that in the Cubans the Soviets have an effective proxy force for which the West has no counterpart.

While the use of proxies in major conflicts by both superpowers and particularly by the Soviets has proved highly effective, one should be careful not to exaggerate their overall importance. Several factors exist that limit the utility of proxies by the superpowers in the Third World. Only by understanding these limitations can it be possible to evaluate the significance of the proxy instrument in Third World wars for the future.

Neither superpower is likely to use large numbers of proxies against the important interests of the other superpowers. Proxy wars are initiated in political vacuums. If there is a strong likelihood that the use of proxies by one superpower would provoke a military or otherwise significant reaction from the other superpower, the use of proxies would probably be forestalled. This is especially true if there is a clear imbalance of interests whereby the initiator of the proxy war is less committed than the superpower that must respond to the potential proxy threat. Neither Angola or Ethiopia was in the U.S. sphere of influence at the time of the Soviet-Cuban proxy intervention. As for Zaire, the Soviets were sufficiently distanced from the Katangese rebels to claim credibly noninvolvement.

The United States and the Soviet Union are also unlikely to depend on proxies against capable and effective indigenous opposition. This is especially true for the United States, which lacks a potent proxy on the level of the Cubans that could confront a significant adversary. Even the Soviets, however, are also likely to resist getting into a major conflict against a determined and sophisticated opponent. Both superpowers realize that their control over proxies is limited. Should they face a conflict that is likely to be long, bloody, and perhaps unwinnable, it would probably not be worth the cost of a rupture in the proxy relationship or of the future use of the proxy to intervene. It is noteworthy that in the cases of proxy wars considered in this study, all of the opponents were relatively weak and quickly succumbed to the superior fighting abilities and firepower of the proxies. Where such weakness is not evident, proxy wars are not probable.

The political context of a Third World conflict can further constrain the use of proxies by the superpowers. In general, the United States and the Soviet Union would only seek to use proxies where such use can be defended politically. This means responding to the requests of the existing Third World government and/or using the proxies for defensive purposes. Employing proxies in a manner that is seen as illegitimate or offensive is bound to create regional opposition, resulting in political costs that outweigh the benefit of the superpower-proxy intervention. In Zaire and Ethiopia, proxies were used to defend the existing regime from outside invasion. The use of proxies in Eritrea and in Angola before independence was not as defensible politically, but the absence of significant Western opposition and (in the case of Angola) the participation of South African troops against the Soviet-backed forces eliminated the prospect of serious political difficulties. Where such difficulties are expected to arise (for example, using a proxy force to overthrow a regime), proxies will probably not be utilized.

Finally, the low incidence of major conflicts in the Third World will constrain the use of proxies in "proxy wars." Although the Third World is a violent place, the actual number of interstate wars, large-scale rebellions, and other major conflicts where a proxy army can make a decisive difference remains relatively small. While one's attention is diverted by the armed strife in Zaire, Angola, and Ethiopia, most changes in the Third World of relevance to the superpowers stem from coup d'état or assassinations. With few major wars ongoing at any given time, the opportunities for large proxy interventions will most probably stay limited.

Conclusions

That proxy wars might not be as numerous as otherwise expected does not mean that the United States can ignore their implications when they do—or should—arise. The potential for increased use of proxies and the Soviet proclivity for exploiting this area make it imperative that the United States prepare for future proxy contingencies. Based on the proxy war cases considered in this study, the following points should guide U.S. policy.

Most important, the United States will have to accept the fact that it cannot match the Soviet capability to use proxies. The structure of the Soviet alliance relationships and the availability of the Cubans are factors that the United States cannot equal, and it should be under no illusions that it will be able to do so in the future. Nevertheless, there is much the United States can and should do to mitigate the Soviet proxy threat.

First, the United States should increase its efforts to counter Soviet proxies with proxies of its own. Even if the United States' proxies are not equal to the Soviet-backed forces, the Kremlin must understand that it cannot win a "cheap" victory. U.S. proxies would ideally operate in their own regions. Possible choices include Egyptians, Jordanians, Pakistanis, Moroccans, and South Koreans. Discussions about future proxy operations with these and others should begin well in advance of their use as proxies. In return for their cooperation, political support, military aid, and direct logistical assistance should be provided as long as these measures do not interfere with more important U.S. interests.

Second, the United States should work more aggressively to get Third World countries and organizations to condemn the use of proxies in local conflicts. While this type of condemnation could also be used against the United States, the greater importance of proxies to the Soviet Union ensures that an overall limitation of their use would eventually work in the U.S. interest.

Third, in certain situations the United States ought to link the Soviet use of proxies to other aspects of the U.S.-Soviet relationship. This does not mean that every Soviet or Cuban advisor should be allowed to disrupt trade negotiations or undermine arms control negotiations. Rather, it suggests that the Soviets be made aware that they cannot radically change the nature of a Third World conflict without paying some price. Such a policy of linkage will not remove Soviet proxies from countries where they have already been sent, but it could inhibit further uses of proxies elsewhere.

Fourth, the United States should consider applying "horizontal escalation" when confronted with a Soviet proxy threat to its interests. For example, Soviet moves in Africa could be countered with increased U.S. efforts against Soviet clients in Afghanistan or Nicaragua. Again, the purpose of these moves would not be to reverse existing Soviet proxy efforts but to deter future ones by raising their costs.

Fifth, the United States should in some cases deal directly with Cuba to inhibit its use as a Soviet proxy. The United States should explore avenues of cooperation (especially economic) that could wean Havana away from its nearly total dependence on the Soviet Union and make it realize it will incur costs if it continues its military adventurism. If this policy is not successful (and it is unlikely that it would be), the United States ought to consider direct action against Cuba when Cuban proxies threaten serious U.S. interests. Such direct actions could include efforts to reverse Cuban gains in Latin America, greater support for anti-Castro groups, and even in extreme circumstances a blockade.

The threat posed to U.S. interests by proxy war is real. The Soviets realize that this is one of the few areas in which they can successfully compete with the United States in the Third World, and they are likely to do their utmost to exploit their advantage. Nevertheless, as detailed above, the proxy war threat is limited by many factors, the most important of which is the fear of provoking a violent reaction from the other superpower. So long as the United States demonstrates a willingness and capability to resist Soviet proxy threats in the less important Third World states, and demonstrates that it is prepared to act forcefully and directly in the more important Third World states, the Soviet use of proxies in major Third World conflicts can be contained to tolerable levels.

Notes

1. The problems of protracted intervention were persuasively made by Samuel Huntington (among others) in, "Vietnam Reappraised," *International Security* 6, no. 1 (Summer 1981): 2–26.

2. Joan Spero, *The Politics of Economic Relations* (New York: St. Martin's Press, 1981), 142–43.

3. For a good account of what the United States can do to lessen its dependence on imported raw materials, see Michael Shafer, "Mineral Myths," *Foreign Policy* (Summer 1982): 154–71.

4. Richard K. Betts makes this point in, *Soldiers, Statesmen and Cold War Crises* (Cambridge: Harvard University Press, 1977).

5. This section draws on two excellent accounts of the Shaba crises: Peter Mangold, "Shaba I and Shaba II," *Survival* 21, no. 3 (May–June 1979), and "Zaire," in *Africa Contemporary Record: Annual Survey and Documents, 1977–1978*, ed. Colin Legum (New York: Africana Publishing, 1979), B589–B611 (hereafter cited as *ACR*).

6. *The Guardian,* Mar. 26, 1977.

7. *New York Times,* May 23, 1978.

8. *ACR, 1977–78,* B594.

9. *New York Times,* May 23, 1978.

10. Mangold, "Shaba I and Shaba II," 112.

11. For a good analysis of what to do in the long term in Zaire, see Crawford Young, "Zaire: The Unending Crisis," *Foreign Affairs* 57, no. 1 (Fall, 1978): 184–5.

12. William Durch, "The Cuban Military in Africa and the Middle East: From Algeria to Angola," *Studies in Comparative Communism* XI, nos. 1–2 (Spring–Summer 1978): 64–67.

13. Stephen T. Hosmer and Thomas W. Wolfe, *Soviet Policy and Practice toward Third World Conflicts* (Lexington, Mass: Lexington Books, 1983), 82.

14. Hosmer and Wolfe, *Soviet Policy and Practice,* 83.

15. For details of the airlift, see *ACR, 1977–1978,* A44; *Strategic Survey 1978,* 13; and Hosmer and Wolfe, *Soviet Policy and Practice,* 92.

16. *New York Times,* June 11, 1978.

17. Young, "Zaire," 170.

18. *New York Times,* June 11, 1978.

19. *New York Times,* June 16, 1978.

20. *New York Times,* July 11, 1978.

21. *New York Times,* July 11, 1978.

22. *Nathaniel Davis, "The Angola Decision of 1975: A Personal Memoir," Foreign Affairs* 57, no. 1 (Fall 1978): 120.

23. *ACR, 1975–1976,* A15.

24. *ACR, 1975–1976,* A20.

25. *ACR, 1975–1976,* A14, A15.

26. *Newsweek,* December 29, 1975, 25.

27. For additional lessons of the Angolan and Ethiopian experiences, see Hosmer and Wolfe, *Soviet Policy and Practice,* 84–85, 94.

10

Conflict Termination in the Third World: Theory and Practice

William O. Staudenmaier

O f the many aspects of war, none is more important or less understood than that of war termination. Shrouded in semantic confusion and shunned by most liberal political scientists lest they be accused of condoning war, the topic has languished in relative neglect compared with the more popular and voluminous research into the causes and prevention of war. Nevertheless, in recent years some excellent work has been done on war termination, although most of this research is based on wars waged by the so-called great powers.[1]

For the past five hundred years, the Western experience with war has largely been within the framework of the great power system. During this period, about a dozen states, usually European, dominated the political and military landscape.[2] Wars among the great powers were formally declared, fought by professionally led armies seeking decisive victory in battle, and generally ended in negotiated peace treaties. Such of course is not the case today—either among the great powers or among Third World states. Although the long-term trend in the frequency of wars between the great powers has been downward—over 75 percent of great power wars occurred before 1735—they have tended to become more violent and to last longer as the technological and managerial innovations of the Industrial Revolution were applied to military operations.[3] The development and deployment of nuclear weapons in the past forty years has had a further dampening effect on the willingness of the great powers, especially the superpowers, to engage in interstate war.

But the decline in wars among the great powers has been more than matched by the turmoil created by the collapse of Europe's colonial empires after World War II. New states were violently carved from the former European colonies at accelerating rates until, by December 1985, the world community consisted of 169 more or less independent states.[4] This uninterrupted proliferation of nations since 1945 has complicated the international system, both in a regional and global context, resulting in the creation of a large number of nations that

The views expressed in this chapter are those of the author and do not reflect the official policy or position of the Department of Defense or the U.S. government.

are small, weak, and vulnerable. The dilemma of most of these new nations is that their limited power potential restricts them to a peripheral role in world affairs; nevertheless, their vulnerability serves as an invitation to political, economic, and military penetration by other nations or by internal dissident groups. This phenomenal growth in the number of nation-states has led to a shift not only in the pattern of conflict—from the great powers to the Third World—but in the form of conflict as well—from high-intensity wars to low-intensity wars—that has had consequences for the ways in which wars end.

Prior to World War II, interstate war was the predominant type of warfare. Since then, however, approximately 85 percent of wars have been intrastate or colonial wars, and over 95 percent of the wars have been fought outside of Europe—the traditional center of the great power system. The forms of the wars have also changed.[5] Overwhelmingly, wars since World War II can be classified as guerrilla insurgencies that do not normally begin or end amidst much formality, and which are seldom quickly resolved. As Robert Harkavy points out, most major conflicts in the Third World tend to linger on.[6] This observation has widespread consequences for war termination and military strategy.

War Termination and Military Strategy

Contemporary nations exist in a state of international anarchy. Because there is no supranational authority that can impose solutions to disputes among the members of the international community, nations seek to maximize their power in order to ensure their survival as well as their prosperity. Often sovereign nations quarrel over rival national interests, and when this occurs military force is frequently invoked to resolve the dispute. The nation also has authority over its internal affairs; when this authority is challenged from within, civil war may result. A nation may also have its authority challenged externally by a political or social group that is not recognized as a member of the state system, such as the Palestine Liberation Organization (PLO), or it may become the target of terrorism supported by a rival state. In all cases, nations often use military power when it appears that political or diplomatic action will not realize their political goals peacefully. The plan that guides such use of military force is called strategy.

An underlying premise of strategy is that its aim is not solely to achieve peace (as commendable an objective as that is) but to win something. That "something" is normally expressed in political terms. In the Iran-Iraq war, Iraqi war aims were threefold: first, to gain control of the Shatt-al-Arab and certain disputed border territory and islands; second, to establish Iraq as the leader of the nonaligned movement; and third, to overthrow the Ayatollah Khomeini.[7] In the instance of Nicaragua during 1978–79, the objective was the ouster of the Somoza government and its takeover by the *Frente Sandinista de*

Liberación Nacional (FSLN). In neither case was peace the primary objective, but rather the achievement of political goals that could not be realized without the use of military force. Implicit in this conception of strategy is the rational notion that when the costs of war exceed its benefits, the war should be stopped. The benefits of course are the political values for which the war is being fought, and the costs are established on the battlefield. This rational approach to conflict or war termination is yet another underlying premise of military strategy.

Military strategists assume that decision makers on both sides of a dispute will behave rationally when establishing war aims and choosing war policies and strategies. Decision makers, it is believed, will behave rationally whether deciding to continue a war or to end it. If a strategist believes that the enemy will act in a rational way, the path is open to manipulation and control. To believe otherwise would circumvent the strategic process.

There are four salient assumptions with regard to strategic rationality that are important to our discussion of war termination.[8] First, all the necessary data relevant to the strategic problem to be solved is assumed to be available. That means that the payoffs of the strategist's various alternatives are known, as well as those of his opponent. Second, it is assumed that all the possible options are carefully considered. Third, it is assumed that each strategic problem can be afforded the time and attention it requires. Finally, it is assumed that each problem can be examined in its totality, without stress or emotional bias affecting the result.[9]

This approach is not without its detractors, particularly with respect to conflict termination. Critics of the strategic-rational model argue that decisions to stop wars are not made by unitary actors, but through a political process that involves many competing power centers. The result often is not a pristine solution, but a sordid compromise based not on rational choice but on bureaucratic bargaining. The critics also contend that neither side has comprehensive knowledge about its own objectives and values, let alone about those of its adversary. Nor is it possible to compare the costs and benefits of war in any meaningful way.[10] What, they ask, is the benefit of an anti-Communist Vietnam compared with the cost of over fifty thousand American lives?

But surely rationality can be *characterized* in less stringent terms. As Robert Gilpin has noted, "Rationality applies only to endeavor, not to outcome; failure to achieve an objective because of ignorance or some other factor does not invalidate the rationalist premise that individuals act on the basis of a cost/benefit or means/ends calculation."[11] Defining rationality in this way brings it closer to normal usage and still allows insights into the war termination process.

A rational strategist will be one who knows that his initial information may be erroneous with respect to understanding the relevant interests that are at stake for both sides, and he understands that he may not even know what all of the major options are, but he will correct his initial poor judgments when better data become available. On the other hand, an irrational actor will refuse to adjust his initial interpretations in the light of new evidence that conflicts with his "rigid belief system." Faced with data that threaten his beliefs, he will either disregard the information, believing it to be false, or he will force the facts to "fit" his preconceived notions.[12]

The strategic-rational model that will be introduced shortly will assume rationality even though it is fully understood that often all of the required information will not be available, that all possible alternatives cannot be considered, and that irrational factors such as ideological or emotional biases may enter the analysis. The decision that awaits impeccable data is a decision that will never be made.

A Strategic-Rational Model of Conflict Termination

The strategic-rational model examines war termination concepts from a systems perspective. It may be divided into three interactive segments: input, conversion, and output (see figure 10–1). The inputs are political disputes that may be either domestic or international, and the outputs are resolutions of these conflicts. The conversion from input to output takes place on the battlefield in the interaction between contending parties. If war does not resolve the political issues for which it is being waged, or if new issues arise out of the passion of battle as often happens, the system is closed by these unresolved issues' becoming inputs to a new cycle.

Substantively, this heuristic, multidimensional war termination model is composed of three major elements. First, the input into the system is some type of political conflict, either internal or external, that will require the use of military force to resolve. Second, once the decision to use force has been made, the dynamics of the battlefield take over as the conflicting parties combine strategy and violence to resolve their political differences. The third major

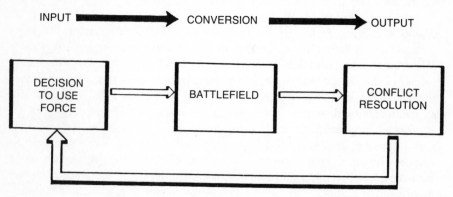

Figure 10–1. Conflict Termination Model

factor—conflict resolution—begins with a Clausewitzian assessment of the value of the political interests for which the war is being fought measured against the costs of the war in blood and treasure, includes a rational choice among alternatives ranging from escalation to surrender, and ends with a consideration of the ways in which conflicts can be terminated and resolved. This latter point requires further elaboration.

As was discussed earlier, the aim of war is not primarily peace, but the resolution of some political issue that cannot be solved through diplomacy. Since the advent of the total war concept, exemplified by World War I and World War II, many analysts doubt the efficacy of war in resolving political problems. This is especially true with regard to nuclear war, but it is no less valid for wars of the Third World. For example, Israel has had at least five instances of war termination, but none of war resolution. Despite scoring seemingly decisive victories over the Arabs in 1948, 1956, 1967, 1973, and again in Lebanon in 1982, Israeli statesmen have been unable to find a solution to the deep political, social, and cultural differences that separate them from their Arab neighbors.[13] In the Falklands war, the British were able to restore militarily the status quo ante, but the political issue that precipitated that war still persists—Argentina still contests the British claim to sovereignty over the Falkland islands. While one hesitates to predict how the Gulf war will end, stalemate rather than a decisive victory of one side over the other seems to be a possible if not probable outcome. If so, the smoldering animosities that would be the legacy of such an outcome would surely sow the seeds of yet another round of conflict in the Gulf. War must result in something more than an uneasy, unsatisfying peace; strategy must direct military operations in such a way that resolution of political issues takes precedence over merely bringing the fighting to an end, as important as that may be.

Conflict Input and Battlefield Conversion

One of the major reasons that war is considered an inadequate political instrument today is that few battles are decisive. In the past, when the statesman opted for war, he implicitly agreed to accept the outcome of battle as the final arbiter of the political dispute. Clausewitz was among the first to perceive that battle was the means by which political ends would be met. His advice was to seek great battles in order to achieve great success.[14]

Evidence, however, is accumulating that suggests that it is becoming increasingly difficult in the twentieth century to achieve decisive success on the battlefield. At one extreme, nuclear weapons circumvent traditional battle strategy by striking deep at civilian population centers, thereby forfeiting their political utility, serving only to deter the use of other nuclear weapons.[15] At the other extreme, political terrorism and guerrilla insurgencies—the forms of warfare most frequently encountered in the Third World—are methods that have great political effectiveness, although they too avoid the test of the traditional battlefield.[16] Political terrorists shun the traditional battlefield altogether.

There has also been a decline in the number of traditional battles or campaigns that can be judged decisive. Despite several years of war, there are no decisive results as yet in the Gulf war or in Afghanistan. While the British reasserted their sovereignty over the Falklands, the Argentines remain politically opposed. The conflicts in the Horn of Africa, the Western Sahara, and Central America are still being contested. This is not to deny that there have been decisive battles fought in the past forty years (the North Vietnamese campaign against Saigon was decisive by anyone's standards); it is only to say that there are fewer such battles. One reason to account for this trend is the change in the forms of war that avoid traditional battles, and another is the enormous cost of modern conventional weapons that seem to favor the defense, making traditional battles difficult to sustain or win, particularly for Third World states.

Nevertheless, battles do occur, and if their impact is seldom decisive, they are nonetheless significant events. The battlefield still is the military catalyst that helps to establish the relationship between costs and benefits of a war that Clausewitz argued should be the measure of when it should be ended. When costs exceed benefits—for example, when the costs of the war exceed the value of the political interest at stake—then the war should be stopped.[17] Although the pain thresholds of nations and insurgent political groups vary, it is remarkable how much suffering can be endured in the name of political or social progress. All of the case studies in volume 1 of *The Lessons of Recent Wars in the Third World* attest to the validity of this observation.

Conflict Termination

Although there are many issues that flow from a consideration of the input and conversion segments of the strategic-rational model, it is the output that we wish to bring into sharper focus.[18] A prior condition of conflict resolution is conflict termination, because—as Iklé so cogently reminds us—"every war must end." The war termination process begins with an evaluation by the policymaker of the costs of the war compared to the value of the political interest at risk. Earlier, under conditions of great uncertainty, in opting for war the decision maker estimated the value of the political interest at stake, calculated the risks involved in using force, and arrived at some expectation of success. Once the battle had been joined, the social, political, and economic costs of the war were unveiled. The policymaker then related these costs to the value of the political interest at risk in order to decide upon future military operations.

The essential choices open to the decision maker at this juncture in the war are to continue the war at the same intensity, to escalate or deescalate, or to quit. Although our primary concern is with the latter option, regardless of which alternative the decision maker chooses, his choice will be based on his perception of the course of the war. The problem can be stated quite simply: Are we winning or losing? Stating the problem is the easy part; the difficult part is measuring success or failure in war. In the Falklands, it was rather easy. The progress of the British combat units could be followed on a map and the surrender of the Argentine garrison at Stanley clearly marked the end of the war. It is not as easy a task when a conventional war, such as the Iran-Iraq war, becomes stalemated. Body counts are neither accurate nor humane indicators of success or failure, as the United States learned in Vietnam and as the Soviets are undoubtedly learning in Afghanistan. Yet there is no suitable substitute in an insurgency such as those in El Salvador or Guatemala. In any event, this interaction of political value, cost, risk, and expectation will influence the decision maker in his deliberations relating to the future course of the war.

If the war is progressing satisfactorily and the strategist foresees that it will end favorably, the war would probably be continued at the same intensity. This appears to have been the case with the Chinese incursion into Vietnam in 1979. The Chinese fought a limited war for limited objectives, and when these objectives were secured, they withdrew back into China. The Chinese strategy in the Sino-Vietnamese war replicated the pattern of conflict behavior that they followed in five earlier crises, including the Korean War and the Sino-Indian and Sino-Soviet border clashes. These incidents revealed that Chinese conflict behavior followed a discernible pattern that encompassed sequential phases of probing, warning, demonstrations, attack, and détente. The Chinese actions in 1979 indicated that their objectives were limited, and the intensity of the conflict was decided upon early and adhered to throughout the crisis. When their objectives were accomplished, they ended the war—unilaterally.[19]

If the war situation requires escalation but the strategist does not have the necessary resources to escalate, as is often the case with Third World nations that are striving to sustain modern warfare, then the choice is between continuing at the same intensity and deescalation. When Somalia began losing in Ethiopia, its economy did not enable it to compete with the mighty infusion of Soviet and Cuban military aid to Ethiopia. It eventually withdrew from active operations. Because the *Polisario* did not meet with success in 1983, and subsequent operations by Morocco seem to be winning the countryside back, the insurgents may be required to retrench. For a guerrilla, deescalation is a major setback, for by its very nature an insurgency must continue to escalate or it will fail.

Revolutionary warfare is conducted in three phases, each phase being more violent than the one preceding it, culminating in a final stage of mobile warfare designed to overthrow rapidly the existing regime. The *Polisario* in the mid-1970s was in the first or organizational phase; escalated to the second or expansion phase during which sabotage, terrorism, and bold, small unit actions reduced the control of the governing authorities; and by 1983 were moving into phase three—mobile warfare—using tanks, artillery, and modern air defense weapons. Events since 1983 suggest that this decision to engage in mobile warfare was somewhat premature. The guerrillas in El Salvador appear to be stalemated in phase two, while those in Guatemala have been beaten back to phase one.

By far, the phase that lasts the longest in an insurgency is phase two. The organization phase may also be long, but the threat is usually not recognized until phase two. Phase three is short by design. The North Vietnamese offensive against Saigon in 1975 is an excellent, perhaps textbook, example of phase three of a revolutionary war. Insurgencies normally do not end in phase two. If the insurgents lose, it will usually be in phase one when they will either be eliminated by the government—such was the case with Che Guevara in Bolivia—or they will simply fade into the hills or jungles. If the insurgents win in a classical guerrilla campaign, it is generally the result of mobile operations in phase three, although it sometimes happens that a government will collapse unexpectedly, and an insurgency will be ended without resort to mobile warfare.

A rational decision maker might decide to quit when the cost of war exceeds the value of the political interest or if he believes that he will not win militarily. In either case, the war is ended. Before examining the various mechanisms that have been used to end wars in the Third World, two points must be made. First, it is not normally the military that initiates the process to end a war. This is certainly the case in the United States. In the United States, the military is frequently opposed to the use of force initially, but once committed, it favors escalation over withdrawal, believing that the application of additional military power will eventually result in winning.[20] It is not certain that these views are held by the military leaders of the Third World, but since many of them were trained in the West, it is at least a reasonable hypothesis that merits further research.

Second, the role of peace parties in the war termination process is not clearly understood. We must discover what causes them to emerge when they do and how they can be used to end wars. Since most Third World countries do not have much of a tradition of democracy, often the part played by peace parties in the industrialized nations is replaced by coups d'état in developing countries. When the fortunes of war turned against Mauritania in the Western Sahara in 1978, the result was the overthrow of the Mokhtar Ould Daddah regime, which led directly to the withdrawal of Mauritania from the war with the *Polisario.* In Nicaragua, the alliance of the "moderates" with the FSLN in 1978 led to the ouster of Somoza in 1979. Had the moderates backed Somoza during the critical 1978–79 period, it is possible that the outcome might have been different. A losing cause can also lead to serious political repercussions. The Galtieri government in Argentina fell as a result of losing the Falklands war. Even winning causes are sometimes traumatic affairs, as the political turmoil in Israel since the 1982 invasion of Lebanon demonstrates. The emergence of peace parties or political factions opposed to the conduct of the war or its results seems to be a major strategic factor in most war situations. Strategists must devise methods to prevent the emergence of peace parties in their own nation and exploit them in the enemy camp.

Once the decision to end a war has been made, then the mechanisms through which this can be accomplished become operative. There are six major ways in which wars may be ended. First, there are armistices, truces, and cease-fires. The common element among these concepts is that they all aim at ending the fighting between opposing armies. Surrenders are usually preceded by a cease-fire or an armistice. In the Falklands, a cease-fire that took effect locally enabled the surrender negotiations at Stanley to be conducted. These negotiations led to a general de facto armistice in the South Atlantic between the military forces of the United Kingdom and Argentina. In 1978, the *Polisario* declared a unilateral cease-fire with regard to the forces of Mauritania that lasted for one year and was suspended only when the *Polisario* believed it necessary to put additional pressure on the Mauritanian leaders to convince them that it was time to quit the war. In the Gulf war, cease-fires have been observed to celebrate religious holidays and to limit damage against cities and commercial shipping.

Each of these cease-fires has been of limited duration only. It may be unilaterally declared or by mutual consent. Christmas cease-fires have been observed in El Salvador by both sides; and in Afghanistan, the Soviets arranged a local cease-fire with rebel leader Ahmed Shah Massoud in the strategic Panjsher Valley that lasted fifteen months. However, none of the cease-fires resulted in a permanent end to hostilities, except in the Falklands and Mauritanian cases. Frequently, cease-fires result from third power pressure to contain a local war, to prevent it from becoming something much more serious. Several of the Israeli unilateral cease-fires were of this type, usually induced by U.S. diplomatic pressure.

Second, in the past, great power wars usually ended in formal peace treaties. Although joint political agreements, cease-fires, and armistices still have relevance for ending wars, formal peace treaties have become passé. The Falklands war is interesting in this regard. When the Argentine garrison surrendered in June 1982, there was no assurance that hostilities would end in the South Atlantic; so, the British withheld the repatriation of one thousand high-ranking Argentine POWs in an unsuccessful attempt to force the Argentine government to declare formally an end to hostilities. Argentina never formally declared "peace," but the British finally accepted Argentina's statement that "a de facto cessation of hostilities" was in effect—the Falklands war simply faded away.

While peace treaties are seldom used today to end wars, the same cannot be said of joint political agreements—the third mechanism for ending war. Joint political agreements are contractual engagements between contending parties that are of a bilateral or multilateral nature. An excellent example of this instrument for ending wars is the "Agreement on Ending the War and Restoring Peace in Vietnam" that provided for a cease-fire throughout Vietnam, withdrawal of U.S. troops, release of prisoners of war, restoration of the demarcation line between North and South Vietnam, and the creation of an international body to supervise the truce.[21] The *Polisario* also signed a joint political agreement with Mauritania to end that nation's participation in the Western Sahara war. "The Definitive Peace Agreement," as it was called, stipulated that Mauritania would renounce all claim to Tiris el-Gharbia and would withdraw its army from the Western Sahara. It is curious to note that in each of these examples an ally that quit first was able to negotiate its way out of an insurgency. Morocco declared that Mauritania had no right to withdraw from the war and quickly occupied the Tiris el-Gharbia, thereby frustrating the *Polisario*'s apparent victory in southern Western Sahara.

One reason that peace treaties are no longer used as a means to end wars, especially in the Third World, is that internal wars, which are endemic in the newly emerging nations, are all-or-nothing affairs. The very survival of the government is at stake. Usually internal wars end in the death or in the flight into exile of the government leader in the event the insurgents win, or in the guerrillas' fading into the jungles or mountains if the government is victorious. In either event, there is normally no one to negotiate with, so the winner unilaterally declares victory and the war ends. This fourth method of ending hostilities—unilateral declaration of victory—was used by Nicaragua in 1979, by the British in the Falklands war (since Argentina would not acknowledge defeat), and by Iraq unsuccessfully several times during the Gulf war.

Capitulation is the fifth method that has been used to end the fighting in wars. A capitulation puts an end to the fighting through a mutual agreement that is reached entirely within military channels by military personnel. Its purpose is normally to arrange for the surrender of armies in the field. The victorious commander promises some sort of quid pro quo to the commander of the defeated army if he will surrender his command. There does not seem to be any unequivocal example of a capitulation in the case studies under consideration.[22]

Finally, a war may be ended by one party's simply unilaterally withdrawing from active campaigning in the theater of operations. Somalia's withdrawal from Ethiopia in 1978 and China's retirement from Vietnam in 1979 are cases in point. Insurgencies that fail often end in this manner as well. A withdrawal in an interstate war is sometimes accompanied by a unilateral declaration of victory.

Conflict Resolution

Earlier the point was made that the output of the strategic-rational model is conflict resolution. Thus far, our emphasis has been on conflict termination.

Of the few instances of war termination that our study includes, there are fewer still of war resolution. Wars in the Third World seldom resolve the issues for which they were begun. In the case of the Sino-Vietnamese War, the political issue of Vietnam's drive for hegemony in Southeast Asia is still unresolved, although China claimed that its objectives in that war were met.[23] The issue of Falklands sovereignty is still present despite the British military victory. The Israeli incursion into Lebanon to expel the PLO does not seem to have made Israel more secure. Even the unconditional victory of the FSLN in Nicaragua seems threatened by the Contras.

Certainly a case can be made that China's, Britain's, the FSLN's, and Israel's use of military force had some short-term political benefits. Although war continues in Indochina, Vietnam suffered economically as a result of the Chinese invasion and Thailand could not have been anything but heartened by it. For Britain's part, the war has at least restored the political status quo in the Falklands, albeit at some considerable continuing cost. The FSLN won a nation. Israel, if it did not totally destroy the PLO, at least dealt it a serious blow—and Israel continues to survive. Perhaps the lesson is that war does not settle everything forever.

Observations

This brief survey of how wars end in the Third World leads to two major observations. First, interstate wars in the Third World end in very much the same way as do contemporary wars involving the great and the near great powers. There is no longer any "rite of passage" when crossing the threshold from peace to war anymore than there is when we retrace our steps from war to peace. Declarations of war are as rare in the post–World War II era as formal peace treaties to end wars. In fact, war and peace are no longer considered to be polar opposites, but hopelessly entangled. War and peace coexist in a troubled partnership in which force is used in situations short of war, such as coercive diplomacy, military interventions, guerrilla insurgencies, state-sponsored terrorism, and proxy wars. The significance that this circumstance holds for strategy is great. In the past, declarations of war served to lay out the grievances that the war was to eradicate. The peace treaty not only signaled the end of the war and the return of normal diplomatic relations between the belligerents, but it also strove to resolve the grievances for which the war was fought, although not always successfully. Strategy bridged the gap between the declaration of war and the signing of the peace treaties by focusing on ways to defeat and destroy the enemy army decisively.

Second, as we have seen, it is becoming increasingly difficult to wage decisive war militarily. Moreover, in the intrastate wars in the Third World, the aim of strategy has shifted from its classical focus on the defeat and destruction of the enemy army to the almost total aim of changing the social order. The aim of most revolutionary insurgencies in the Third World is the overthrow of the incumbent government and the radical restructuring of society. These are not issues that admit of much compromise—it is winner take all. The nature of these wars is such that they are not resolved quickly—often lasting for a generation or more. When they end, there is usually no one with whom to negotiate.

We may conclude from this that interstate wars in the Third World, like their great power counterparts, tend to be both militarily and politically indecisive; whereas, intrastate war, which may be militarily indecisive for decades or more, is usually politically decisive in the end.

Notes

1. For a discussion of war termination, see: Fred Charles Iklé, *Every War Must End* (New York: Columbia University Press, 1971); "How Wars End," William T.R. Fox, ed., *Annals of the American Academy of Political and Social Science*, November 1970 (Philadelphia: The American Academy of Political and Social Science); Paul Kecskemeti, *Strategic Surrender: The Politics of Victory and Defeat* (Stanford, Calif.: Stanford University Press, 1958); Herman Kahn, *On Escalation: Metaphors and Scenarios* (New York: Frederick A. Praeger, 1965); Bernice A. Carroll, "How Wars End: An Analysis of Some Current Hypotheses," *Journal of Peace Research* 4 (1969): 295–320; Michael Handel, "The Study of War Termination," *Journal of Strategic Studies* 1 (May 1978): 50–75; Stuart Albert and Edward C. Luck, eds., *On the Endings of Wars* (Port Washington, N.Y.: Kennikat Press, 1980).

2. Jack S. Levy, *War in the Modern Great Power System, 1495–1975* (Lexington: University Press of Kentucky, 1983), chapter 3.

3. Ibid., 116–17.

4. Telephone interview, Office of the Geographer, U.S. Department of State, December 11, 1985.

5. See Harvey Starr and Benjamin A. Most, "Patterns of Conflict: Quantitative Analysis and the Comparative Lessons of Third World Wars," in *The Lessons of Recent Wars in the Third World, vol. 1* eds. Robert E. Harkavy and Stephanie G. Neuman (Lexington, Mass.: Lexington Books, 1985), 38–50.

6. Robert E. Harkavy, "The Lessons of Recent Wars: Toward Comparative Analysis," in *The Lessons of Recent Wars in the Third World*, vol. 1, eds. Robert E. Harkavy and Stephanie G. Neuman (Lexington, Mass.: Lexington Books, 1985), 22–23.

7. William O. Staudenmaier, "Iran-Iraq (1980–)," in *The Lessons of Recent Wars in the Third World*, vol. 1, eds. Robert E. Harkavy and Stephanie G. Neuman (Lexington, Mass.: Lexington Books, 1985), 217.

8. Trevor C. Salmon, "Rationality and Politics: The Case for Strategic Theory," *British Journal of International Studies* 2 (October 1976): 293–310.

9. Ronald Rogowski, "Rationalist Theories of Politics: A Midterm Report," *World Politics* 30 (January 1978): 296–323.

10. Michael Handel, "The Study of War Termination," *Journal of Strategic Studies* 1 (May 1978): 50–75.

11. Robert Gilpin, *War and Change in World Politics* (New York: Cambridge University Press, 1981), x.

12. Glen H. Snyder and Paul Diesing, *Conflict among Nations: Bargaining, Decision Making, and System Structure in International Crises* (Princeton: Princeton University Press, 1977), 333–39.

13. Certainly Israel's wars have had the considerable benefit of enabling it to survive in these tumultuous last forty years—no small accomplishment given Israel's precarious strategic circumstances.

14. Carl von Clausewitz, *On War*, ed. and trans. Michael Howard and Peter Paret (Princeton: Princeton University Press, 1976), 258.

15. This is not to deny that diplomacy uses military threats and posturing to further its aims. Diplomacy is part and parcel of strategy in peace and war. Our emphasis, however, is on the use of force in war.

16. By traditional battle, we mean warfare as it was conducted in the Napoleonic era and since. Battle is sought in order to destroy the will of the enemy in a swift, climactic battle.

17. Clausewitz, *On War*, 92.

18. For a more extensive treatment of the input and conversion segments of the model, see William O. Staudenmaier, "Conflict Termination in the Nuclear Age," paper presented at the Conflict Termination Conference, Naval War College, September 22–24, 1985.

19. For a discussion of Chinese conflict behavior, see Steve Chan, "Chinese Conflict Calculus and Behavior: Assessment for a Perspective of Conflict Management," *World Politics XXX*, no. 3 (April 1978): 391–410. For the application of Chan's argument to the Sino-Vietnamese war, see Edward W. Ross, "Chinese Conflict Management," *Military Review LX*, no. 2 (January 1980): 13–25. *Together, these articles support the belief that the Chinese did achieve their limited goals of that war.*

20. Richard K. Betts, *Soldiers, Statesmen and Cold War Crises* (Cambridge: Harvard University Press, 1977), chapter 1.

21. The signing of a joint political agreement is no assurance that both sides will abide by its terms. The North Vietnamese used the agreement with the United States as a cover to reinforce their military forces in the south, thereby setting the stage for the final offensive against Saigon two years later. Cease-fires have a similar history of being used to gain military advantage.

22. The surrender of eighty British Royal Marines in the Falklands war may be one such example, since they were quickly repatriated to the United Kingdom. But the involvement of the political governor of the Falklands in the surrender negotiations technically takes it outside strictly military channels.

23. International Institute for Strategic Studies, Strategic Survey, 1979 (London: International Institute for Strategic Studies, 1980), 59.

11
Lessons Learned, Insights Gained, Issues Raised: Summary and Agenda for Further Research

Robert E. Harkavy

In the summary chapter of *The Lessons of Recent Wars in the Third World*, volume 1—that devoted jointly to methodological approaches and case studies—some preliminary conclusions and/or recurrent themes were presented according to the following outline:

1. Questions of method
2. Types of war
3. Factors determining how wars are fought and their outcomes
   a) Strategy, operations, and tactics
   b) Logistics
   c) Internationalization of conflict

In this, our second volume, we intended to move beyond (never quite resolvable) methodological arguments and also beyond the essentially inductive approach provided by our case studies. To that end, we chose a number of comparative dimensions that we felt could fruitfully be analyzed so as to provide further illumination of the fundamental themes included in the above outline. In some cases, those dimensions rather clearly constitute, roughly speaking, "independent variables" in relation to these themes. The chapters on geography, culture, and economics, for instance, were intended primarily to shed light on how wars are fought and their outcomes—in short, who wins or loses. Those on security assistance, Third World arms production, and surrogate forces were intended mostly to illuminate aspects of the "internationalization of conflict," that is, the linkage of Third World conflicts to the overarching, superimposed one between the superpowers and/or their respective alliances. On the other hand, some of our comparative chapters may be seen as related in important ways to more than one of these themes. Those on strategy and tactics, war termination, and the "human factor" have a lot to say about how wars are fought and about their outcomes, but necessarily also about classifying types of war. The chapter on termination is also linked to questions about the internationalization of conflict. Generally, in one way or another, if only by implication or in the interstices between analyses devoted to other questions, each of our chapters has either addressed or at least illustrated one or more aspects of each of the major themes from the given outline.

Most of the critical methodological issues involved in the study of "lessons learned" were covered, in considerable detail, in the first volume. That was done deliberately, in part because many of those issues were perhaps more applicable to interpretations of case studies than they would be to interpretations of analyses of various comparative dimensions. Among the issues covered: the uses and limits of quantification; various levels of analysis problems (strategic, operational, and tactical); trade-offs among various types of comparative analysis (case studies, functional/comparative, and longitudinal); the contributions and limitations of various disciplinary perspectives (military history, political science, sociology, and so forth); the problem of time perspective or hindsight; ideological, political, and national perspectives—that is, the issue of parochialism; negative versus positive lessons; losers' versus winners' perspectives, and so on. Above all, an elaboration of these various problems was intended as cautionary, providing a checklist of the various lenses through which lessons are viewed; or the various angles from which they can be viewed. Unavoidably, those lenses will exist in an edited volume in which there can be only one author per topic, an obvious result of space limitations.

A review of the various selections in volumes 1 and 2 seemed to us, however, to highlight two particular methodological or conceptual points, one of which involves the issue of quantification, and the other the very validity of the concept of lessons learned. On the first point, it is very clear that whereas numerous extensive attempts have been made to quantify the various dimensions of war on a *macro*level—how many wars in what time periods, how divided by regions, durations of wars, and so on—very little has been done at a *micro*level, where the central questions have to do with how wars are fought and who prevails and why. In part, this may have to do with the relative availability of data and with the inherently more objective basis of the classes of data used in macrolevel studies such as the Correlates of War (COW) project at the University of Michigan.[1]

But then one might also suggest that there is an ideological component to this question: academics, predominantly liberal or left in their modal political orientation, are most interested in the causes of wars and their possible solutions or cures. Indeed, a review of the introductions of the various works devoted to macrolevel analyses of war will reveal this prescriptive or reformist intent very clearly. Not surprisingly, the one major attempt at quantifying war at a more microlevel was made by a military man, Trevor Dupuy, perhaps understandably more interested by profession alone in the question of who prevails. But then the question of who prevails, involving such subjective matters as geography, culture, and human will, is by its nature far less easy to subject to quantitative analysis. Or is it? All in all, our work seems to indicate the need for far more serious empirical work on the various elements determining success and/or failure in warfare, be they the "givens" of geography and demography, or the far more variable, ephemeral elements such as morale, will, nationalist fervor, and so forth. The latter elements, of course, do feed back into macrolevel questions such as, for instance, the average duration of wars.

Lessons Learned, or Issues Raised?

Otherwise, concerning methodological and conceptual matters, it is clear that virtually all of the contributors to our two volumes—across the board from case studies to comparative analysis, and spanning all of the various approaches—are inclined to caution if not outright pessimism about the possibilities for drawing inferences that might rightfully be defined as "lessons." In varying degrees, the very concept of lessons seems subject to questioning as being too self-consciously and optimistically didactic, too prone to conveying a (not easily deserved) sense of certainty, and too apt to be frozen in time but also subject to endless revisions. The *pro forma*, catchy title of the two volumes notwithstanding and the ritual nature of "lessons learned" exercises within the national security milieu aside, there is general agreement that the subject simply is too complex, too daunting, to allow for definitive conclusions. Insights gained, yes, perhaps, tentatively so. Issues raised, yes, galore. In part this renders our work, unavoidably, largely heuristic, that is, one that can merely point toward further, more focused analysis. Clearly, a large number of very important issues have been raised, some of which are, directly or indirectly, points of contention between our authors, and some of which may not easily be resolved by any level of research effort, given the inherent limitations of comparative analysis and the obvious difficulties of requiring inferences from a statistically limited and varied (like apples and oranges) number of cases.

One of the more interesting points of contention—if only one of nuance and interpretation—concerns the real distinction, for analytical purposes, between conventional and unconventional warfare. As noted elsewhere in this book, these have long been considered very distinct realms of analysis with very separate traditions of scholarship—few national security or military history scholars have dwelt in both worlds. For that reason, we had originally commissioned a separate chapter on unconventional strategies, tactics, doctrines, and weapons. Unfortunately, it was not completed in time for publication.

In our first volume, however, Neuman questioned whether in reality, over the long run, this distinction is wholly valid. In that regard, she cited the uniform dominance of land warfare, the consistent dominance of defense, the protracted nature of virtually all of these wars, and the inherently mixed (conventional and unconventional) nature of wars such as those in Lebanon, the Horn, the

Western Sahara, and that between the PRC and Vietnam. In all cases, the historical distinction between peace and war was seen to have become blurred.

Others, however, have insisted upon hewing to the older distinction. The format of the macrodata chapter in volume 1 by Starr and Most maintains it; in the process, it is indicated, as it has been elsewhere, that the post–World War II period has seen an ineluctable trend toward revolutionary/unconventional/ guerrilla/low-intensity warfare, most of it within the Third World and mostly involving internal insurgencies. Staudenmaier too accepts this common and almost universally accepted generalization, stating in this book,

> This phenomenal growth in the number of nation-states has led to a shift not only in the pattern of conflict—from the great powers to the Third World— but in the form of conflict as well—from high-intensity wars to low-intensity wars—that has had consequences for the ways in which wars end.
>
> Prior to World War II, interstate war was the predominant type of war- fare. Since then, however, approximately 85 percent of wars have been intrastate or colonial wars, and over 95 percent of the wars have been fought outside of Europe—the traditional center of the great power system. The forms of the wars have also changed. Overwhelmingly, wars since World War II can be classified as guerrilla insurgencies . . . [2]

Cohen, however, who focused more on the very recent wars among our case studies rather than on data aggregated over a longer time span, sees some still newer developments. He sees several of the recent wars as fitting the rubric of "postcolonial" or even "post-postcolonial." Generally, this appears to him to herald a new era of increased conventional interstate warfare between Third World states and a relative lessening of intrastate wars of national liberation. Further, he sees a return in some respects to patterns earlier familiar in eighteenth- or nineteenth-century Europe—that is, long-term enmities and coali- tion wars that have "usually taken years or decades to run their course; often they come to inconclusive ends. . . . As in the wars of the eighteenth century, short periods of intense fighting punctuate much longer periods of uneasy truce, during which the primary antagonists (in the eighteenth century, England and France) rebuild their forces and attempt to attract new allies."[3]

Cohen also avers, on another note, that the artillery round remains the great killer in modern warfare—presumably, that claim would apply far more to conventional than unconventional warfare. Or would it?

Clearly, the above discussion—involving the tangential analyses of several authors—raises several separate but related questions concerning the nature of modern war or, specifically, the divide between the conventional and the unconventional. One set of questions—Neuman's seem pointed in this direction—relates to *how* the wars are fought: moving, identifiable fronts, massed formations versus smaller and more dispersed units, number of forces involved, the role of heavy weaponry such as armor, and so on. Another set involves trends, such as they are, toward or away from interstate versus intrastate warfare, the latter assumed inherently to lean more toward unconventional tactics and operations (the Chinese civil war in the late 1940s was one exception). Still another set of questions relates to the duration of wars and the extent to which they tend to have definitive endings—that is, formal peace agreements—and the extent to which evolving trends are historically novel or, contrariwise, reminiscent of past eras, say, the eighteenth or nineteenth century in Europe.

Generally, there is little disagreement that contemporary war has become largely a Third World phenomenon. Some (Cohen, for example), see European military history—at least in some respects—about to be repeated in the Third World, which will now see long-term, serial, and (primarily) conventional conflicts. Others (Staudenmaier, for instance) tend to see modern Third World practice as somewhat unique and not necessarily transitory, involving a predominant emphasis on unconventional operations and tactics and the absence of definitive conclusions. Still another view (Neuman's for example) tends to see European conventional warfare and Third World guerrilla warfare as partially merged, for a variety of reasons involving geography, technological constraints, and systemic factors ("moods") that allow for total warfare. Curiously, Cohen gives short shrift to some writings that stress the limited if not chivalrous nature of war in the Europe of the classical system—which is still another subject involving a complex mix of political/systemic and technological questions.[4]

Still another point that might be considered at least partly at issue is that made by Cohen pertaining to the dominance of land warfare in the Third World. Is that the case *relative* to the recent history of warfare in Europe, or does it contrast at least with planning for such a war? The point appears to reinforce others that have to do with the constraints imposed on Third World combatants by their limitations in dealing with advanced technology, which limitations would, of course, asymmetrically apply to air and naval warfare.

But one should also point out that one reason for the relative lack of importance of air and naval capabilities in Third World wars is the simple fact that external logistics are handled by major power arms suppliers, most often where the "implicit" rules of engagement proscribe interference with those operations. U.S. movement of men and materiel to Europe in World Wars I and II had to contend with all-out submarine and surface naval warfare. By contrast, the rival U.S. and Soviet air- and sealifts to the Middle East in 1967 and 1973, and Soviet airlifts to Vietnam (1979) and Ethiopia (1977–78) all went totally unopposed and allowed for almost no role for the air and sea forces of the combatants themselves. Hence the asymmetric emphasis by the latter on ground forces is not surprising.

Still, air power has been important to Israeli dominance in the Middle East in 1967, 1973, and 1982, it being kept in mind that Israel's extreme sensitivity to casualties dictates the need for quick and relatively costless offensives that can be eased by air power's role in destroying enemy armor, contributing to the overall shock effect necessary to *blitzkrieg* warfare, and providing reconnaissance.

Air and naval power were, of course, vital to the outcome in the Falklands (one of whose combatants was not an LDC). And even in the bogged-down Iraq-Iran land war, which by 1986 had become virtually a *sitzkrieg,* air power had come to play a prominent role (whether significantly deadly or not may be open to debate) in the war of nerves in which both sides, but primarily Iraq, strove to fray the will and nerves of the other so as to produce a favorable negotiated outcome, if not a political collapse or an internal upheaval. And in the Horn, some battle reports spoke of the extensive use of "vertical envelopment" operations, featuring helicopters, by the Cubans aiding the Ethiopians as having been vital to the ultimately successful counterattack that drove the Somalis back out of Ethiopia.

At the traditional core of military historical analysis are the interrelated issues of offense and defense; weapons, tactics and operations; wars of maneuver and of attrition; *Niederwerfungsstrategie* (the strategy of overthrow) and *Ermattungsstrategie* (the strategy of exhaustion). Here too some important issues have been raised in our two volumes, with some disagreements and/or differing explanations.

Perhaps the central point to emerge from our studies is that of the absence of successful, decisive, offensive, long-distance power projection by the Third World antagonists; hence, the seeming dominance of *Ermattungsstrategien.* Only the Israeli *blitzkrieg* during 1967 (and to a lesser degree its Sinai campaign in 1973 and the conventional phase of the 1982 Lebanon war) and India's decisive advance into East Bengal in 1971 stand out as exceptions; perhaps also, on a smaller scale, Britain's rapid reconquest of the Falklands once a beachhead was established. The war of 1967 is hence, sometimes referred to as "the last battle of World War II," an ironic tip of the hat to the legacy of Guderian and Patton. India's success, much less often commented upon or used as an historical guidepost, is often attributed—rightly or not—to the presumed collapse of a demoralized Pakistani Army, whose professionalism was claimed to have been compromised by its slaughter of civilians in what was to become Bangladesh.

But several other conventional wars in the recent period have taken on the character of relatively stationary attrition wars or have merely seen initial offensive thrusts stalled well short of decisive victories: Iraq's stalled advance into Iran and Somalia's failed offensive into Ethiopia. China's costly "lesson" to Vietnam was brief but in the nature of a "meat grinder" conflict. Israel's failure to conduct a decisive counterattack toward Damascus from the Golan Heights in 1973 might also be said to fit this pattern.

This is not to say, however, that wars of attrition need necessarily exclude decisive outcomes. The two world wars were, ultimately, decisive attrition wars. For the Iraq-Iran war in particular, the jury is still out.

Before comparing our contributors' explanations, however, it might be appropriate to suggest at least one (tentative) caveat. It should be stressed that we are dealing with a small number of cases. Just as earlier so much was (perhaps wrongly) inferred from the 1967 and 1973 wars regarding weapons and operations, so too of late it is possible that, in particular, too much is being read into the Iran-Iraq war by way of general lessons.

The contrasting (or in some cases, nuanced and varying) explanations are nevertheless instructive. Cohen focuses on the seeming frequency of wars of limited objectives (more precisely, the "limited objective surprise attack"), of seize-and-hold strategies geared to producing "new facts" on the ground, if not decisive victories. Egypt in 1973, Iraq in 1980, China in 1979, and Somalia in 1977 are all claimed to have fitted this pattern. The reasons for it are moreover seen as broadly "systemic", having to do with "rules of the game" as now played: norms of "international order" claimed nowadays virtually to preclude wars of annihilation, as well as the elimination of sovereign states, related constraints imposed by superpowers worried about escalation toward their own direct involvement, and so forth. Yet one is also compelled to ponder whether the war aims of Egypt, Somalia, and Iraq really were all that limited; that is, are we inferring a strategy from an outcome? If any of these nations had scored a decisive breakthrough, would it not have exploited that breakthrough, even if ultimately, some territorial gains might have had to be returned? And in all of these cases, did not military planners overestimate what they could have achieved, even if their aims may not have been those of total victory?

Creveld, by contrast, appears to attribute the trend (if that is what it is) to *Ermattungsstrategie* and stalemate wars primarily to logistics. Generally, he sees the vastly increasing ratios between "tail" and "tooth" so limiting the forces available for actual combat as to limit more or less automatically the possibilities for sustained, offensive operations. This thesis requires, of course, further analysis according to, in various situations, the basic facts of population, forces-in-being, mobilizable reserves, and so on.

Creveld, it may be noted, also dismisses altogether attempts at generalizing about the impact of changes of weaponry on advantage to offensive or defensive warfare. O'Sullivan, if only indirectly, offers still another explanation. He points to the critical absence of road networks and other modes of transportation and communication in the Third World as limiting mechanized, offensive operations. This may suggest, somewhat paradoxically, that much of our intellectual baggage involving the critical relationships between weapons, tactics, and strategies—including the basic assumptions about what in specific epochs gives advantage to the offense or defense, or compels either strategies of maneuver or attrition—has been inferred *from* the experience of the two world wars on the plains of Europe *to* other arenas in the Third World. Indeed, O'Sullivan points out that in all of our major cases—the Euphrates delta, northern Vietnam, the Ethiopian uplands, Lebanon—the prospects for rapid maneuver warfare were dimmed by imposing geographical and/or meteorological barriers. But then what about Rommel and Montgomery in North Africa?

Kennedy's contribution on economics provides still another angle on the contemporary balance of usage of attrition and maneuver strategies. To a degree, in some cases, economics has dictated such strategies. Israel's extreme sensitivity to the economics of attrition warfare (shutdown of economy due to reserve mobilization, loss of tourist revenue, need to replace expensive weaponry, and so forth—the 1973 war lost almost one year's GNP in twenty-two days) obviously dictates maneuver warfare, insofar as possible (and vis-à-vis Syria and without use of Jordanian or Lebanese territory, that is indeed difficult). If it is not possible, the alternative may be economic attrition from the air. Iraq, whose war effort has been underwritten by massive grants from Saudi Arabia and other Arab Gulf States (to the tune of $25 billion plus), has thus been able to carry out a strategy of attrition (both on land and against Iranian oil installations), even despite its numerical disadvantage and the (now seemingly overrated) dangers of internal disarray in connection with ethnic and religious divisions. Jencks hints at China's inability to sustain a long attrition war in Vietnam in which its much smaller foe might receive massive external aid; in part that may have dictated a quick *blitzkrieg* followed by withdrawal. All in all, Kennedy suggests that lengthy attrition wars in which massive amounts of materiel are expended are the most costly and hence may redound to the advantage of the wealthier side or that availed of the most outside aid—Iraq, Ethiopia, and the United Kingdom seem to have fit that bill, to one degree or another. The Arabs have not yet prevailed on that basis, though one might argue that in some respects, 1973 was for them a successful attrition war.

Sereseres meanwhile in volume 1 notes that the very nature of guerrilla war (the need for huge numerical advantages by the counterinsurgent side and the latter's asymmetrically large expenditure of materiel) tends to constitute a war of economic attrition against the incumbent. The Central American states and Morocco have thus required external aid to sustain their efforts, though the direct link between the actual available amounts and the strategies and tactics used remains hard to pin down.

Creveld provides another connection derived from economics. He points to the pressures on the Israeli reserve system caused by the increasing complexity of weapons, which, he says, dictates the need for a larger number of technical specialists. If this means that in many armies there will be a requirement for larger standing forces, it is hard to say what impact will be wrought on strategy and tactics, particularly in (relatively) outnumbered countries. It may militate toward a still greater imperative to preemptive warfare.

Some of our other selections have provided still other angles of vision on these crucial questions. Rothschild, clearly aware of the current temptation to read a cultural explanation into the Arab armies' failure to prosecute offensive wars (Egypt and Syria versus Israel, Iraq versus Iran), reminds us of the early *blitzkrieg* reputation of (largely Arab) Islamic armies. Other possible cultural explanations for strategies and tactics abound, though it will be noted that all of our authors have remained, cautiously, on the side of cultural relativism.

Creveld in particular cautions about generalizations that might tend to attribute inherently superior fighting qualities to one or another people, noting that such generalizations may be subject to rapid alteration. Rothschild, however, noting the example of the American Civil War and no doubt with Israel in mind, reminds us that mere reputations for superior fighting ability can be important and durable, sometimes even intimidating. This involves a peculiar paradox, which may ramify into the very basis for measuring combat effectiveness in the manner assayed by Dupuy.

The standard current gauges used to measure the average *qualitative* capacity of armed forces tend all, in one way or another, to correlate with per capita GNP, that is, with levels of economic development. In turn, that tends to correlate with educational levels and to ramify into the ability to handle high technology. By that line of reasoning, it is not surprising that Israel's and Britain's forces, man for man, count for more than the Arab or Argentine forces.

But Rothschild, in pointing to a (paradoxically) opposite line of reasoning, reminds us of the Confederacy's qualitative advantage based on the South's rural, martial tradition as compared with the lesser fighting abilities of the Union's conscripted urban rabble. And, indeed, in recent decades, the best soldiers from the U.S., British, and German armies have always been assumed to come from the rural areas, from cultures that stress the outdoors and hunting; it is the ancient myth of the "sturdy yeomanry."

In a curious way, Creveld returns to this for the Israeli case. In the past, the kibbutzim had produced an outsized number of the most outstanding Israeli soldiers and military leaders. Now, Israel having become increasingly urbanized, there are hints of a diminished martial spirit, which is perhaps thereby reflected in the higher rates of dissidence and also of psychiatric casualties exhibited in Lebanon. Israel (and consider also the U.S. experience with its middle-class draftees in Vietnam) now has an army drawn from an advanced consumer, suburban society, a milieu *not* normally associated with traditional martial virtues. Just how this is balanced by the higher capacity to utilize high technology also related to a high standard of living (not only in Israel's case) and how that all translates into a combined assessment of combat effectiveness clearly is an important and apt subject for further research.[5]

Several of our authors have dwelt on the now popular issue of unit cohesiveness and on the linkage between social structure and the quality of junior commanders—that is, the capacity for low-level initiative and the disaggregation of decision making in fast-moving combat situations. These issues were raised in bold relief, earlier, by the U.S. experience in Vietnam. Generally, our collective research appears to indicate that in democracies with high levels of education (for example, the United Kingdom and Israel), this kind of disaggregation and the presence of highly competent junior commanders provides a significant advantage. The opposite appears to obtain for authoritarian/totalitarian polities or in nations with low average levels of wealth and education, as witness, for example, the Soviet and Iraqi performances in their respective wars. On this issue, there is indeed little debate—the seemingly stark contrast between Israel's citizen army and Britain's professional cadres seem overshadowed here by larger societal forces. On the issue of unit cohesion, however, Cohen's view contrasts somewhat with the standard view of Creveld and others. He suggests that Western observers may underestimate the force of nationalist and ethnic fervor in maintaining élan and discipline, entirely aside from the issues raised by U.S. analysts of Vietnam (too much individual rotation of troops and officers) and also by Creveld (the loneliness of battle).

The above discussion converges upon the very important issue of the alleged debellicization of modern societies, a theme advanced in one form or another by Rothschild and Creveld. The theme has recently derived considerable prominence from discussions related to the large-scale slaughter of the Iran-Iraq war (hundreds of thousands are assumed to have been killed on each side), as that compares with the presumed low pain threshold exhibited by the United States in Vietnam (also by contrast with the clearly much higher pain threshold exhibited by the North Vietnamese). These matters, in combination generally with trends in the West toward pacifism, neutralism, "arms-controlism," and so forth (often referred to sarcastically by the U.S. Right as the "Scandinavianization" of the West), have given rise in turn to more strictly military questions about the relationship between pain thresholds, culture, and the pursuit of certain kinds of strategies along a spectrum from attrition to maneuver warfare. Only Islamic fanaticism, with its foundation in the religious cult of martyrdom, so it is often said, could nowadays sustain the level of slaughter exhibited along the Shatt-al-Arab. But the Chinese appear to have suffered proportionately huge casualties in three weeks in 1979 against an opponent that had sacrificed millions in interminable warfare stretching back over some forty years, suggesting a broader phenomenon, perhaps more easily explicable in light of a combination of nascent Third World nationalism, large populations, and the absence of effective intellectual or public dissent. Rothschild appears to accept this thesis, that Third World nations can and will sustain large-scale attrition wars while more developed societies perhaps no longer can do so. Creveld, on the other hand, sees this alleged debellicization of the West as likely more transitory, subject to sudden change.

Linkage Politics: The External Context of Third World Wars

Three of our chapters—those on military assistance, Third World arms industries, and surrogate forces—cluster about the external relationships of the various combatants, both to the major powers and to other Third World states. In combination and in relation to some of our other comparative dimensions such as geography and culture, these chapters have raised some additional interesting questions about the nature of contemporary warfare.

Describing the myriad security assistance relationships of Third World antagonists, Neuman has asserted a central thesis, namely, the overwhelming of both the quality and quantity of transferred technology by the so-called human factor. With specific application to security assistance, this otherwise refers to the severe constraints imposed upon Third World military forces by the problem of "absorption," though more broadly speaking, the "human factor" here refers to tactics, strategy, training, operability, battle management, technical skills, logistics, and so forth. These factors are seen by Neuman to operate both in conventional and unconventional wars, despite the different mixes of technology involved.

Essentially, Neuman's point is that little can be made from the raw numbers of arms inventories and resupply transfers by way of predicting outcomes. Quantitatively inferior forces seem to win more often than not; standard inventories of weapons in Third World arsenals vastly exaggerate in relation to the "real" inventories, that is, those of operable equipment or systems that can be used to real effect.

Still, as Dupuy, Handel, and others have reminded us by analogy in other contexts, sheer mass may still at some point overwhelm qualitative advantages.[6] This may be difficult to discern in Third World contexts. Far more research needs to be done on Third World wars to assess the relative weights of quantitative (weapons) versus qualitative (human) factors so as to provide some explanations, if not the basis for predictions. Such research would, further, take into account the numerous criteria provided by Creveld, Rothschild, and others, particularly those centered on the critical nexus of culture/economic development and the capacity to deal effectively with weapons technology.

Regarding newly arisen arms industries in the Third World, a couple of major points appear to emerge from Neuman's and other contributors' analyses.

First, with the sole exception, as usual, of Israel's performance in Lebanon, it is clear that nascent Third World arms industries cannot easily succeed in producing high-performance systems (attack aircraft, helicopters, missiles, tanks, and so on). Argentina's "indigenous" aircraft (themselves chock full of foreign licensed technology) were virtually irrelevant to the Falklands conflict. As Neuman points out, the limited capabilities of Third World industries, combined with superpower embargoes and third party transfer restrictions on major systems, have often determined the level of technological sophistication at which recent wars have been fought.

More problematic is the question of whether at the level of so-called consumables—ammunition, quartermaster supplies, spare parts, and so forth—

indigenous industries can be important to sustaining conflict and to providing the basis for Third World combatants' circumventing of embargoes and/or political pressures applied by major power mentors. Israel appeared to learn that lesson in 1973 and subsequently made a major effort at stockpiling. Argentina may have derived a similar lesson from 1982. But on the other hand, Iran seems to have had few problems acquiring such consumables despite being embargoed by major powers. Perhaps the differences between these cases have largely to do with matters of time urgency and volume requirements—Iran has been able somewhat to control the pace of a long but sporadically fought war. These questions deserve further research.

Some Third World arms industries have themselves become important for providing security assistance to other Third World states in combat. Iran, Iraq, Morocco, Argentina, Ethiopia, and Somalia all received significant degrees of such assistance. But none of this kind of assistance has involved major systems—those remain under the control of the major powers. Rather, nations such as Brazil and the two Koreas may sustain an Iraq or Iran with quartermaster supplies and ammunition, supplies otherwise available from numerous sources.

The material on surrogate forces also raises some interesting questions, perhaps not easily answered given the lack of extensive historical perspective.

First, it is clear that what we think about this as a possibly emerging, significant contemporary trend is based on a fairly limited number of *major* cases: the Cubans in Angola and Ethiopia, Moroccans in Zaire. Will the coming years see more such cases, or will these later on appear anomalies, a phenomenon restricted, accidentally or not, to one era of the Cold War?

Whatever the answer to that question, David's chapter raises some very interesting questions about measuring combat capability in relation to Dupuy's and others' work. David demonstrates that the insertion of a relatively small number of forces from a more advanced LDC can overwhelm or destabilize a military balance (or slight imbalance) between less advanced LDCs. Cubans and South Africans in Angola, the former in Ethiopia, immediately had a major impact on the course of combat. This appears to indicate the need for the type of research on combat effectiveness (either with actual numbers or perhaps on a less ambitiously empirical basis) conducted by Dupuy in connection with Europe or the central Middle Eastern conflict, but applied to nations at much lower levels of development and, hence, of effectiveness in conducting modern war. Are Dupuy's methodologies applicable at these levels? Is there the same relationship between terrain and technology, the same role for surprise?

At the risk of some repetition, it would appear by way of summing up some "issues raised" in regard to how modern wars are fought, that further attention needs to be paid to dominant images or paradigms that determine how patterns of warfare are interpreted. This in turn brings us back to the "levels of analysis" dilemma raised in our introduction: what kinds of lessons are to be gained and for whom? As scholars, we seek empirically based lessons, whatever the degree of difficulty involved and the tendency toward caution in interpretation. But at another level—or from another vantage point—defense planners may perceive their own lessons and plan, acquire weapons, and deploy forces accordingly.

Planners before 1914 were obsessed with the possibilities for offensive wars of maneuver, as successfully demonstrated by Prussia in 1870 and perhaps too by Sherman's forces driving through the Confederacy. The Maginot line imagery of the 1930s (matched, incidentally, the early phase of World War II notwithstanding, by the German *Westwall*) is too well known to require further comment, and likewise, the British plan to defend Singapore from Japan. Later, by the early 1970s, some commentators were to see the Israeli blitzkrieg imagery from 1967 as so firmly entrenched that it apparently provided the inspiration for Pakistani plans to launch a deep ground strike into the heart of India.[7] After 1973, new imagery arose, that of the dominance of precision-guided munitions (PGMs), particularly antitank and surface-to-air missiles (SAMs), thought jointly to have brought on a new era of attrition, stalemate warfare. And indeed the Iran-Iraq war, even if fought in a manner entirely different from that in 1973, seemed to reinforce this imagery, which was only slightly altered by Israel's conduct of the 1982 war in Lebanon.

From the vantage point of 1985–86, this writer is of the opinion (granted, a tentative and not altogether tenaciously held one) that the current dominant imagery of conventional warfare is that of high attrition, defensive warfare. The wars of 1973 and between Iran and Iraq have established that image. Much of the scenario writing for Central Europe (granted, mostly that part of it that is optimistic about NATO's ability to hold the line against a full-scale Soviet assault) seems to accept the same imagery.

The latter imagery has apparently been reinforced by the futile (so far) Soviet experience in Afghanistan, by the tenacity of the several (past and present) Central American insurgencies, also by the tenacity of Angola's UNITA, the Eritreans, southern Sudanese, anti-Vietnamese Cambodian groups, and others. That is, the dominant imagery of unconventional war appears to be that of the common failure of counterinsurgency strategies, with the exception of Morocco.

Carrying this point one step further, it would appear clear that as concerns dominant imagery, there is one rather fundamental distinction between conventional and unconventional warfare analysis. Commentaries about how conventional wars have been or ought to be fought assume a certain symmetry beween the combatants: both sides must wrestle with the impact of current weaponry upon offensive or defensive operations, either of which they may be required to conduct. Germany and France both assumed an offensive advantage in 1914; Egypt and Israel have had to wrestle more or less equally with the impact of PGMs. (By way of exception one might point to Swiss or Swedish defense planning, which need be done only from a strictly defensive perspective.)

On the unconventional level, however, the respective insurgents and counterinsurgents appear to deal with a wholly distinct set of historical images, which in turn translate into preferred strategies and tactics. Hence, the historical progression from Malaysia to the U.S. effort in Vietnam to the Soviet effort in Afghanistan involving the various types of counterinsurgency tactics or of various mixes of military and political instruments: fortified hamlets, spread effects, civic action to win over local people, search and destroy, and so on. On the other side, insurgents deal with a different set of historical guidelines and imagery: *foco insurrecional* versus *guerra prolongada*, and variations upon the Mao/Giap policy of gradual escalation from harassment and political action through guerrilla warfare to a final thrust with conventional offensive forces.

The core of analysis regarding conventional warfare has to do with the nexus among weapons, tactics, operations, and strategies; introduction of new weaponry such as was done by the Arabs in 1973 or Israel in 1982 is assumed, at least potentially, to change the very basis for successful conduct of war. Regarding unconventional warfare, however, one might speculate that geography rather than weaponry predominates as the key variable determining types of wars and their outcomes. Weaponry receives little attention, save with respect to the quantity of small arms and ammunition available to insurgents (the Afghan rebels' problems in acquiring SAMs to combat Soviet helicopters may be one exception here). Generally, the success or failure of counterinsurgency appears to hinge crucially on the cover provided by vegetation and/or topography, that is, on the barriers posed to counterinsurgency (COIN) forces in finding and targeting insurgents. Not accidentally, Morocco's COIN policy in the Western Sahara has been relatively the most successful of those we have observed.

Conventional wars clearly lend themselves to overall strategies of limited victories, based on surprise attacks and seize-and-hold strategies. In unconventional wars, however, the existence of sanctuaries and the often-seen ability of counterinsurgents to control the pace of war make for wholly different strategic assumptions. Unconventional wars are often long, very long. They are also, by their nature, usually ultimately conclusive.

Summary

In a review of the first of our volumes on lessons of recent wars in the Third World, Edward Luttwak made a number of points that address what remains to be done in this area, but that also supported and reinforced the initial thrust of our undertaking. Generally, he advocated a far more ambitiously inductive approach to the subject through expanded case studies, and following that, an effort at historical analysis, whether or not to be made explicitly comparative.

In his words,

Instead, the initial investigation must be all-inclusive and uncritical, in the manner of those local histories written by amateurs for local circulation that seek to record every fact of note in full detail, without trying to explain anything or substantiate any developmental vision. In other words, the first stage must be antiquarian (or "annalist" to use the technical term) rather than historical. Only in a second stage, after full familiarization with the events of the case, including those seemingly trivial or accidental, can one begin the historical analysis as such, whereby questions are asked to prove or disprove specific propositions. It then turns out, quite frequently, that the seemingly trivial was actually very important, and the seemingly accidental was to the contrary a pre-ordained result. In this two-stage process, therefore, the fact-gatherers of intelligence in all its forms and the analysts, i.e., the serving officers of each branch and in the doctrine commands, must collect and sift through a great quantity of information to obtain that very small fraction which is true, not previously known, and also relevant. But of course things are no different in extracting mere grams of rubies and diamonds from tons of alluvial deposits—and usable data paid for by the blood of others is more precious than rubies or diamonds. The process is elaborate but so obviously rewarding that it seems unthinkable that it should have less than the highest priority.

But that, notoriously, is not so. Military institutions that deem it proper to spend millions to obtain some fractional improvement in a secondary weapon scarcely attempt to collect, analyze, and disseminate information on contemporary wars except in a most superficial manner, often limited to cursory accounts such as one might find in a newspaper article, and in statistics always so unrevealing in themselves. In the same vein, millions might be spent to obtain technical intelligence on this or that Soviet weapon, whereas hardly anything is done to inform serving officers about the use and misuse of that same weapon in action in Afghanistan.

In the most serious case of neglect, no sustained effort has been made to disseminate information about the military experiences of the modern and semi-modern armed forces that have fought on a large scale in recent years, notably the Indian, Iraqi, Pakistani, and Syrian.[8]

If our two volumes have at least moved the state of knowledge in this area some distance in that direction, our purposes will at least to some extent have been fulfilled. Much clearly remains to be done, not least—as Luttwak argues—by way of far more detailed individual war histories and accompanying lessons learned exercises.

The value of such careful study—including allowance for greatly varying military cultures within the Third World—was nowhere better illustrated than in an article by John Kifner on the Iraq-Iran war in February 1986, at a point some military observers had begun to anticipate, rightly or wrongly, a possible Iraqi collapse. According to him,

Those who have seen the war from both fronts find the armies a study in contrasts.

The Iranian front lines tend to be scenes of chaos and dedication, with turbaned mullahs, rifles slung on their backs, rushing about on brightly colored motorcyles encouraging the troops. Religious slogans are posted everywhere, and sometimes reinforcements arrive cheerfully carrying their own coffins as a sign of their willingness to be "martyred." There is little sign of military activity behind the combat area itself.

In Iraq, by contrast, the military zone extends for dozens of orderly miles of defenses behind the front with tanks and artillery dug into the dirt along side the roadside, elaborate World War I–style bunkers and trenches, and dump trucks excavating grid-pattern defenses.

The Iraqis have the reputation of being the best trained force in the Middle East after the Israelis and the Jordanians. Military police man the intersections, uniforms and even footwear match, somewhat unusual among many Arab armies, and officers receive snappy salutes.

"They look sharp, well turned out and superficially disciplined," a Western career officer said. "But it's only superficial. When the chips are down, then the problem begins.

"The senior commanders here must realize by now that the people who have to do the dirty work—the grunts—are not steadfast in action," he went on. "The landings the Iranians just made demonstrate this: the lads manning the positions downed tools and ran away."

Typical Iranian tactics, military experts say, include waiting in a foxhole with an RPG-7 and blasting an oncoming tank at close range. The Iraqis, by contrast, rely on vast artillery fire from great distances and fortress-like defenses.

Some military experts here traced the lack of enthusiasm among the soldiers to two major political factors: what they saw as a lack of a strong, clear sense of Iraqi national identity, and ambivalent feelings about the Hussein Government and the Baath Party.

Like other Middle Eastern countries, with the exception of Egypt and Iran, Iraq is not an historic entity, but a set of lines drawn on a map by European powers, first as semicolonial mandates after the Ottoman Empire fell in World War I and then as independent countries after World War II. Iraq has had 22 "revolutions," most of them coups, since 1920. It is an ethnically and geographically diverse land.

"They haven't had enough time for people at the extremes of the nation to believe in a unity for which to sacrifice themselves," a diplomat here said of the Iraqis. "I doubt whether the veneer of nationalism is very thick or very substantial."[9]

The foregoing commentary underscores, if nothing else, the very subjective nature of interpretations of war. There is much that is dimly understood, all the more so outside what is familiar within the Western world. The conjunction of weapons technology, cultural nationalism, and geography provides, in a way, something very specific to each war. And yet it is only by some effort at comparative analysis that such things can be understood, however tentatively. There is a real need for further analysis.

Notes

1. The results from this project may be seen in Melvin Small and J. David Singer, *Resort to Arms: International and Civil Wars, 1816–1980* (Beverly Hills, Calif.: Sage, 1982).

2. William O. Staudenmaier, "Conflict Termination in Wars of the Third World," in *The Lessons of Recent Wars in the Third World*, vol. 2, eds. Stephanie G. Neuman and Robert E. Harkavy (Lexington, Mass.: Lexington Books, 1987).

3. Eliot A. Cohen, "Learning from Distant Battles: Strategic and Other Lessons from Wars in the Third World," in *The Lessons of Recent Wars in the Third World*, vol. 2, eds. Stephanie G. Neuman and Robert E. Harkavy (Lexington, Mass.: Lexington Books, 1987).

4. The common generalizations about the claimed limited nature of warfare during this period may be learned from K.J. Holsti, *International Politics*, 2d ed. (Englewood Cliffs, N.J.: Prentice-Hall, 1972), chapter 2.

5. For a promising start in this area, see Barry L. Scribner et al., "Are Smart Tankers Better? AFQT and Military Productivity," *Armed Forces and Society* 12, no. 2 (Winter 1986): 193–206.

6. In addition to Dupuy's chapter in our first volume, see Michael Handel, "Numbers Do Count: The Question of Quality vs. Quantity," *Journal of Strategic Studies* 4 (September 1981): 225–60.

7. See Gen. D. Palit, *The Lightning Campaign: The Indo-Pakistan War, 1971* (Salisbury: Compton Press, 1972), 77.

8. Edward Luttwak, review of Harkavy and Neuman, eds., *The Lessons of Recent Wars in the Third World: Approaches and Case Studies,* in *Parameters,* journal of the U.S. Army War College, 16, no. 1 (Spring 1986): 87.

9. "Iraqis Stalled by a Tenacious Enemy," *New York Times,* Feb. 28, 1986, p. A3. Copyright © 1986 by The New York Times Company. Reprinted by permission.

Index

Page number in *italics* indicates figure.
"t" after page number indicates table.

About the Contributors

Eliot A. Cohen is Secretary of the Navy Senior Research Fellow at the U.S. Naval War College, where he teaches in the Strategy Department. Formerly a member of the Faculty of the Harvard University Department of Government, he has served as a consultant to both government and industry. He is the author of *Citizens and Soldiers: The Dilemmas of Military Service* (1985); articles in *International Security, Foreign Affairs, Commentary,* and other journals; and a monograph on elite military units in modern democracies.

Steven R. David is an assistant professor of political science and coordinator of the International Studies Program at The Johns Hopkins University. He has written widely on Third World security issues in such journals as *International Security* and *The Washington Quarterly* and in his book *Third World Coups d'Etat and International Security* (1986).

Gavin Kennedy is professor of defense finance at Heriot-Watt University, Edinburgh, Scotland. He is the author of *The Military in the Third World* (1974), *The Economics of Defence* (1975), *Burden Sharing in NATO* (1979), *Defense Economics* (1983), and numerous articles on defense finance and economics. He regularly lectures at U.K. service colleges and has given evidence to the House of Commons Select Committee on Defence.

Patrick O'Sullivan is professor and chairman at the Department of Geography, Florida State University. His research interests include geopolitics, military geography, and regional identity. He is author of *The Geography of Warfare* (1983) and *Geopolitics* (1986).

Joseph Rothschild is Class of 1919 Professor of Political Science at Columbia University. His teaching and research interests focus on the politics of polyethnic states and on East Central European studies. He is the author of, among other books, *Ethnopolitics* (1981), *East Central Europe Between the Two World Wars* (1974), *Pilsudski's Coup d'Etat* (1966), *Communist Eastern Europe* (1964), and *The Communist Party of Bulgaria* (1959).

William O. Staudenmaier is a colonel in the United States Army and the director of strategy for the Center for Land Warfare, U.S. Army War College, and he holds the George C. Marshall Chair of Military Studies at the U.S. Army War College. Colonel Staudenmaier served in combat in Vietnam as a district advisor and in various staff assignments in Washington, D.C. His articles have appeared in *Foreign Policy, Orbis, Naval War College Review, Military Review, Army,* and *Parameters.* He is co-author of *Strategic Implications of the Continental-Maritime Debate* (1984) and co-editor of *Military Strategy in Transition: Defense and Deterrence* (1984) and *Alternative Military Strategies for the Future* (1985).

Martin van Creveld teaches history at the Hebrew University, Jerusalem, and is currently employed at the National Defense University in Washington, D.C. His principal publications are *Supplying War* (1977), *Fighting Power* (1982), and *Command in War* (1985). He is currently working on a book about technology and war.

About the Editors

Stephanie G. Neuman is a senior research scholar at Columbia University's Research Institute on International Change, and the director of the Comparative Defense Studies Program. She was on the Graduate Faculty of the New School for Social Research from 1972 to 1983 and now teaches Third World security issues at Columbia University. Dr. Neuman's recent publications include: *Military Assistance in Recent Wars: The Dominance of the Superpowers,* The Washington Papers, no. 122 (Washington, D.C.: Center for Strategic and International Studies, Georgetown University, with Praeger Publishers, 1986); "International Stratification and Third World Military Industries," *International Organization,* winter 1984; "The Arms Trade and American National Interests," in *Power and Policy in Transition,* ed. Vojtech Mastny (1984); and "Third World Military Industries and the Arms Trade," in *Arms Production in Developing Countries: An Analysis of Decision Making,* ed. James E. Katz (1984). Dr. Neuman has also coedited and contributed to other books on Third World security issues and has published articles in other academic and popular journals and newspapers. She is currently a consultant to the Department of State.

Robert E. Harkavy is a professor of political science at The Pennsylvania State University, specializing in national security policy, arms control, and U.S. foreign policy. He earlier served with the Atomic Energy Commission and the Arms Control and Disarmament Agency. He has been a senior research fellow at Cornell University, a visiting research professor at the U.S. Army War College, and an Alexander von Humboldt fellow at the University of Kiel, Germany, and a Fulbright Research Scholar in Sweden. Professor Harkavy is the author of *The Arms Trade and International Systems* (1975), *Spectre of a Middle Eastern Holocaust* (1978), and *Great Power Competition for Overseas Bases* (1982). He is coeditor of several other books on national security. He is currently a consultant to the Office of the Secretary of Defense. He is also working on a book to be entitled *Foreign Military Presence.*

WIDENER UNIVERSITY WOLFGRAM LIBRARY CHESTER, PA.

DATE DUE